Sie mir den Tag Ihrer Rückkehr noch-
mals mit. — Täschner gefällt mir gut.
Stella weniger. Ihre Arbeit macht
sich im Atelier viel besser. —
Im ganzen passt die ganze Ausstellung
nicht in den Rahm. Die meisten
Kunsthändlersachen hätte man besser
in die einzelnen Tagdawirtes und
Restaurant's aufgehängt.
Herzlichen Gruss Ihr
[Unterschrift]

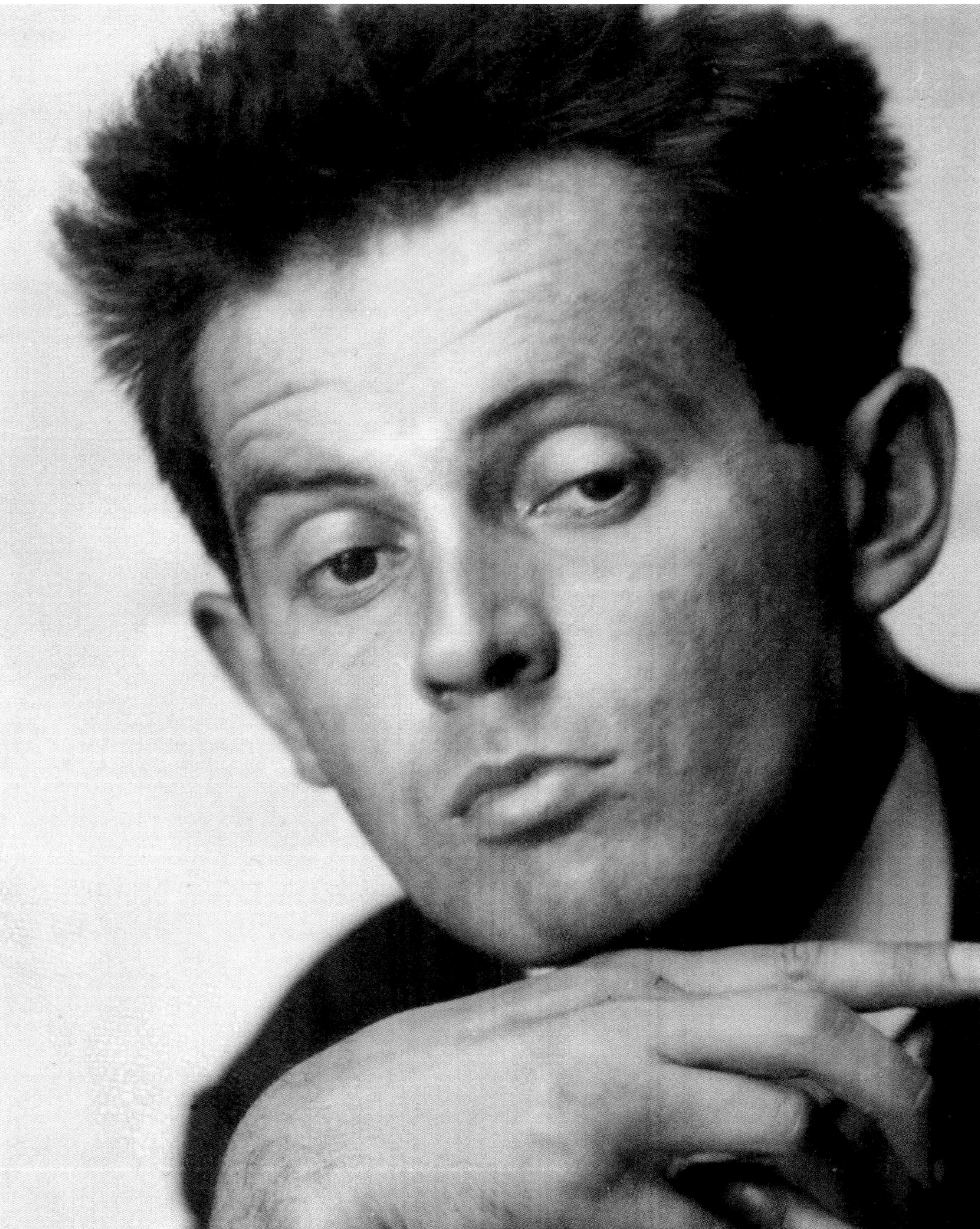

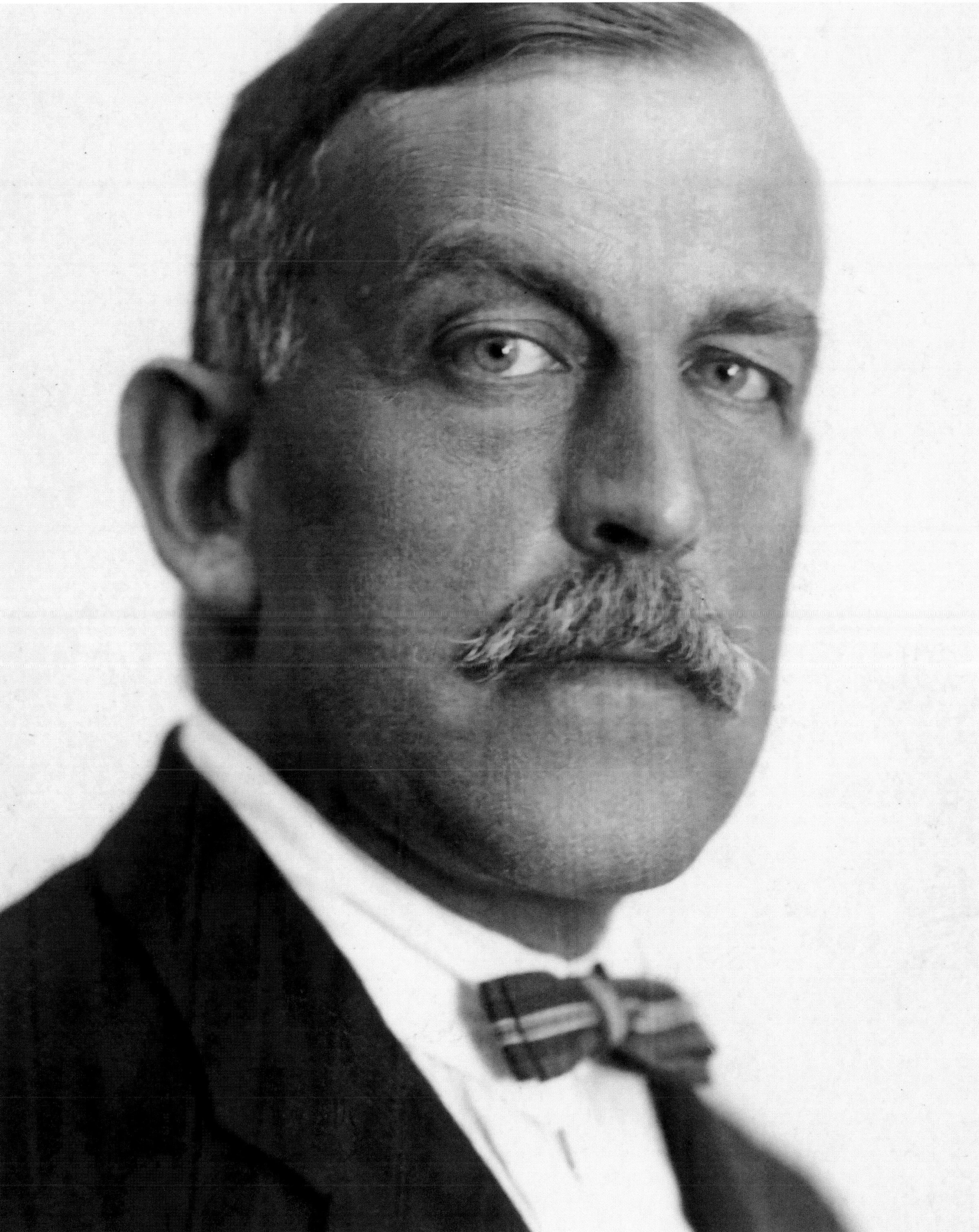

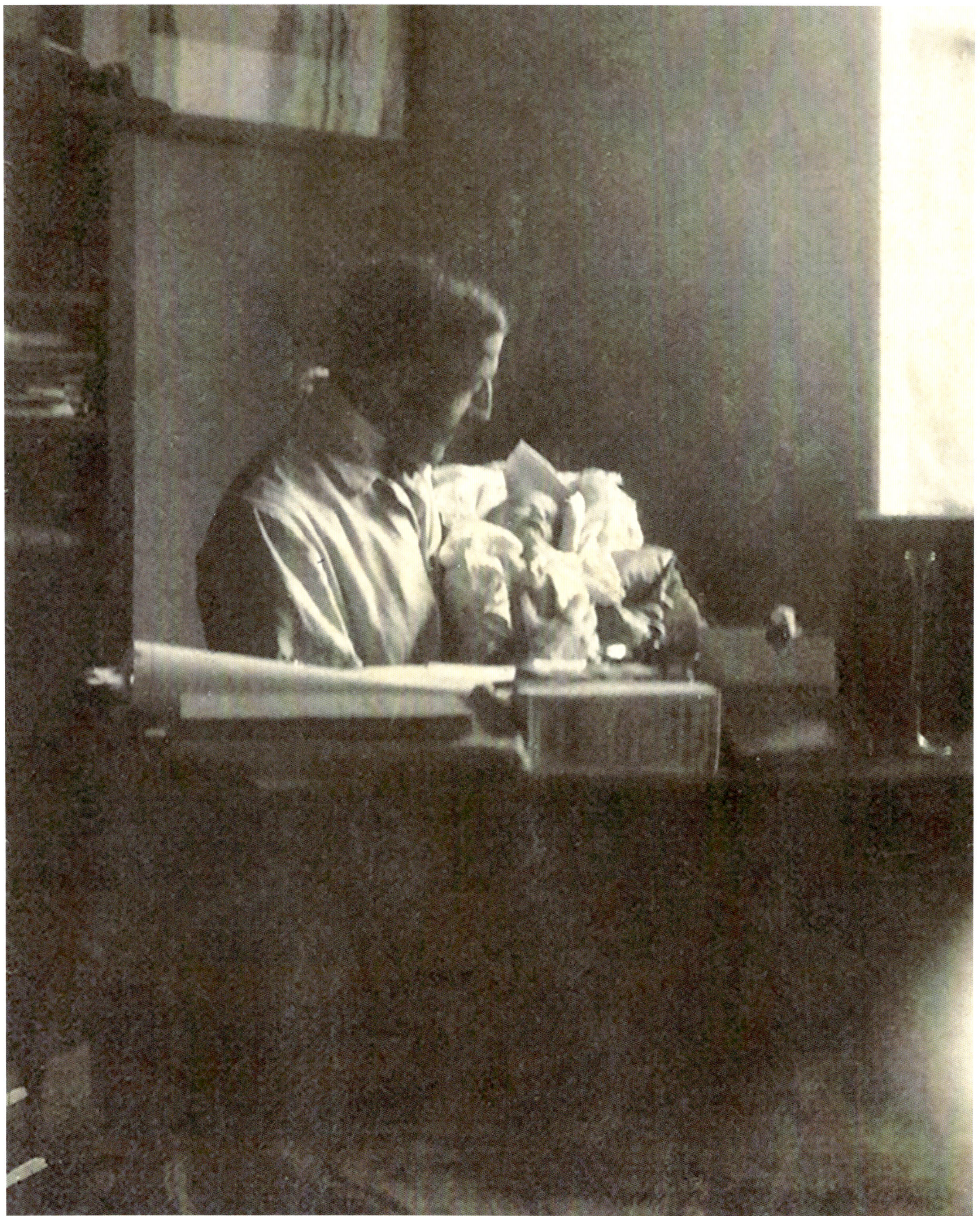

EGON SCHIELE

PORTRAIT OF DR. ERWIN VON GRAFF

ELISABETH DUTZ

PRESTEL

MUNICH · LONDON · NEW YORK

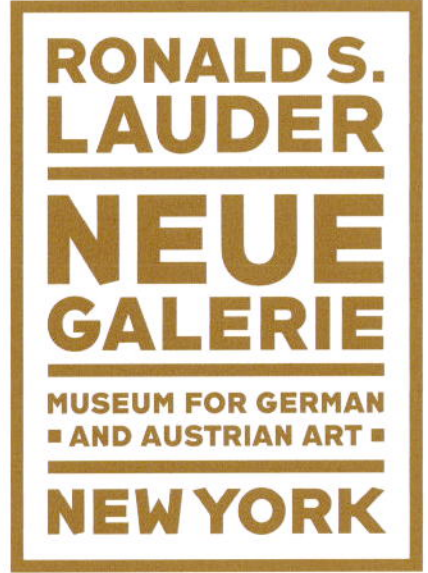

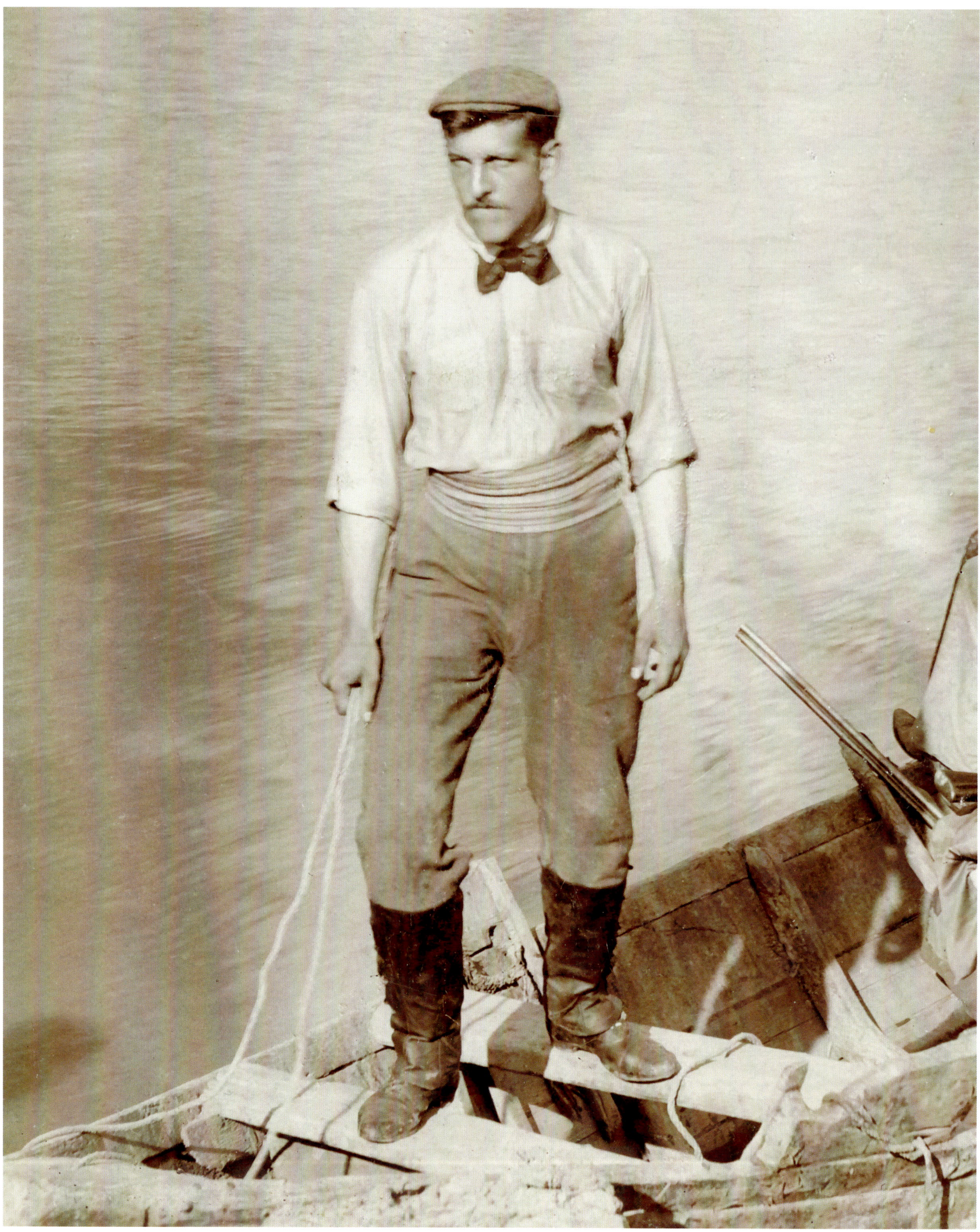

ACKNOWLEDGMENTS

Dina Alexander, New York
Art Installation Design, New York
Colin Bailey, New York
Vivian Endicott Barnett, New York
Christian Bauer, Vienna
Jennifer Belt, New York
Antonia Bryan, New York
Matti Bunzl, Vienna
Sam Cameron, New York
Christophe Cherix, New York
Alice Chumard, New York
Alessandra Comini, Dallas
Emily Cushman, New York
Herwig Czech, Vienna
Shawn Digney-Peer, New York
Elisabeth Draxler, Graz
Rose Durand, New York
Andreas Dutz, Vienna
Martina Effaga, Munich
Linda Mischel Eisner, New York
Michael Freissmuth, Vienna
Jennifer Friess, Ann Arbor
Verena Gamper, Vienna
Ralph Gleis, Vienna
Elisabeth Graff de Pancscova, Vienna
Alexander Graff de Pancsova, Vienna
William M. Griswold, Cleveland
Corey Gross, Ann Arbor
Jeffrey Haber, New York
Max Hollein, New York
Gerhard and Ingrid Jenisch, Strobl
Kerstin Jesse, Vienna
Jane Kallir, New York
Cheryl Karim, New York
Evelyn Kelley, New York
Herbert Kiss, Vienna

Marissa Klein, New York
Ursula Kreuzbauer, Vienna
James Kohler, Cleveland
Daniela Kumhala, Vienna
Michael Lesh, New York
Steven Lindberg, Berlin
Jill Lloyd, London
William Loccisano, Sarasota
John Manley, Scarsdale
Susanne Manley, Scarsdale
Peter Marino, New York
Cassie Mazzucco, New York
Caroline McGuckian, New York
Claire McGuckian, New York
Gretchen Shie Miller, Cleveland
Sonja Niederacher, New York
Mauricio Olivares Díaz, Vienna
Christina Olsen, Ann Arbor
Olaf Peters, Halle (Saale)
Ernst Ploil, Vienna
Vivian Pomerantz, New York
Brandi Pomfret, New York
Ellen Price, New York
Jerry Rivera, New York
Stella Rollig, New York
Jackie Scalisi, New York
Brigitte Schwarzer-Daum, Vienna
Arlene Shaner, New York
Marcella Sigmund-Graff, Bad Fischau
Christa Simon, Vienna
Harald Sitte, Vienna
Katie Stadtmiller, Ann Arbor
Elizabeth Szancer, New York
Jack Zinterhofer, New York
Will Zinterhofer, New York
Tom Zoufaly, New York

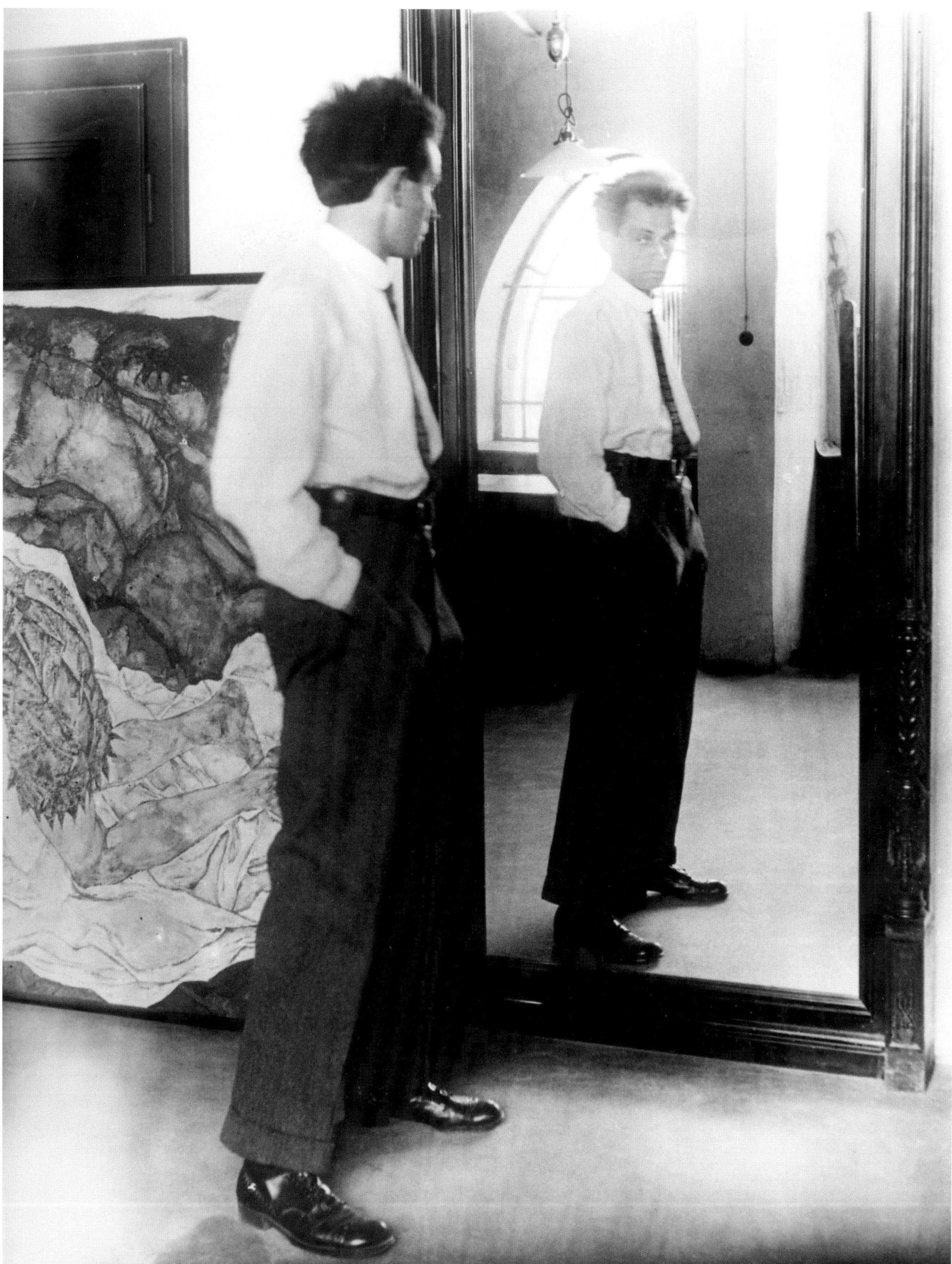

FOREWORD

Egon Schiele is one of the greatest artists in the collection of the Neue Galerie New York. We have proudly presented a number of major exhibitions on Schiele over the years, surveying his extraordinary portraits and landscapes, as well as other aspects of his brief but brilliant career.

With this publication and accompanying small exhibition, we are focusing on a single work, along with some related drawings and paintings: the *Portrait of Dr. Erwin von Graff* from 1910. This was the year Schiele really came into his own as an artist, and we consider the von Graff painting to be one of the most important works in the extended collection of Neue Galerie.

Schiele completed this portrait of a surgeon at the Second University Women's Clinic at the age of twenty. The painting of the striking thirty-two-year-old doctor somehow manages to portray the subject looking both friendly and slightly menacing, with his warm smile, but also darkened complexion and bandaged finger. Dr. von Graff, who the young artist met in Vienna at the home of collector Carl Reininghaus, became a confidant of Schiele. Von Graff generously treated, cared for, and paid the hospital bills of Schiele's pregnant friend Liliana Amon.

The doctor was among the very first to recognize Schiele's great talent, allowing the artist to visit the clinic to draw pregnant women and newborns. This was quite an uncommon practice and a sign of respect and trust between the two men. It was clear to von Graff that Schiele was deeply interested in the life cycle, which he honored with his artworks. This portrait and several works on paper were given by Schiele to the doctor in gratitude for his service.

Von Graff remained a good friend of Schiele until the very end. He even attended to Schiele in his final hours, giving him an injection to ease his suffering, as he tragically succumbed to the global flu epidemic in 1918 at the age of twenty-eight—just three nights after Edith Schiele, his six months' pregnant wife, passed away, also a victim of the epidemic.

For this publication, Dr. Elisabeth Dutz, Chief Curator of the Graphic Art Collection at the Albertina Museum in Vienna, has drawn on new research and photo material to give an in-depth overview of the von Graff painting and to provide additional context for the work. She has done a wonderful job of illuminating the close relationship between Schiele and von Graff, showing us artist and patron in spirited dialogue. We wish to thank her for her outstanding work on this publication, part of a Neue Galerie book series devoted to superb individual paintings in the collection. Our thanks also go out to Janis Staggs, Director of Curatorial and Manager of Publications, who has gathered the works on display, as well as to designer Bill Loccisano, for their important contributions.

Ronald S. Lauder
President and Co-Founder, Neue Galerie New York

Renée Price
Director, Neue Galerie New York

EGON SCHIELE ■ PORTRAIT OF DR. ERWIN VON GRAFF

I. EGON SCHIELE'S *PORTRAIT OF DR. ERWIN VON GRAFF*

> *Professor Dr. Erwin Graff, of large stature, has a cameo or, better still, Caesar's head with powerfully curving eyebrows, flashing blue eyes, powerful nose, face shaved smooth, and energetic chin. His closed mouth with a delicate mustache has something severe about it.*

This description was given by Dr. Adolf Kronfeld (1861–1938), an Austrian physician and writer, of his professional colleague Erwin von Graff in a 1927 newspaper article. By this juncture Graff had already been employed at the II. Universitäts-Frauenklinik (Second University Women's Hospital) for nearly twenty years, had gained experience as a pathological anatomist, a surgeon, a gynecologist, and in radiation therapy, and had been an "*ausserordentlich*"[1] professor at the Universität Wien (University of Vienna) for about a year.

1. Egon Schiele, *Portrait of Dr. Erwin von Graff*, 1910, oil, gouache and charcoal on canvas, 100 × 90 cm (39 $^3/_8$ × 35 $^3/_8$ in.), Kallir P161. Private Collection

Kronfeld's impression from 1927 could almost describe the large portrait that Egon Schiele painted of Graff in 1910 and that is now one of the most impressive works in the extended collection of the Neue Galerie New York [Fig. 1]. The half-length portrait painting shows Graff standing in a frontal pose. He looks directly and penetratingly at the viewer. At the time of the portrait, Graff was thirty-two years old and a very slim, athletic man.

Graff is dressed in a short-sleeved white shirt with a stand-up collar that covers his entire neck up to his chin. Over it he wears a bright, skin-colored, sleeveless vest. The top of his trousers is also visible. Graff has adopted the white clothing that was common among hospital physicians. Schiele's portrait does not show a physician posed like a scholar at his desk but rather one practicing his profession. Graff appears to have interrupted his activity only briefly to model for the artist and at any moment could put on a white surgical coat and hurry off to an intervention. At the time of the portrait, Graff was primarily a surgeon and had begun working as an auxiliary doctor at the Second University Women's Hospital just two years earlier after training in pathological anatomy and surgery. Not until 1911 did he become an assistant physician and begin training as a gynecologist.

Graff holds his right arm upward and bent diagonally across his chest, as if attempting to keep it sterile. Surgeons today also keep their arms above their hips to avoid touching something unintentionally and coming into contact with germs. Graff, who had received his first surgical training from Anton von Eiselsberg (1860–1939) in Vienna, had certainly been drilled in aseptic procedures because Eiselsberg was a student of the famous physician Johann von Mikulicz (1850–1905), who had undertaken pioneering work on asepsis.[2]

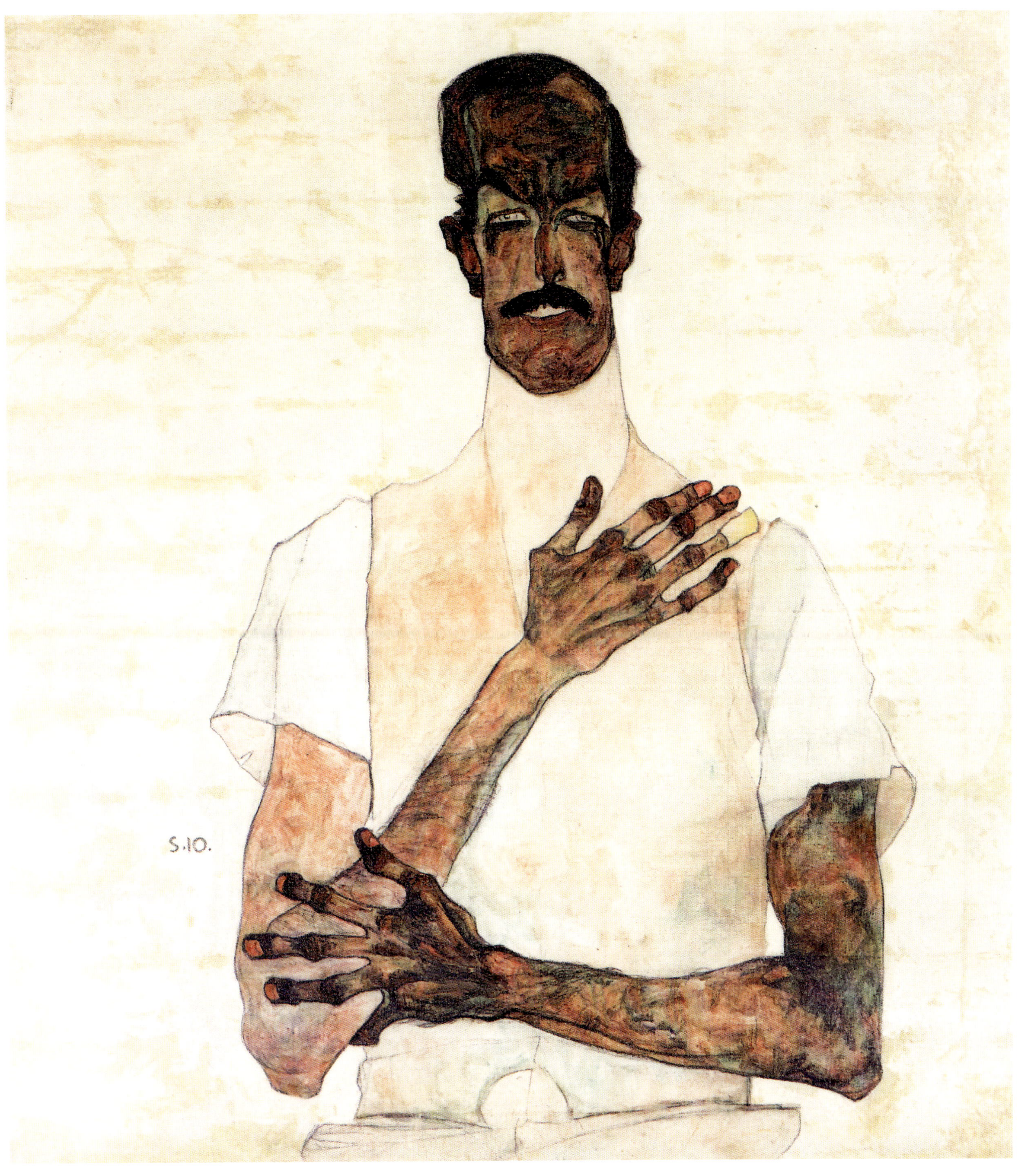
S.10.

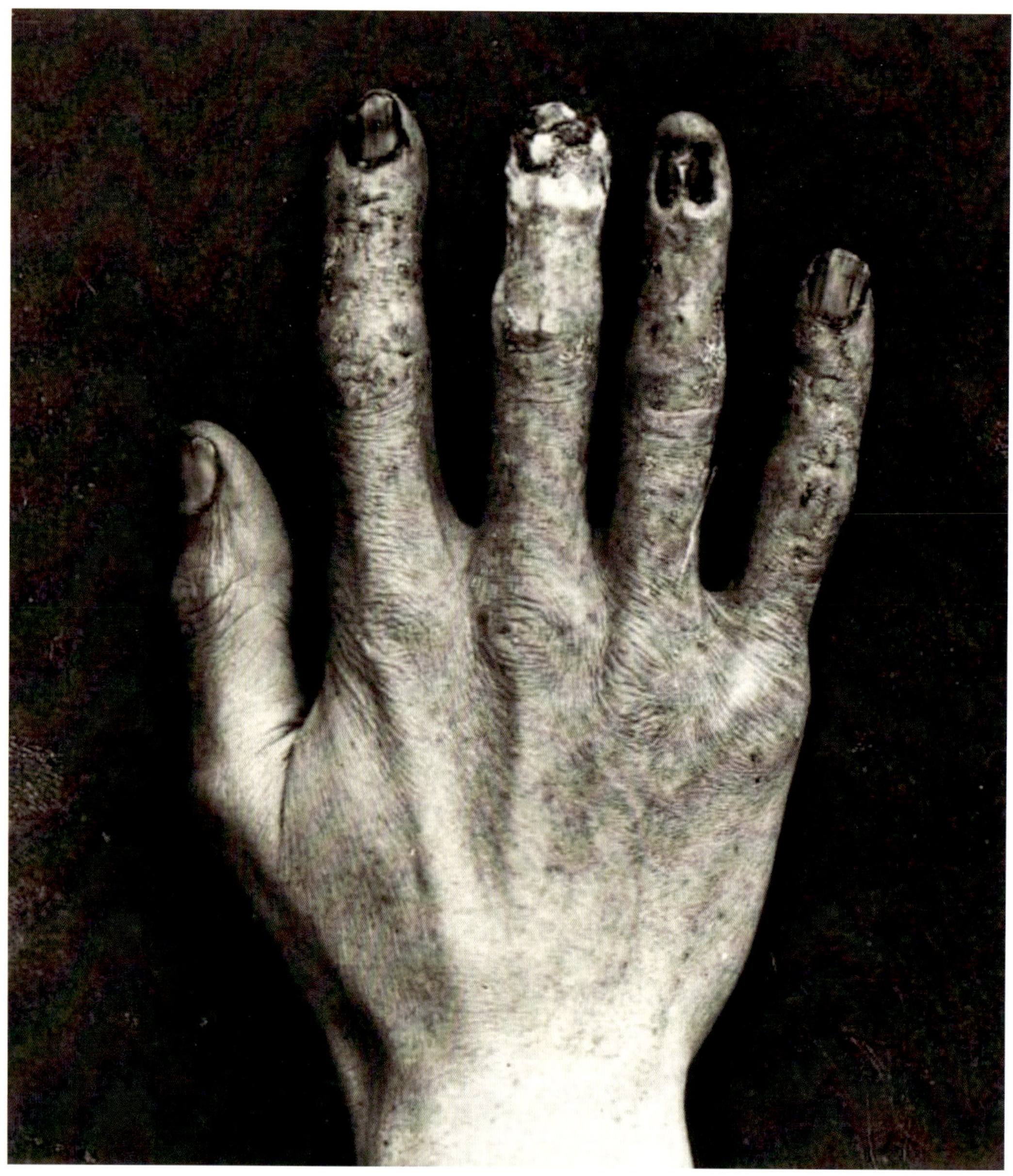

One is struck by the extraordinarily dark color of Graff's hands and forearms, especially with regard to his left arm. Graff has a large bandage on the tip of his right ring finger, which lends an even more determined quality to the physician's self-confident appearance. His trade is bloody. Graff's face is also somber, almost black. The area around his radiantly blue eyes, which seem to flash out between the blackened lids, and the teeth beneath his mustache are rendered as bright points of contrast within his face. His skull is elongated, angular, and deformed slightly to the left on top. In several photographs, Graff's head can be seen leaning slightly to the left. His tall brow is furrowed perhaps in anger, making Graff's piercing gaze seem resolute. The outer edges of his eyes point downward, and the lower eyelids are emphatically heavy. The dark areas appear to "run" on the side down to his cheeks and give Graff a demonic appearance. His slim, aquiline nose, crooked mouth and asymmetrical mustache, and long, angular, sharp chin—everything looks slightly askew. His head seems too small relative to his body, as Alessandra Comini observed:

The doctor appears as a shrunken-headed cadaver in a state of rigor mortis. A creamy, lackluster body halo surrounds the figure and in the resultant morbid atmosphere the prominently bandaged finger has the impact of a grim joke.[3]

Where Graff poses is unclear: there is no furniture or interior detail provided to suggest a specific place. This impossibility to localize the portrayed became an essential component of Schiele's art and of modernism in general. His portraits, nudes, and self-portraits appear to float in a void and evoke a feeling of desolation. In Graff's case, Schiele flooded the background with a bright, whitish yellow, a color that establishes a connection to the sterile, washable walls of a hospital.

In 1910, the year he painted this portrait, Schiele began to work very expressively with colors and corporeal expression. He created bodies with unnatural, sick, and decaying colors that have nothing in common with reality. But could Graff's strikingly dark left arm nevertheless be an indication that he was using morphine?[4] Could the bluish discolorations point to intravenous morphine injections that caused morbid changes to the veins? This seems unlikely.

It is very improbable that Graff injected himself intravenously with morphine around 1910, because at the time injections were primarily administered subcutaneously. Intravenous injection was seen as a mistake to be avoided. (Illegal) intravenous injections with morphine are first reported from 1925 onward.[5]

But subcutaneous injections would not have resulted in such a visibly apparent change.

Research indicates that there is indeed a natural explanation for the appearance of Graff's skin.[6] The Graff family records reveal that he suffered from severe radiodermatitis. Already as a young physician, he was fascinated by the possibilities of X-rays and experimented with them. Graff found opportunities to do so in Vienna, which was the site not only of the first clinical use and closer analysis of X-rays by Leopold Freund (1868–1943) but also of the first central facility for X-ray technology in the Allgemeines Krankenhaus (General Hospital), which opened in 1897.[7] Radiodermatitis is the effect from repeated, unprotected exposure to radiation. In the early twentieth century, much higher doses of radiation were used than are today, and radiation damage could occur relatively easily. It results in inflammation of the skin, typically accompanied by the symptoms of redness, swelling, and itching, which can resemble sunburn. It can also lead to hardening and darkening of the skin, especially above joints, and to blistering and even sores.[8] An extreme case of radiation damage can be seen in a photograph of an X-ray technician employed at the Royal London Hospital around 1900 [Fig. 2].

The bandage on Graff's ring finger has prompted numerous attempts to explain it. The New York critic and art historian N. F. Karlins offered this interpretation:

At any rate, in his portrait Dr. von Graff, the gynecologist has a serene yet Mephisthophelean demeanor. The flesh of his face and arms is painted in an intriguing yet unappealing mottled green. He wears a plaster on one finger, which the Schiele catalogue suggests may "cast the doctor's competence into question." I couldn't help thinking it might prove his bravery, faced with a vagina dentata,[9] *especially as it is his ring finger.*[10]

2. Hand of an X-ray technician at the Royal London Hospital, ca. 1900. Source: Historic Vids/X.; oncodaily.com/blog/24512 [accessed August 31, 2025]

As early as 1904, Graff's finger was a recurring item in the correspondence between his mother and one of his sisters: "Erwin had to take his test on Monday, but no one knows the result yet; unfortunately, his finger was still not good yet, as Olga [Erwin's wife] wrote."[11] A few weeks later: "The Erwins [Erwin and Olga] are very content in Vienna, apart from Erwin's finger, which just won't heal properly, which worries me very much, all the more so as he was supposed to perform his first operation these weeks."[12] And again a few weeks later: "Erwin is terribly busy but he is very satisfied with his work and can finally perform operations since his fingers have healed."[13] Over the years, new skin issues occurred repeatedly, but they always healed.

How did the portrait come to be commissioned? As will be shown, the physician played an important role in Schiele's life in 1910. It has been reported that Graff made it possible for the young artist to sketch pregnant women and newborns at the Second University Women's Hospital. And he helped Schiele with a delicate matter. In early 1910, a young pregnant woman was living with Schiele, whom the physician admitted to the clinic in May 1910, paid all her bills, and ensured that she was well cared for until the child was born. In addition, Graff tried to persuade the young woman to leave Schiele so as not to hinder his artistic career. Schiele must have been extremely grateful to Graff and was also in his debt financially. Painting a portrait was an appropriate way of repaying the favor that was acceptable to both parties.

Three preliminary drawings are known, one of which is lost. The drawing *Three Head Studies of Dr. Graff* [Fig. 3] has three sketches of Graff's head from the side and back; he is readily distinguishable by his sharp part and mustache. This may have been a study made when Schiele was sitting behind Graff and at an angle, observing him from an elevated position, perhaps in the hospital's lecture hall.

3. Egon Schiele, *Three Head Studies of Dr. Graff*, 1910, watercolor and charcoal on paper, 44.5 × 31.7 cm (17 $^1/_2$ × 12 $^1/_2$ in.), Kallir D615. Private Collection

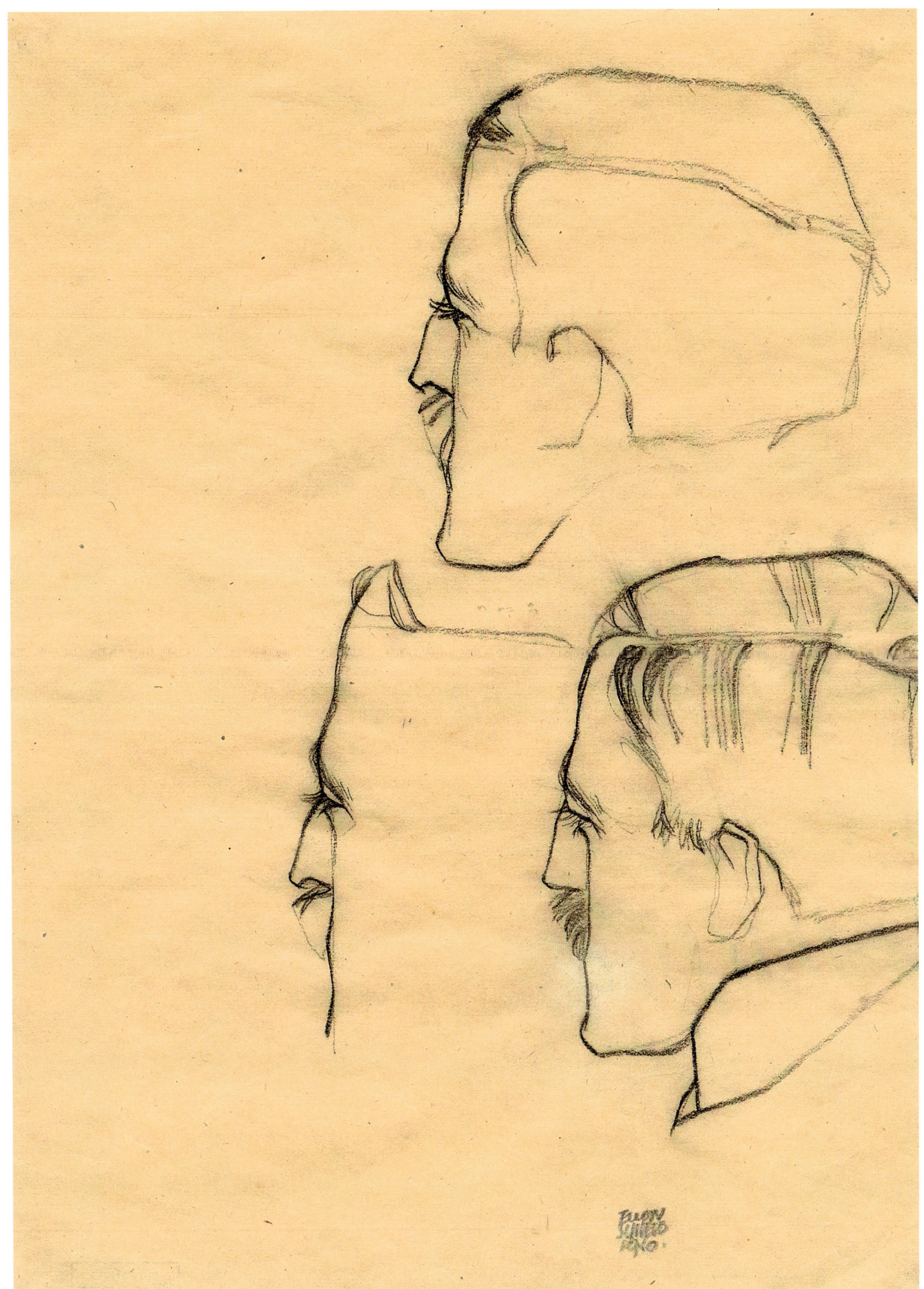

The watercolor *Dr. von Graff* [Fig. 4] reveals clearly how Schiele planned the portrait. Positioned frontally, his head is slender and angular. He has a determined gaze, slightly crooked mouth, and a sloping mustache. It shows an attractive man with nothing of the demonic quality that Schiele imbued into the oil portrait. In the painting, everything appears disjointed: the upper part of the skull curves to the left; the eyes appear bloodshot because of dark spots; his gaze is more penetrating, his chin longer, and the color of his face much darker. These distortions, coupled with the strong contrasts of light and dark, give the sitter an intensity of presence.

4. Egon Schiele, *Dr. von Graff*, 1910, watercolor and charcoal on paper, 44.1 × 30.8 cm (17 $^3/_8$ × 12 $^1/_8$ in.), Kallir D613. Private Collection

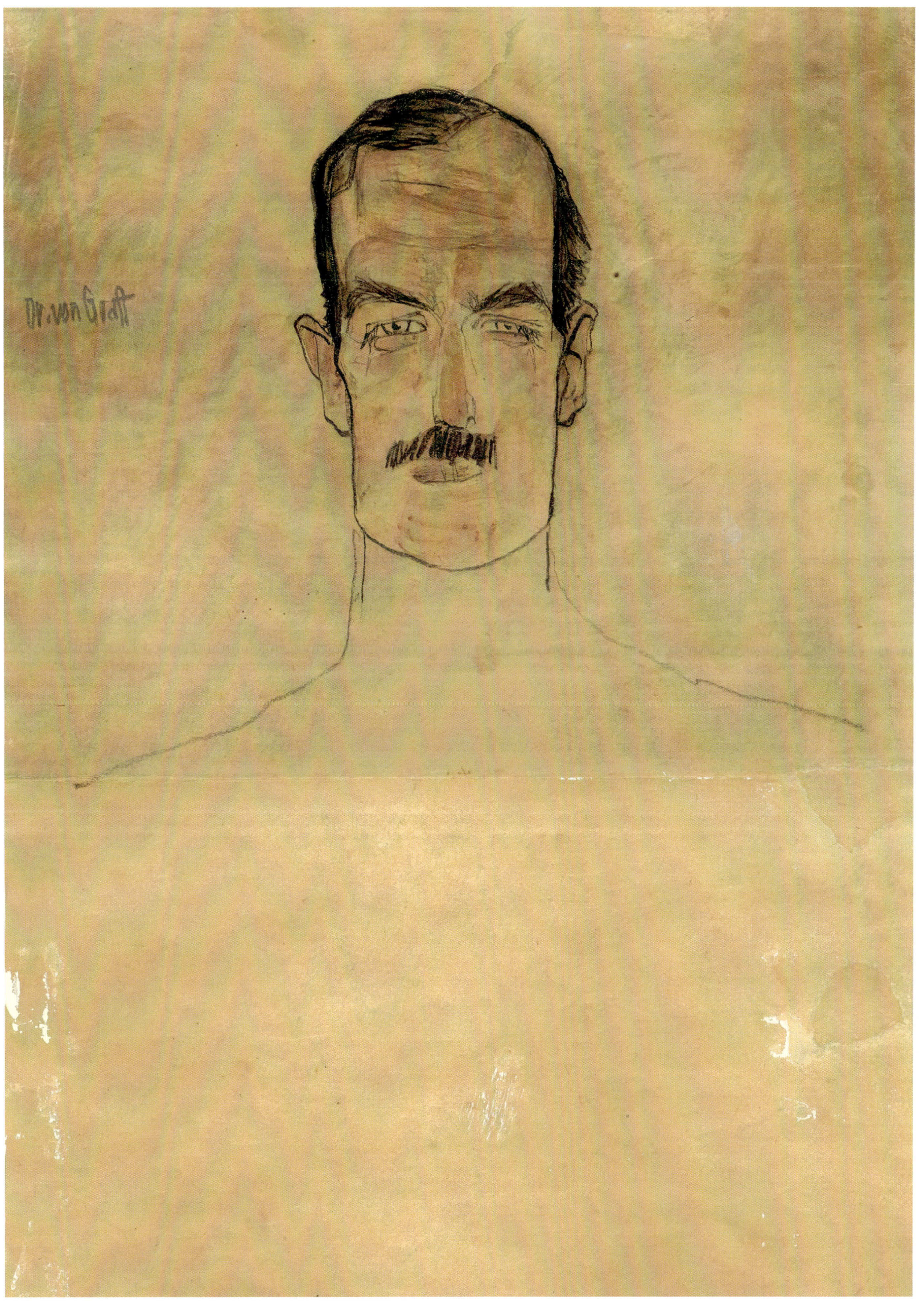

Dr. von Graff

5. Egon Schiele, 1909.
Photographer unknown.
Private Collection

6. Postcard from Erwin von Graff
to Egon Schiele with dancer Elsa
Wiesenthal on the front, March 17,
1910. The Albertina Museum,
Vienna, inv. no. ESA351r+v

The postcard reads:

17. III. 10 Lieber Herr Schiele!
Ich könnte mich Samstag
gegen 12h Mittag freimachen um
Sie zu besuchen. – Bitte Sie mir
auf jeden Fall telephonisch
sagen zu wollen ob es Ihnen passt.
(Tel. 13918 – Klinik v. Rosthorn).
Herzlichen Gruß
Dr. Graff

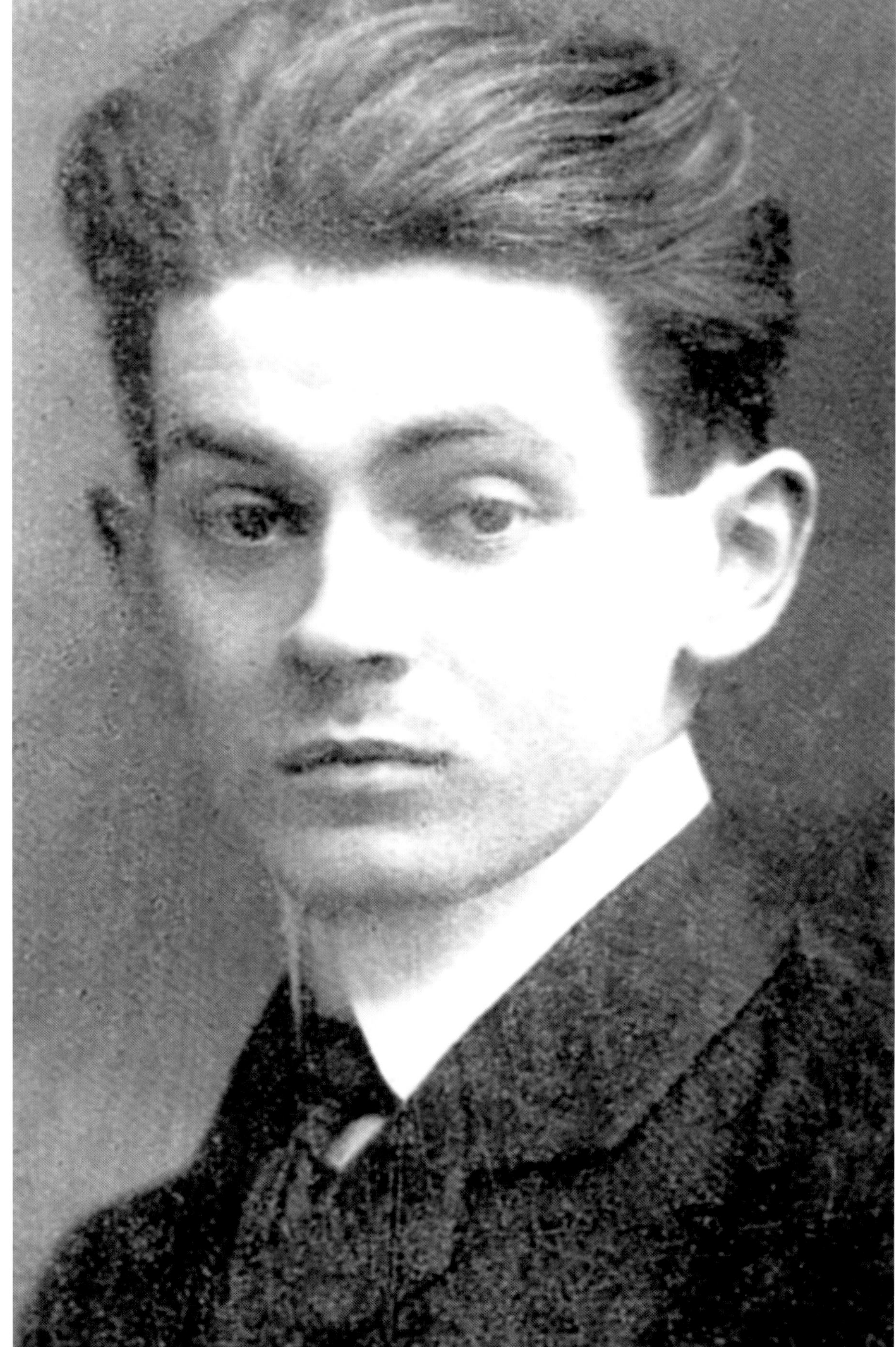

II. THE RELATIONSHIP BETWEEN EGON SCHIELE AND DR. ERWIN VON GRAFF

Meeting in 1910

In 1909, Schiele left the Akademie der bildenden Künste (Academy of the Fine Arts) in Vienna, where he had been accepted in 1906 at age sixteen because of his precocious talent [Fig. 5]. But the academic teaching, and especially his professor Christian Griepenkerl (1839–1916), became increasingly unbearable to him. After leaving, Schiele and like-minded fellow students and friends founded the Neukunstgruppe (New Art Group)—an association of artists seeking new forms of artistic expression. On December 6 of that year, the first exhibition of the Neukunstgruppe opened at the Salon Pisko, an art gallery at Lothringerstrasse 14 on Schwarzenbergplatz in Vienna. At the preview, Schiele made the acquaintance of the art critic Arthur Roessler (1877–1955),[14] who would become an important promoter of Schiele's and a collector and arranger of sales.

Roessler introduced Schiele to friends of the arts and potential collectors, such as the industrialist Carl von Reininghaus (1857–1929), who was from Graz.[15] A shared connection was felt immediately and evolved into a close friendship. Reininghaus acquired several drawings by Schiele at the beginning of 1910 and continued to be a generous patron and collector. Works by living artists were shown at weekly soirées held by Reininghaus.[16] It was presumably at one of these evening events that twenty-year-old Schiele met Graff, who, like Reininghaus, was from Graz.[17] This encounter must have been prior to mid-March 1910, because on March 17, 1910, Graff wrote the following postcard to Schiele [Fig. 6]:

> *17. III. 10 Dear Mr. Schiele!*
> *I could free myself up on Saturday*
> *around twelve noon. Please let me know*
> *by telephone in any case*
> *whether that suits you.*
> *(Tel. 13918—Rosthorn's clinic).*
>
> *Sincerely yours,*
> *Dr. Graff*

It is conceivable that Schiele had invited Graff to his studio when they met, and this was Graff's first attempt to contact him to arrange it. Schiele's studio was at Alserbachstrasse 39, while Graff worked as an auxiliary doctor at the Second University Women's Hospital at Spitalgasse 23, only around twenty minutes away by foot.

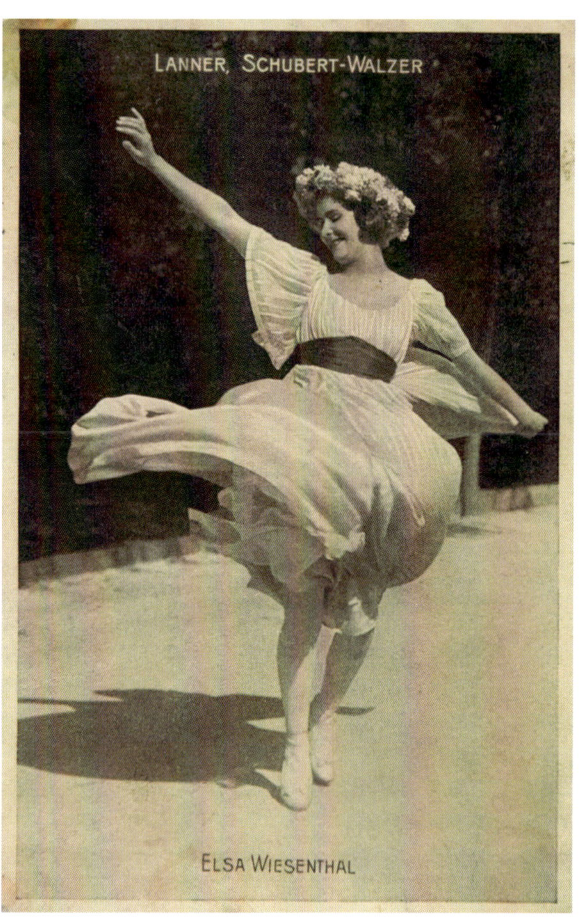

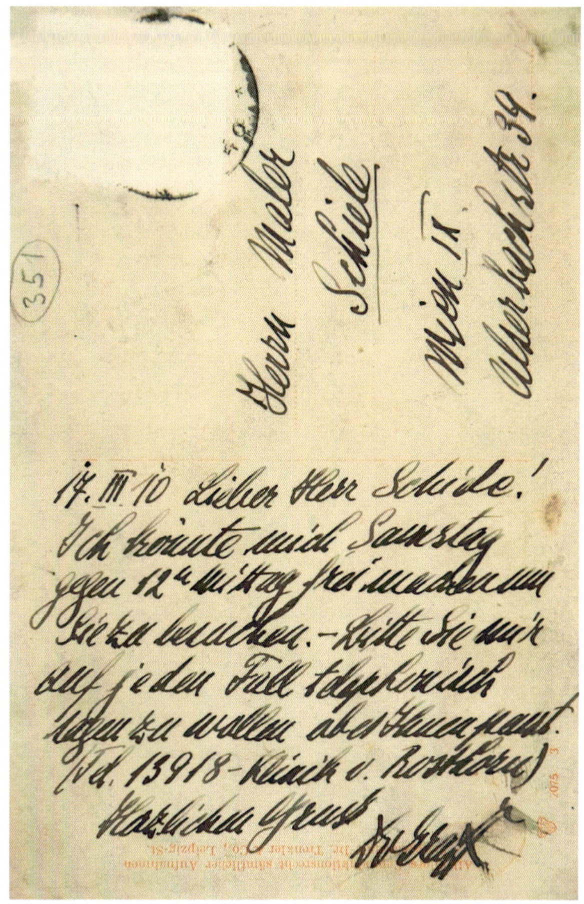

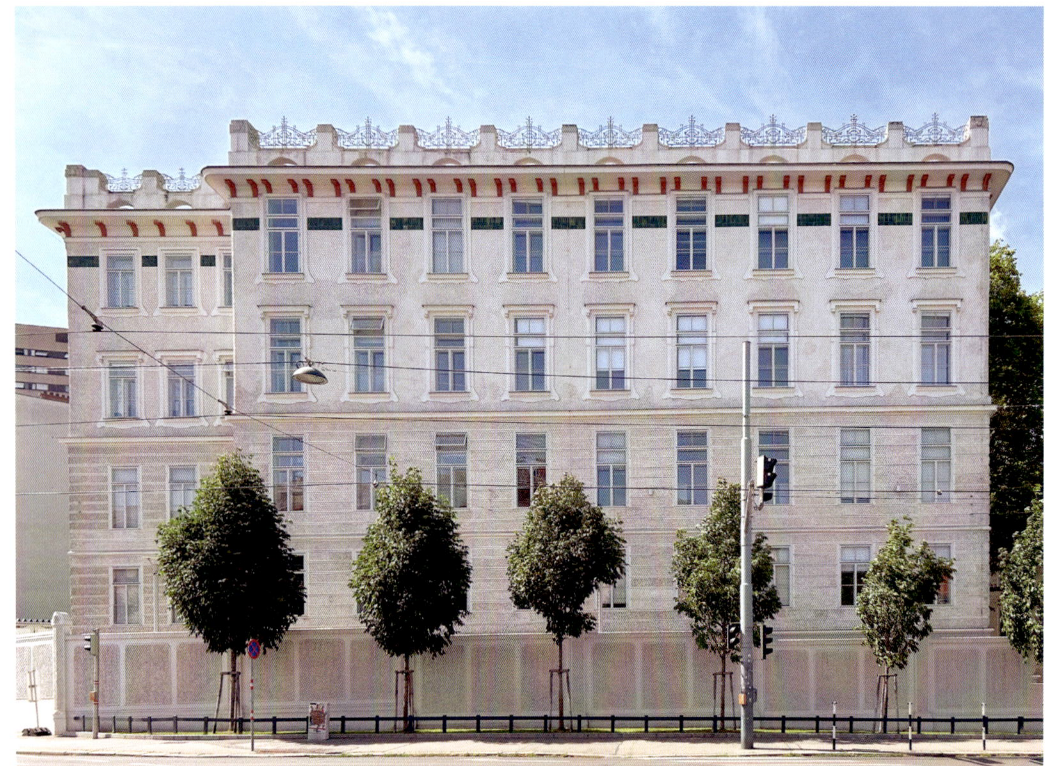

Drawing at Universitäts-Frauenklinik II

Graff and the Second University Women's Hospital [Fig. 7] played an important role for Schiele, since the doctor enabled the artist to come to the clinic to draw pregnant women and newborns. For Schiele, this was crucially important to the artistic evolution he was undergoing in early 1910. He was breaking away from his artistic role model, Gustav Klimt, and from the decorative Jugendstil, and very quickly developed his own uncommonly expressive and radical style. Schiele began to draw many self-portraits in which he tried out various roles and presented himself theatrically: unsparingly naked, ugly, twisted, grimacing, with unnatural skin color intended to reveal the inner state outwardly [Figs. 8–11]. Schiele was penniless. He had left the academy in 1909; his uncle and legal guardian Leopold Czihaczek had resigned as guardian and cut off financial support. Schiele was entirely on his own and therefore spent an excessive amount of time in front of a mirror as his own model since he could not afford to hire anyone to pose for him.

In addition to numerous self-portraits, there is a group of drawings of pregnant women and newborns that are among the first sensational examples of Schiele's new Expressionism and his interest in birth, death, and sexuality. They date from the first half of 1910, probably even from the first months.

Graff came to the Second University Women's Hospital as an auxiliary physician in 1908, just as the clinic was being established. Not until October 1, 1911, did he become assistant physician there and was able to begin his training as a gynecologist.[18]

The First and Second University Women's Hospitals were twin structures built between 1904 and 1908 to plans by Franz Berger and Bartholomäus Pickniczek, and they number among the pinnacles of functional Jugendstil architecture in Vienna. Behind their façades was the *non plus ultra* of modern medicine at the time.[19] With the move into the new clinics, the maternity ward in the old General Hospital was closed. Surgical medicine was given high priority in the new clinics, which was established well into the twentieth century with the treatment options offered by oncology. In 1910, obstetrics was merely a discipline within gynecology.[20] Most births at the time still took place at home with assistance from midwives.

Various questions remain unanswered about where Schiele's drawings were made. Which rooms in the clinic should be considered possibilities? How was it possible that a young auxiliary doctor like Graff could get permission or even provide Schiele with access to the clinic without having received approval? Was it done with the understanding of the patients? What sources indicate that the drawings were done in the clinic?

It was Comini who first pointed out in 1974 that Schiele received permission from Graff to draw in his clinic, specifically pregnant women, newborns, stillbirths, and small sick girls. Comini also wrote that Graff had rejected showing these drawings to his sister-in-law because they were not suitable for women's eyes.[21] As sources for her text on the portrait of Graff, Comini cited personal interviews with Schiele's sister-in-law, Adele Harms, on January 24, 1967, and with the writer Max Mell (1882–1971) on February 26, 1967.[22] Christian M. Nebehay took this information in 1979 and stated that Schiele "drew a great deal in the Universitäts-Frauenklinik in 1910."[23] There are neither tape recordings nor written notes from the interviews that Comini conducted, as she has assured me. The extant tape recordings of conversations with Gerti and Melanie Schiele, as well as Adele Harms, were made later.

There are various possible rooms in the clinic where Schiele could have sketched. The gynecologist Anton Schaller (1933–2018) was the first to consider this question in 2007. He himself had begun training at the Second University Women's Hospital in 1964 and knew the facilities well. Schaller observed "that a clinical auxiliary doctor could grant more or less official permission to an artist friend to draw nudes in the woman's clinic at the university seems prima facie more than dubious."[24] But when searching for the circumstances that could have made it possible, he stumbled across a few notable facts. The head of the clinic at the time, Alfons von Rosthorn (1857–1909), died unexpectedly and suddenly on August 9, 1909. His first assistant, Fritz Kermauner (1872–1931), who was thirty-seven-years-old at the time, was made interim director of the clinic. Not until March 16, 1910, was his successor, Ernst Wertheim (1864–1920), appointed to the board (later succeeded by Kermauner in 1921). According to Schaller, months of uneasiness surely passed in the meantime, and presumably people had other worries than officially facilitating access for an artist. If we assume that Schiele was drawing in the clinic during this period, it must have been before mid-March 1910. But Schaller also thought it possible that Wertheim, who was considered very amenable to the arts, could have granted permission under certain conditions. There may have been personal reasons for this as well. Graff's father, Ludwig von Graff, was a professor for many years at the Universität Graz, where Wertheim's father also had had a chair. Schaller likewise noted the possible influence of Reininghaus, and in whose apartment Graff and Schiele had met.[25] In that case, drawings could have been done after mid-March 1910.

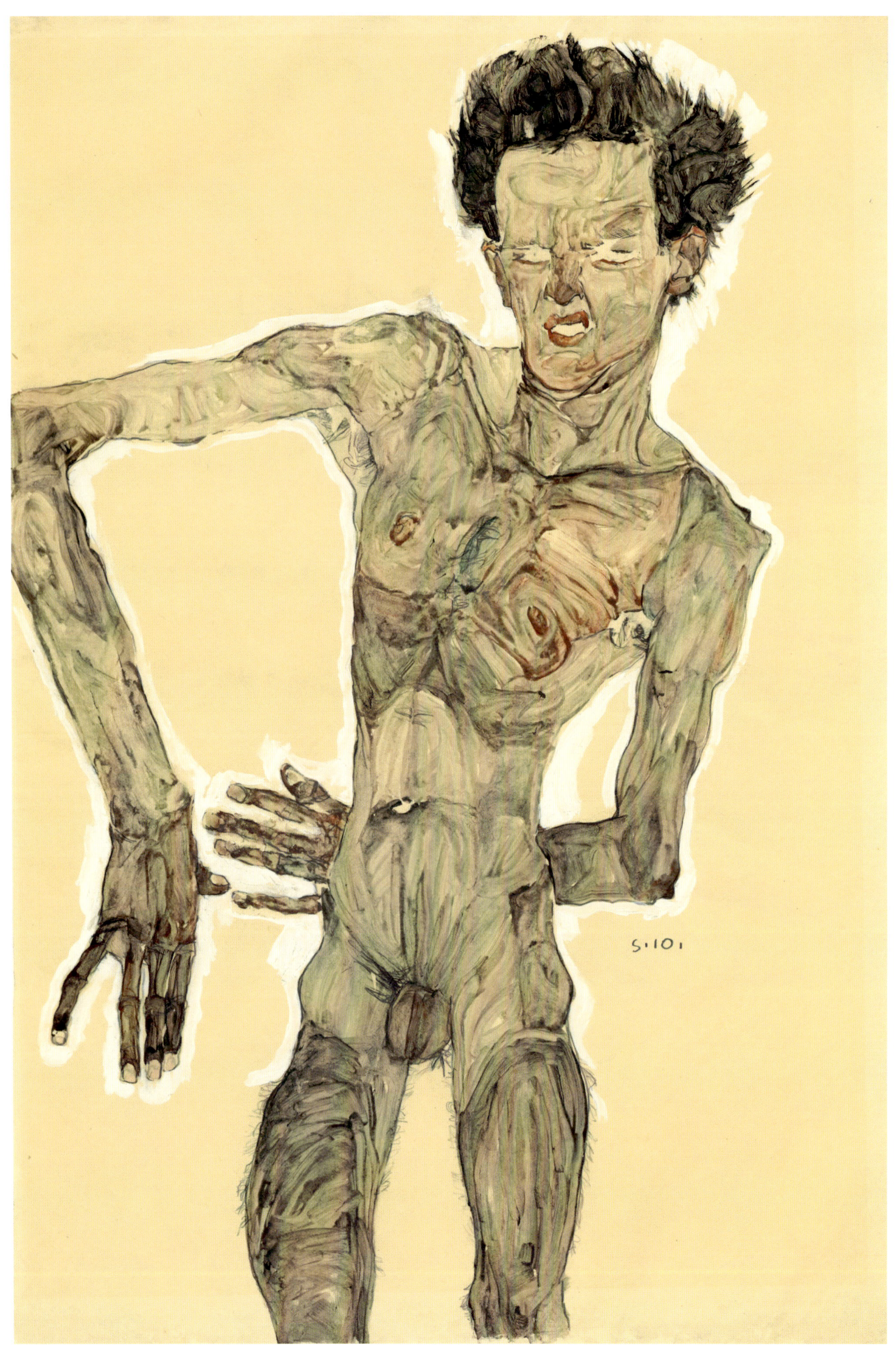

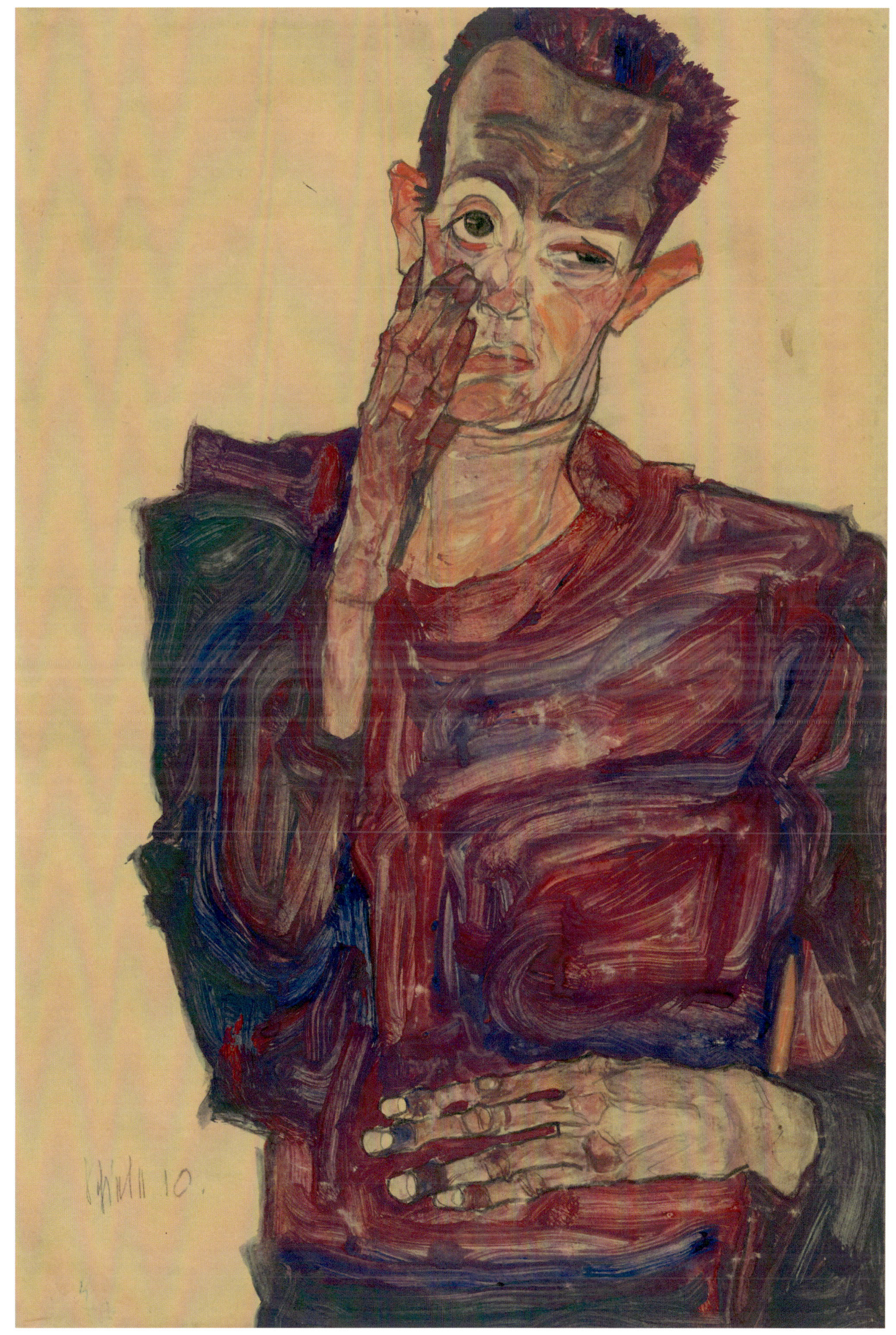

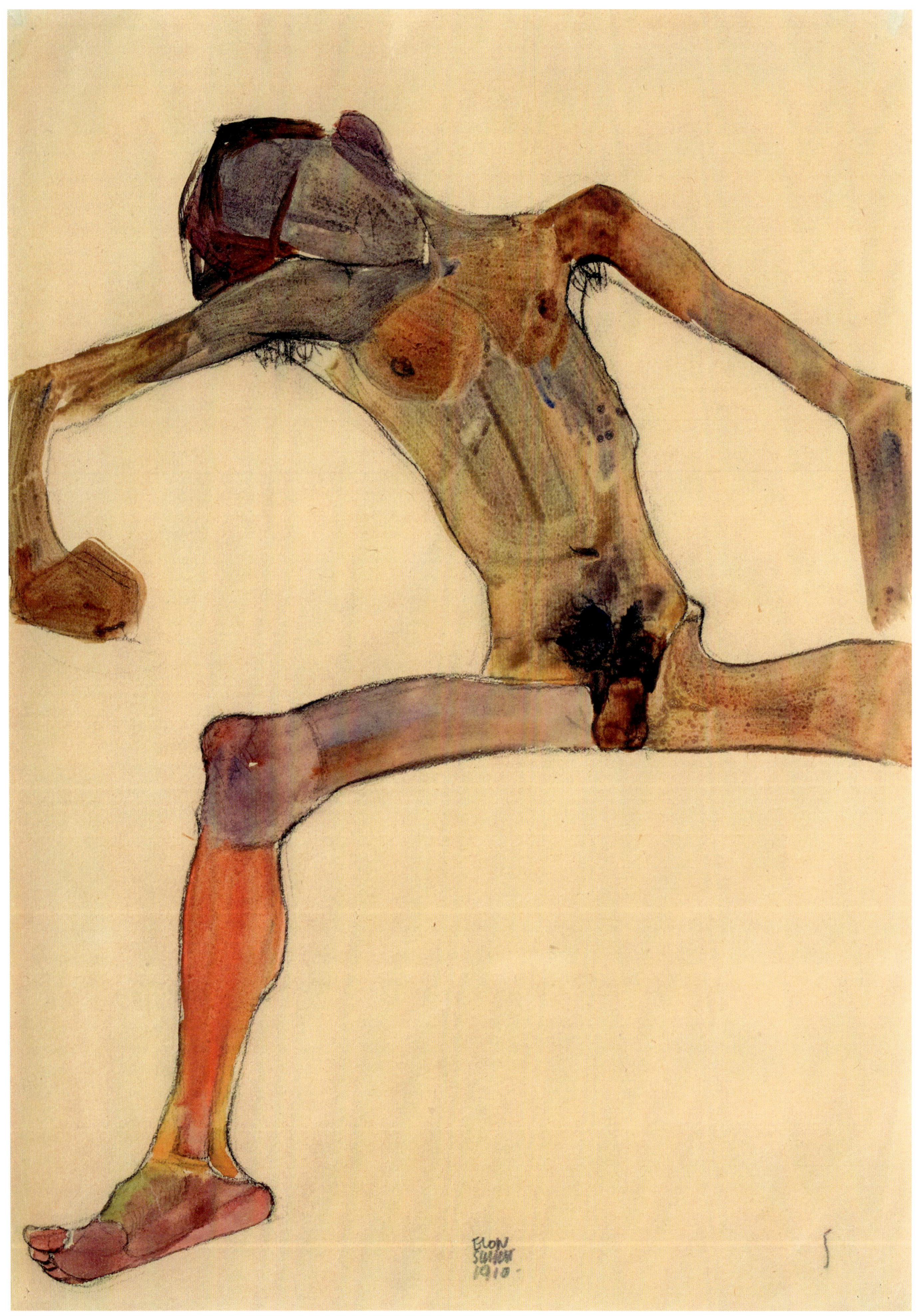
EGON
SCHIELE
1910.

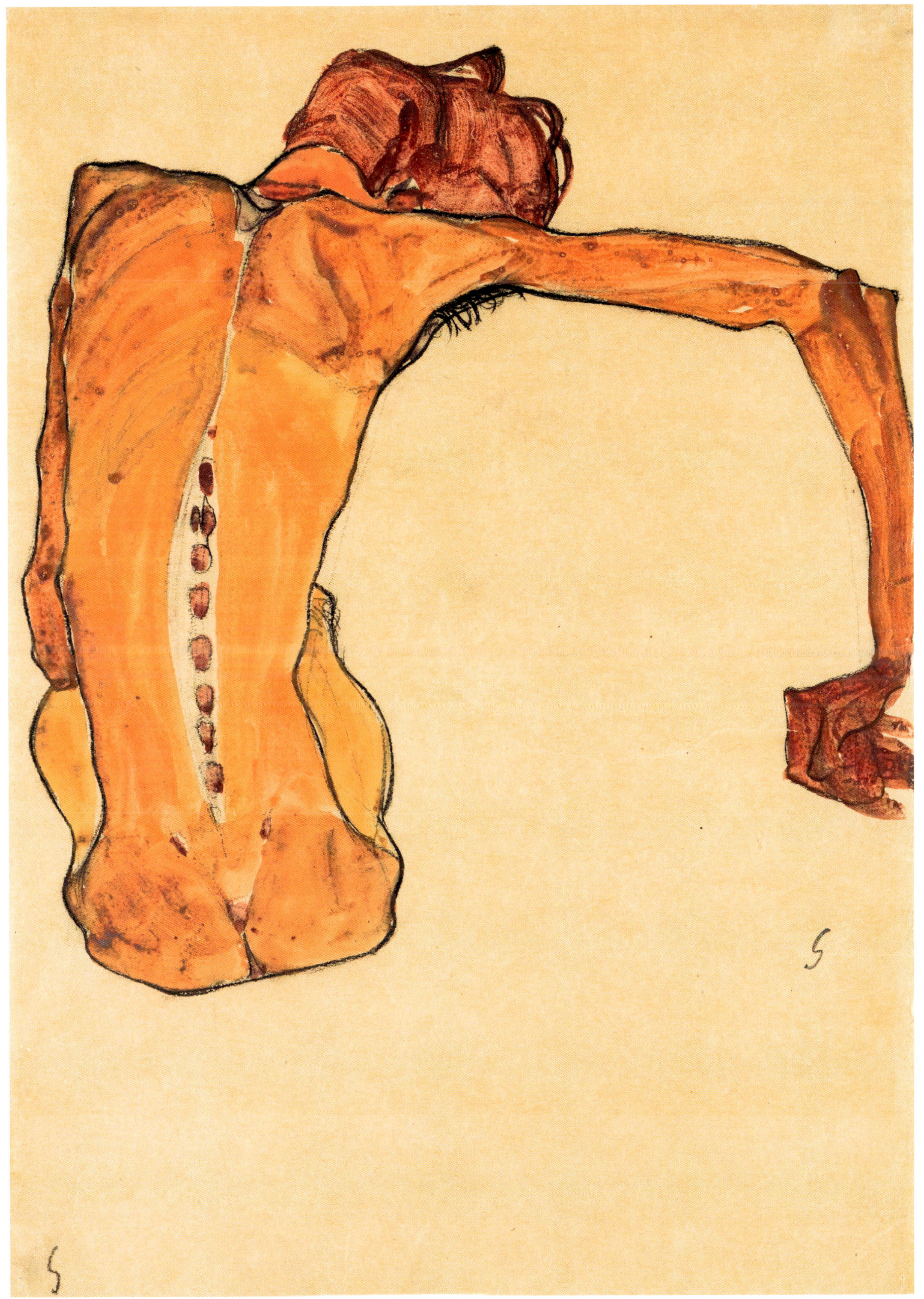

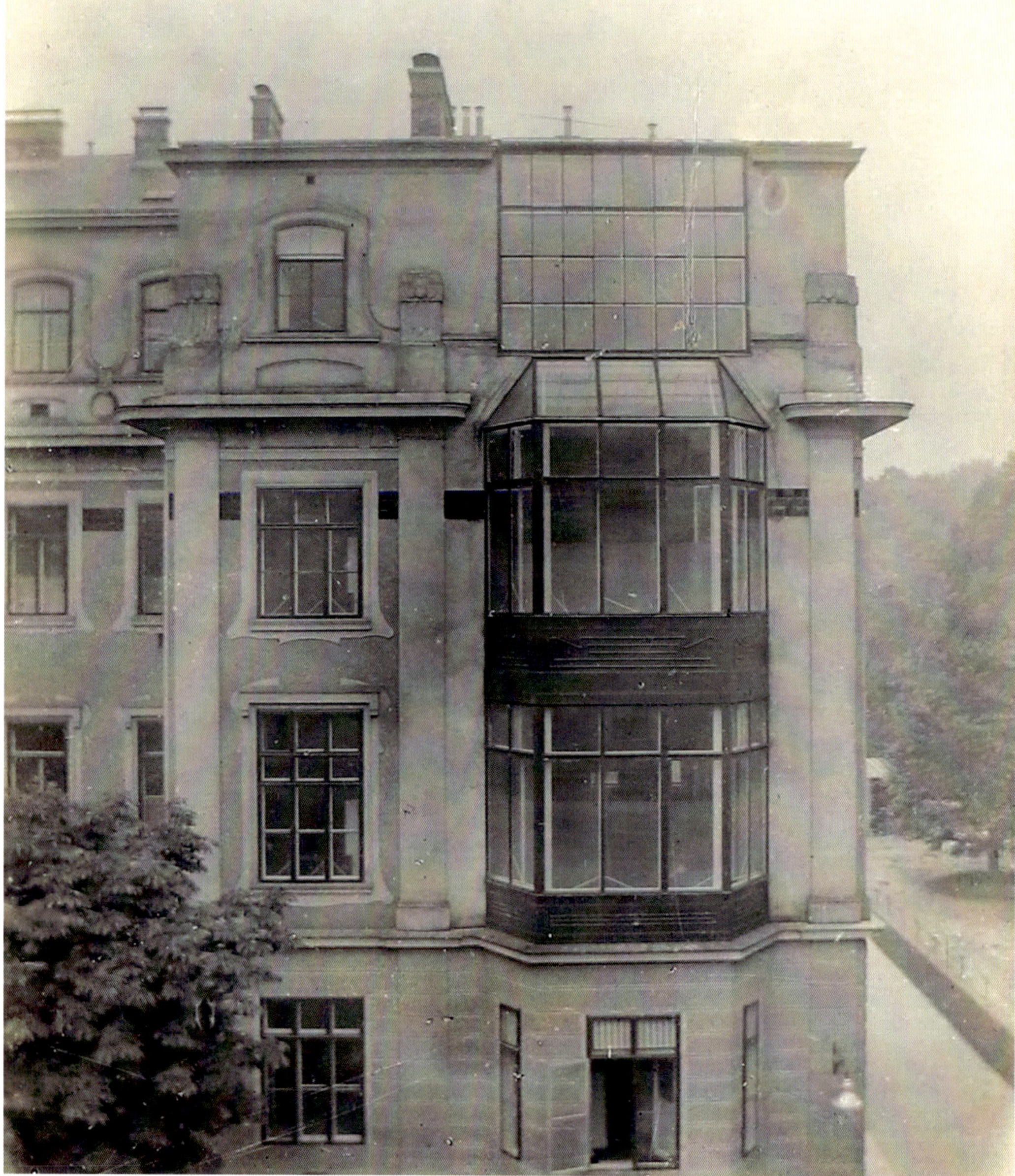

The clinic had its own studio [Fig. 12] located above the two operating theaters.[26] Both the studio and the operating rooms had large windows facing north to provide the necessary daylight. The room was a photographic studio for medical documentation and was somewhat isolated from everyday life in the clinic. It is not known how it was furnished.[27] The studio could be reached directly through a private entrance on the north side of the clinic and via a stairwell without having to pass through the gynecology and obstetrics wards.[28] Graff would have had to speak to the patients to ascertain if they were willing to model (in exchange for payment?) and then send them to the studio or take them himself.

What would have been the situation in an examination room? The presence of a twenty-year-old artist drawing during a gynecological examination is difficult to imagine—even if there was presumably less concern about patients' rights at the time compared to today—unless Schiele had worn a doctor's coat, and the women believed he was one of the medical personnel and the drawings were for medical purposes. It is worth underscoring, however, that Graff was not even an assistant physician yet. Would he even have been permitted to examine a patient alone? And how quickly would Schiele have been able to draw? During an examination lasting around ten to fifteen minutes, he would presumably have had enough time to make sketches quickly that he could then color in the studio.

The clinic also had a lecture hall in which women and their clinical pictures were presented to physicians and medical students. There were not yet sufficient photographs for study purposes. Could Schiele have mingled with the students inconspicuously in order to work? That does not seem impossible, but it would not have gone unnoticed or unremarked if he did draw. Moreover, the perspectives of the known drawings do not correspond to an elevated position in a lecture hall. The rows of seats were arranged to rise steeply. Schiele's drawings in fact show a very close and personal interaction between artist and model.

The patients usually stayed in large confinement chambers and sickbays, which at the time was considered better for adequate lighting and abundant ventilation. It also meant that fewer attendants were needed. Nevertheless, there were also smaller rooms with two to ten beds where married maternity patients could be grouped so they could receive visits from their family members, usually their husbands—which was not permitted in the large, general sickbays.[29] The large sickbays can therefore be ruled out as the site for Schiele's drawings, and the small ones presumably as well, since they would have been occupied only by married women. There were, however, so-called isolation rooms for women suffering from illnesses such as tuberculosis, syphilis, eclampsia, scabies, and so on, were awakening from narcosis, or had undergone difficult surgeries.[30] If one of these rooms had been empty, Schiele could have used it. It would by no means have gone unnoticed, however. In this scenario, Graff must have obtained permission in some form.

That is also true for the situation in a delivery room. It is inconceivable that Schiele would have been granted access to a delivery room, and the result would have been completely different drawings if he had been.

If one considers other areas where the drawings could have been made, leaving the clinic building aside, there are places that would have been less problematic for Graff and Schiele. Looking at the drawings more closely, it is noticeable that the pregnant women do not adopt positions that would be typical for a gynecological examination. Only in the case of two or three drawings, one can imagine an examination chair on which the models sat or reclined. It seems more likely, however, that they were sitting on armchairs or lying relaxed on a sofa. For instance, in the drawings of women with spread legs, they are seated and not in a position that would make a gynecological examination possible.

The drawings also reveal a latent sexual connotation. Schiele neither adopts the perspective of the gynecologist nor shows an examination situation but rather depicts pregnant women as alluring with stockings pulled down, opened blouses, or completely naked [Figs. 22–23]. Usually there is also direct, intense eye contact between model and artist, which would not have been the case in an examination room in the presence of a doctor. Instead, one has the impression that the model and artist were alone.

How could this have been arranged? Graff could have approached patients and arranged separate appointments for Schiele. Two more places are possible for that. For example, he could have arranged for a visit to Schiele's studio. Alternatively, Graff's apartment at Höfergasse 18 would also have been possible, and it was just five minutes by foot from the clinic, but there his wife would have been present—an unlikely scenario. In 1910, Graff did not yet have a private practice.

Graff most certainly spoke to women from lower social classes, whom he probably even paid to model for Schiele. The artist could have returned the favor by giving Graff drawings, which is suggested by the fact that the doctor owned at least eight Schiele drawings from 1910.

All these considerations must remain speculation because neither Graff nor Schiele ever said or wrote anything about the circumstances of a "collaboration."

What interested Schiele about pregnant women and newborns? In early 1910, he was definitively a searcher who felt something great inside himself that would cause a big change in his art. When he met Graff and heard that he worked in a women's clinic, it must have fascinated him extraordinarily. How else, if not through Graff, could Schiele have gained access to pregnant women and newborns? It was the beginning of Schiele's lifelong grappling with the existential themes of life: love, sexuality, birth, motherhood, illness, and death [Fig. 13]. He would have only eight years to explore such topics.

There are twelve drawings of pregnant women whose origins have been ascribed to the clinic.[31] The women are usually seated; as always, Schiele drew only the bodies of the women, typically fragmented, with nothing to indicate their location. *Pregnant Woman* [Fig. 14] shows a seated woman in a late stage of pregnancy who has propped her left and right arms in a very relaxed way on an unseen sofa backrest and allows her forearms to dangle. Her head is tilted slightly to the side and she smiles quietly. She wears black stockings that extend above the knee. Schiele omitted her hands and feet. Although Schiele drew his largest series of pregnant women in 1910, the theme remained of interest to him in later years as well, as evidenced by *Kneeling Pregnant Nude* [Fig. 15].

There are also several drawings of newborns produced in the context of Dr. von Graff and the clinic, such as *Newborn Baby* [Figs. 16–17]. Here, too, the question arises where they were drawn. Schiele's presence in the delivery room can be ruled out. After birth, all the newborns were kept together in the neonatal ward and were brought to the mothers only for breastfeeding. It was certainly not possible for Schiele to access the neonatal ward either. Physicians assured me that the drawings are of skinny newborns who probably had malnourished mothers and who are only a few days old. That analysis is evident from the large reddish scrotum of one. This argues for Schiele somehow having had an opportunity to draw in the clinic.

The drawings show babies who appear to have been placed naked on a pad only briefly for an examination. All the known drawings are of living children, as is clear from the tension in their bodies and their raised arms. Neither the pregnant women nor the newborns show any signs of illness, but they seem undernourished. Schiele's interest here was not in pathological mental or physical states but in the mystery of incipient and newborn life.

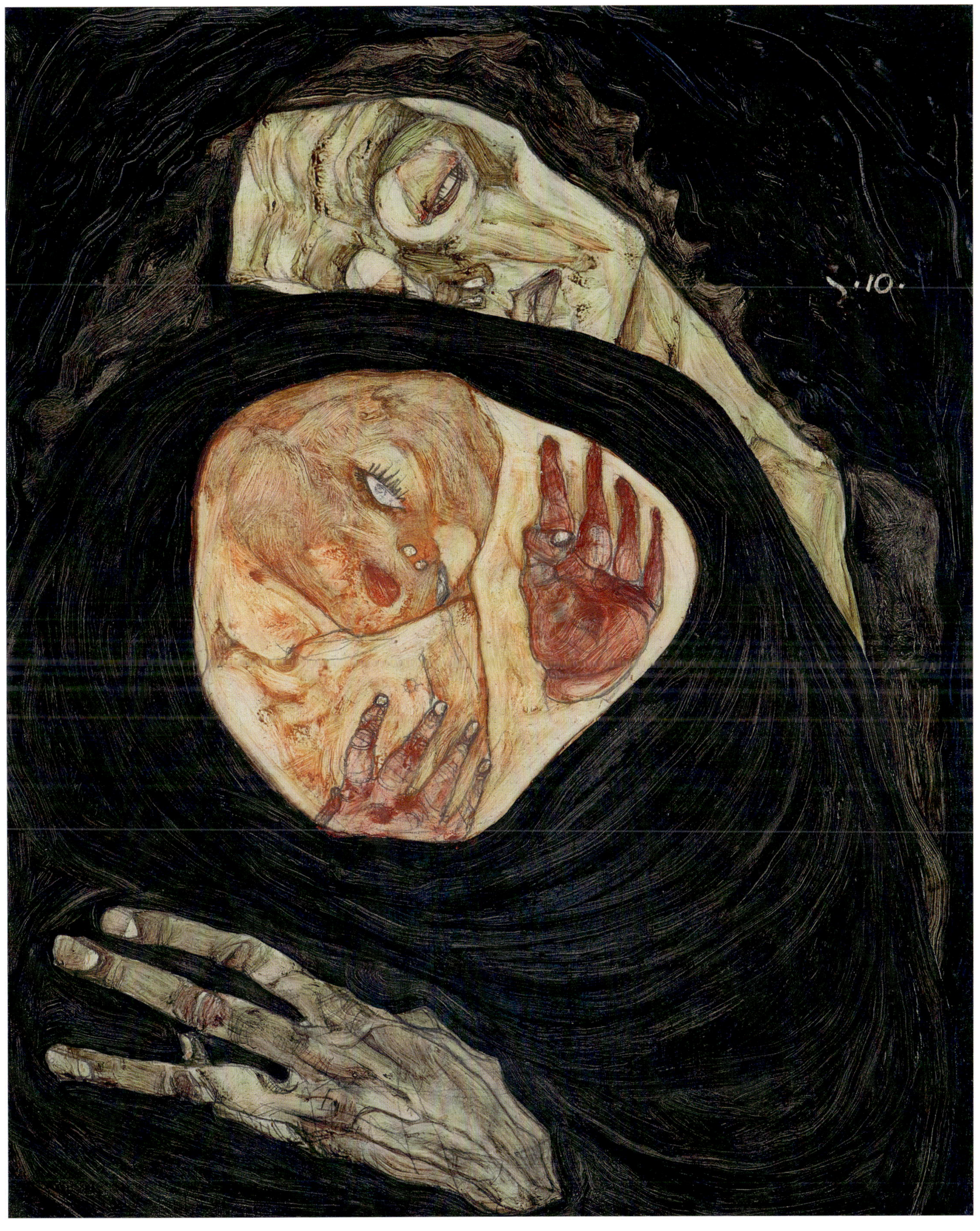

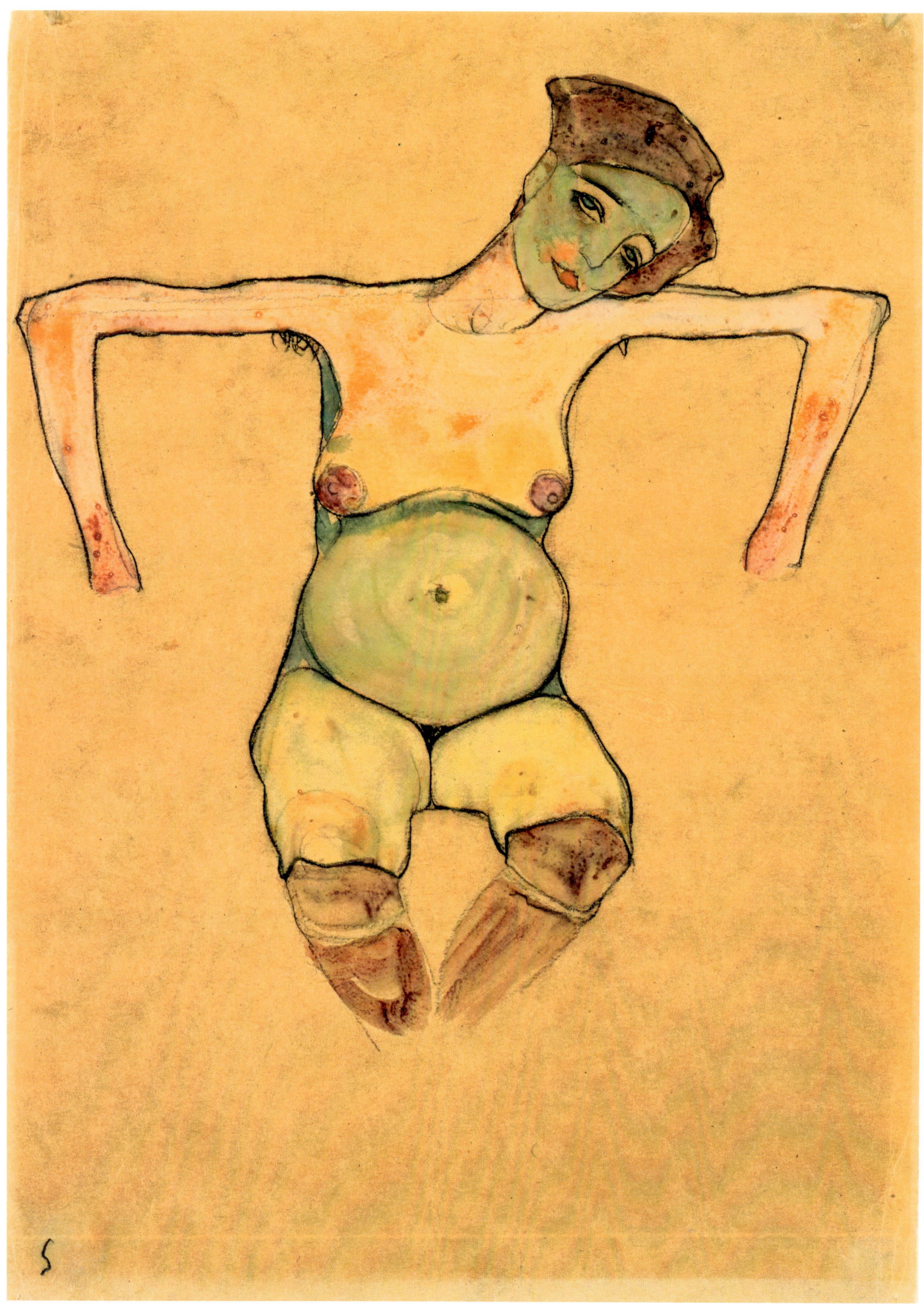

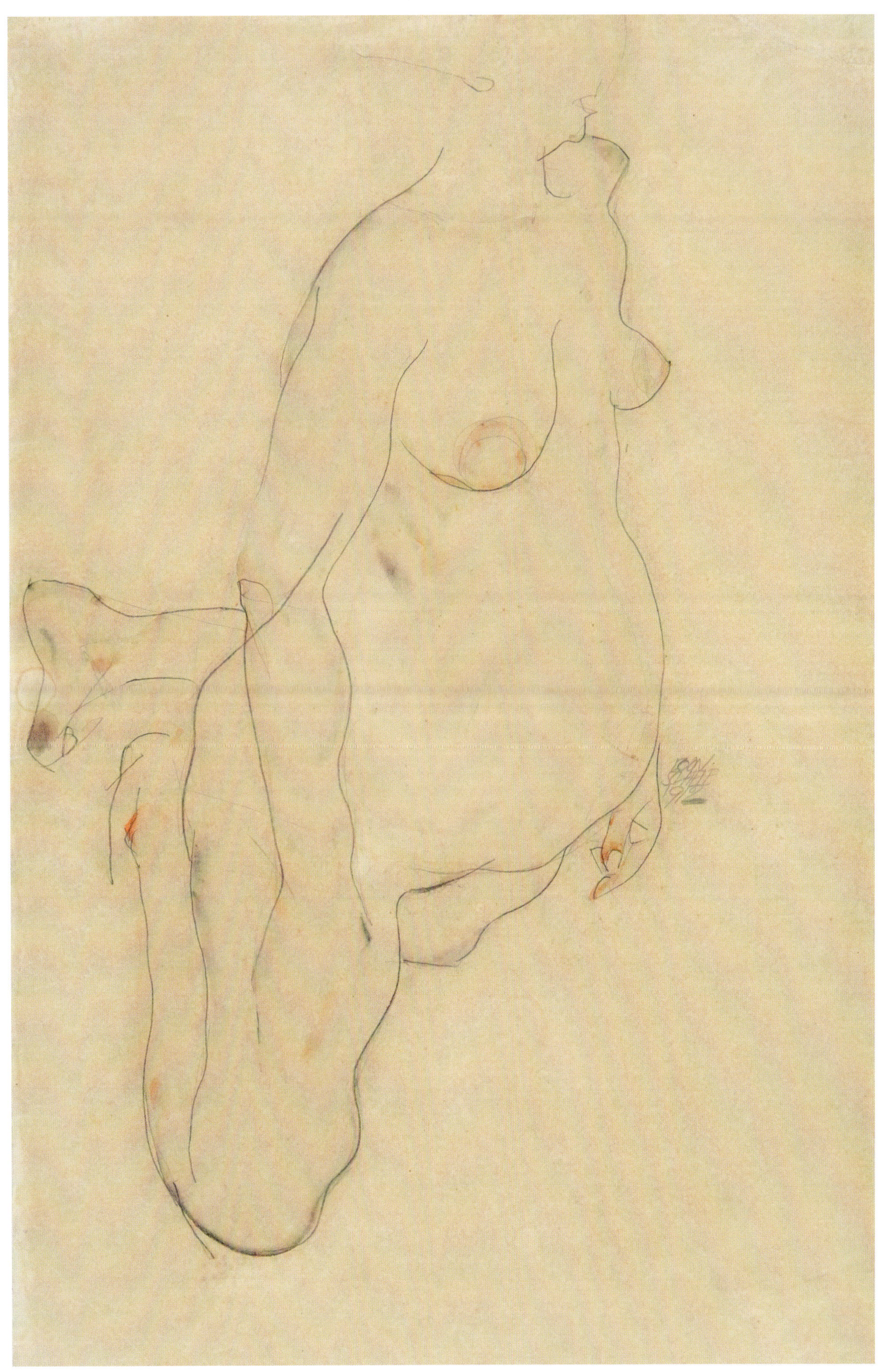

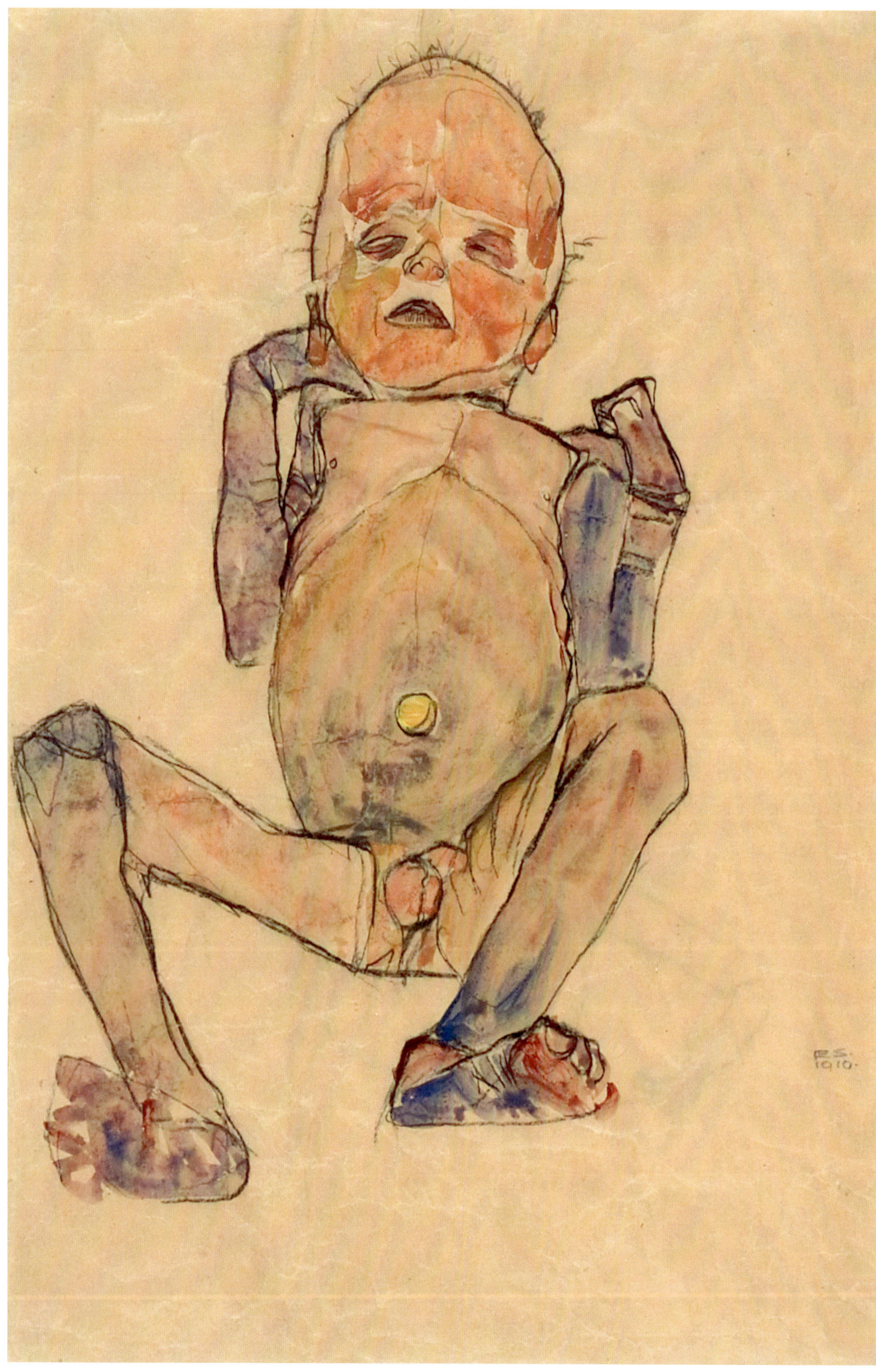

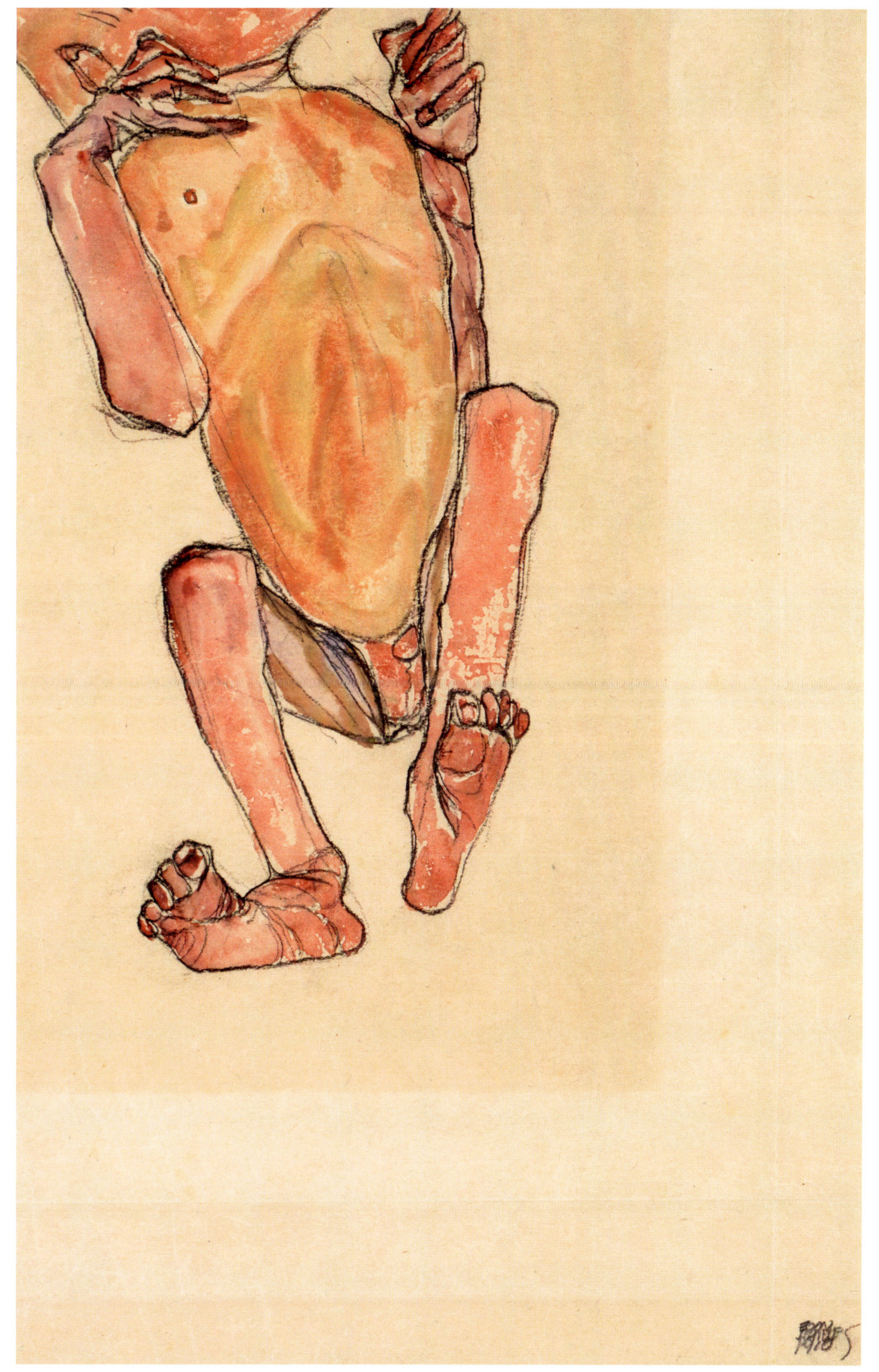

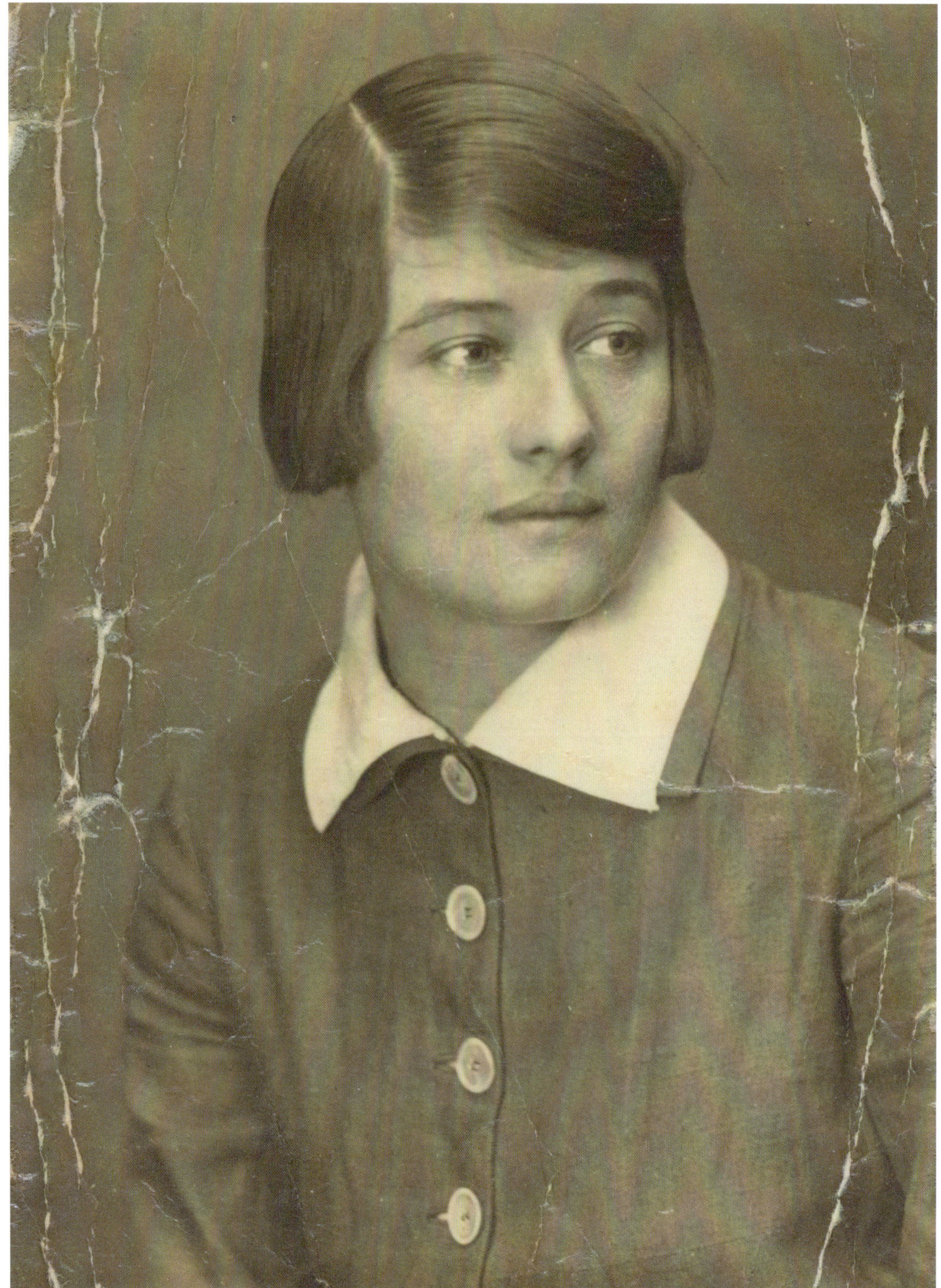

18. Liliana Amon, 1920.
Literary Archive of the
Austrian National Library,
ÖLA 227/L4

In a letter of May 18, 1910 [Fig. 19], from Graff to Schiele, he mentions a patient "L.A." who had a relationship with the artist. For more than a hundred years, no one knew who was behind those initials, but now we know that it was Liliana Amon (also known as Bibiana) [Fig. 18].[32]

Vienna, 18 May 1910.

Dear Schiele!

Sincere thanks for your letter. Yesterday, L. A. came to the clinic and was admitted. She is occupying a room with a second woman and appears to be very unhappy about your infidelity. It is presumably better that way for you and her. The good weather certainly benefited your works, which pleases me. Please give my best regards to Osen and let me know the date of your return again. I liked Taschner very much.[33] Stella not so much.[34] Your work looked much better in the studio. In general, the whole exhibition did not fit in the Prater.[35] Most of the works by artists from the Künstlerhaus should rather have been hung in the individual hunting pavilions and restaurants.[36]

Sincerely yours,

Graff

Liliana Amon was born Maria Liliana Brandstetter on June 23, 1892, at Blumauerstrasse 10 in Linz, as the illegitimate daughter of Zäzilia Brandstetter and Josef Amon. Their son Albert had been born a year earlier. The parents did not marry until five years later, on June 19, 1897, in Linz, where the birth was legitimized and Liliana got the last name Amon.

Amon moved to Vienna at the age of sixteen at the latest. From 1908 onward, she was registered in Vienna at various addresses. It was not until the end of 1909 or early 1910 that she met Schiele, and she wrote a brief chapter about their meeting in her autobiographical roman à clef, *Barrières*, which she published in Paris in 1939 under the name Marie Amon.[37] She is represented by the character Anna in the book, who describes the history of her relationship with Schiele as follows:

She met Egon Sch… on the terrace of a famous artists' café near the Secession.[38] He was twenty, with black, curly hair, the ardent eyes of a fanatic, the triangular face of a small boy, and very bad teeth. He invited her to his studio on Alserstrasse, opened the door, and said: "Don't be afraid, my dear child."

This warning was not unwarranted. What was hanging on the walls seemed more than spooky to Anna, and she almost ran off.

"You cannot understand yet, but I will explain everything to you in time." And he looked at her with his burning black eyes. Gently, he helped her out of her coat, took her beret, and said, "You are truly a beautiful girl."

Almost all the paintings were of naked people with proportional limbs but not one of them had normal skin.

"That can't be! These people have no skin." Anna began to laugh. "Do you know what that reminds me of? A skinned hare." That judgment wasn't so dumb. Egon saw the world in a special way; he saw it, so to speak, under the skin, and painted it green, blue, and red.

And now the positions: women with legs spread, thrusting their genitals at the viewer. Anna stared, stared again, and suddenly it no longer seemed so comical to her; she no longer saw the colors but the brilliant, incredibly true reproduction of the body, and she suddenly exclaimed: "Yes, yes, that's how we are, that's how we squat down, it's true, exactly like that."

Egon S…, who was bound to become famous and died young, never forgot this sentence. Later he said to his wife: "After she had overcome her initial dread, this girl, so beautiful but so stupid, made such childish remarks that I regretted having brought her. Suddenly she said, all dream and almost absentmindedly: 'Yes, yes, that's how we are, exactly like that.' This child carried more weight than all the flattering of my work I heard later, because suddenly I knew I was on the path to truth."

The following morning, Anna had boiled potatoes and a little milk for breakfast with Egon—he had no money at the time—and decided to move in with him. Egon was happy, very cheerful, and took pleasure in his work because she had promised to pose for him.

Anna returned to Karlsstrasse, opened her scapular, took out some money, and closed it again, almost empty. She took her few belongings in the small cardboard suitcase and said goodbye to the proprietor of the room. From now on, she would be staying with a friend.

Anna was one month pregnant by a man whose name she didn't know and whom she never saw again. He had persuaded her to come with him to the hotel; unfortunately, he had lost his key. After getting everything he wanted from her, he said tenderly, "Wait for me a moment, my dear, I'm going to call a friend of mine. I may have left my key at his place." Anna waited in the hotel room until she realized he wasn't coming back.

With a warm blanket and a small pillow that she bought on the way—she had been so cold the night before—she moved in with Egon S... with the certainty that she was now beginning a life in the spirit of Dostoevsky.[39]

Anna vomited after every breakfast, which she attributed to the morning potatoes to which Egon remained faithful. As he claimed, it was the only food that stayed in the stomach for a long time, so

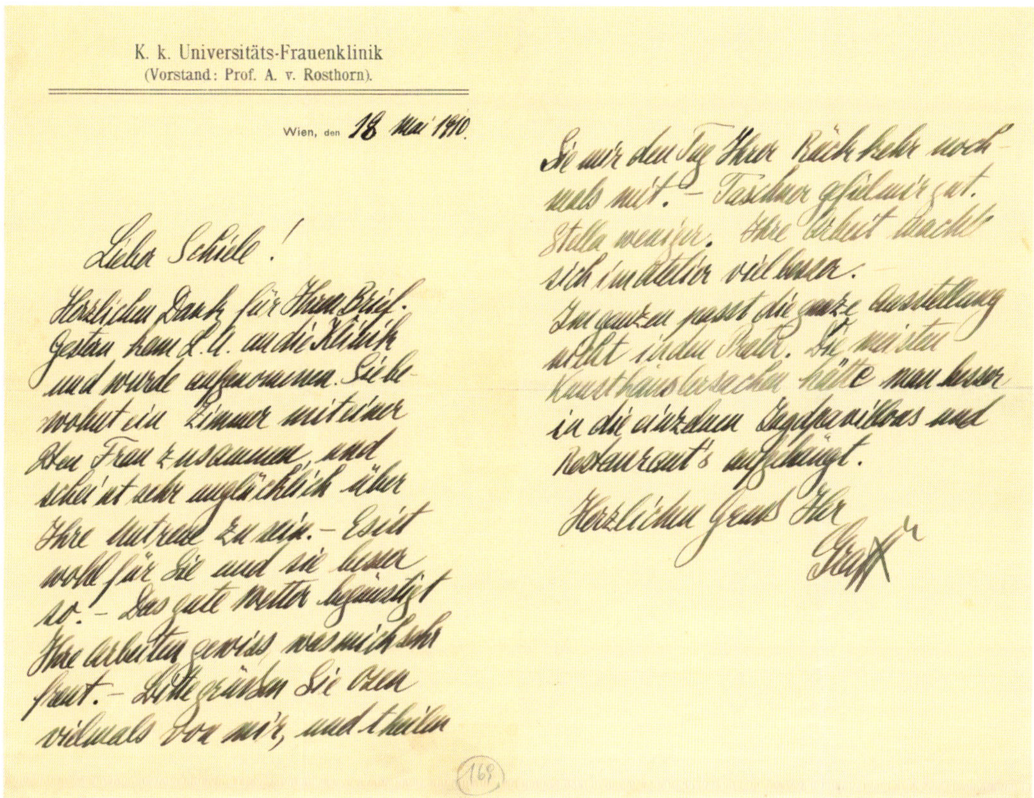

that he would not be distracted by hunger while working. Anna began to have a serious doubt, and when her period did not come, she went to see a doctor.

"No, my dear child, you are not sick; your stomach is fine, but you are pregnant."

Far from weeping or despairing, as the doctor had feared, she asked him with a laugh how much she owed him then for advice on her condition and cheerfully left the examination room.

Back at the studio, she said to Egon, "I went to see the doctor. I'm in good health, but I'm pregnant. It wasn't you. It was a man I don't know, whose name I don't even know. It happened about six weeks ago. It's unfortunate, but what can we do? Tell me honestly, do you want to keep me? If not, I'll leave," and she looked at him questioningly.

"You've gotten yourself into a fine mess; of course you will stay here. We still have time ahead of us. We'll find a way somehow."

It never occurred to either of them, not even remotely, to do anything to prevent it. Anna posed sitting, reclining, standing, in every possible position, sometimes so weakened by hunger and fatigue that everything went black before her eyes and she collapsed like an empty sack. Egon, who was truly working like a madman, only came to his senses when he heard the "boom" of her body falling.

He tenderly reproached her for not letting him know that she couldn't take it anymore, but he got angry when she talked about resting. "Just when I was getting going, she gives up." He would often toss his paintbrush and be in a foul mood all day, cursing his miserable job, or simply go out for a walk. Anna was so malnourished—the child drained all the strength from her body—that she often felt as if she were being eaten alive. At the last moment, rescue came. Egon S... had a friend, a patron, Dr. Graf [sic],[40] who had lived abroad for quite some time and had just returned. Thanks to him, Anna was able to give birth to her child in humane conditions. He believed wholeheartedly in Egon's future and was the only one at the time who recognized his genius. He took them both under his wing, paid Anna's hospital bills so that she would not be used as a guinea pig for gyne-cology students, as was customary, and gave her money to buy the things the child needed. Anna acknowledged that she could not move into Egon's studio with the child. Dr. Graf talked to her at length and said that Egon was too young to take on the responsibility of a family life. As an artist, he had to remain free, otherwise he would come to nothing. She had to understand that. He, Dr. Graf, wanted to give Egon enough money to go to Italy and France, which was necessary for his artistic development, etc.

It was a very hard blow for Anna. Although she accepted it all, she couldn't help feeling bitter at the thought that Egon had dropped her so easily.

He came to the clinic several more times, made a few drawings of the newborn in blue and red, wished her good luck, and left. Anna and her child were placed in a mother-and-child protection facility. She stayed there for three months, learning shorthand and typing during the day. The appointed guardian gave the child to a wet nurse and found Anna a job in an office.[41]

If Schiele met Amon when she was approximately in the seventh week of pregnancy, and her child was born after forty weeks of pregnancy on August 9, 1910, they must have met in mid-December 1909. She moved in with him immediately. If Schiele did in fact draw the pregnant women that Graff arranged for him in his studio, that means that the women were not alone with him but in the company of Amon, another pregnant woman at the start of her pregnancy. It is certain that Amon also modeled for Schiele but not in the late stages of pregnancy, because they were separated by mid-May at the latest. It has not yet been investigated which of Schiele's drawings depict Amon. *Schiele, Drawing a Nude Model in Front of a Mirror* [Fig. 20] could very well be one of them. One model Schiele drew often in 1910 is seen in *Seated Female Nude with Black Stockings* [Fig. 21]. She too should be considered possibly Amon. It is also interesting that Graff possessed a drawing of the model (*Semi-Reclining Nude Girl*, 1910, Kallir D574).

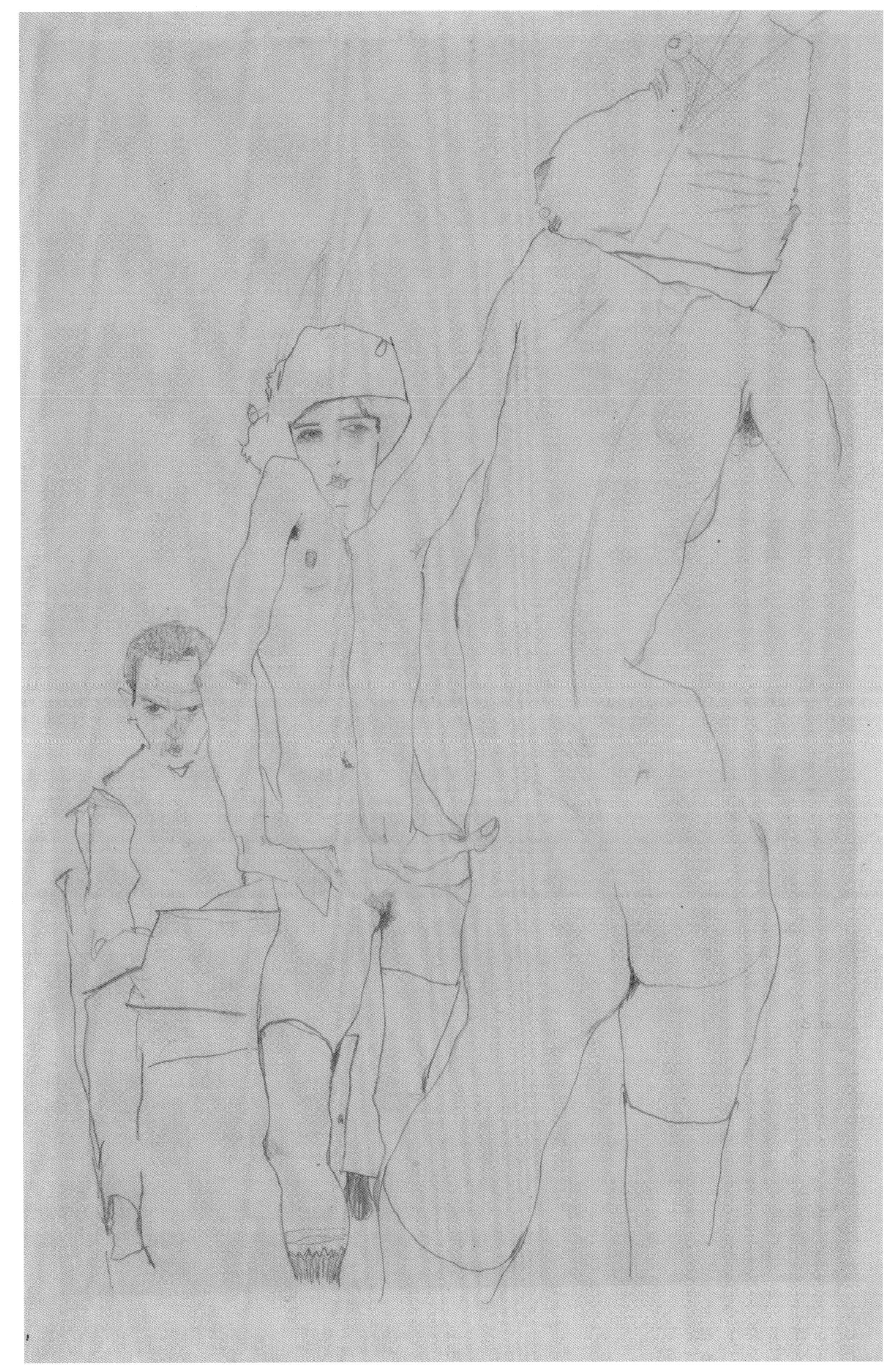

Amon's description permits a more precise analysis of Graff's letter to Schiele. It states that Graff admitted the undernourished pregnant woman to the Second University Women's Hospital on May 17 and took care of her, even paying her hospital bills. He also helped Schiele with the separation by appealing to her conscience, telling her that Schiele was too young to take care of a family that was not even his. And that as an artist he had to be free. Amon decided to give the child up for adoption after the birth. The clinic's admission record bears the stamp "Suitable for admission to the foundling hospital." As early as the eighteenth century, it had been possible to give birth to a child at the foundling hospital in complete anonymity. There was a separate entrance for these patients, no official records were made, and the newborn could be transferred to the foundling hospital within a few hours.[42]

However, no entry for the child in the records of the foundling hospital can be found,[43] so it is reasonable to assume that the statement in the novel that she stayed with her child in a maternity home for three months is accurate.

Graff's sentence "It is presumably better that way for you and her" can only mean that he considered it better that Schiele and Amon should separate. Graff considered it indispensable to the development of the artist-genius that he be free and unattached. It is quite remarkable that Graff was convinced of Schiele's genius already in 1910, when the latter was beginning his transformation from Jugendstil painter to rebellious Expressionist.

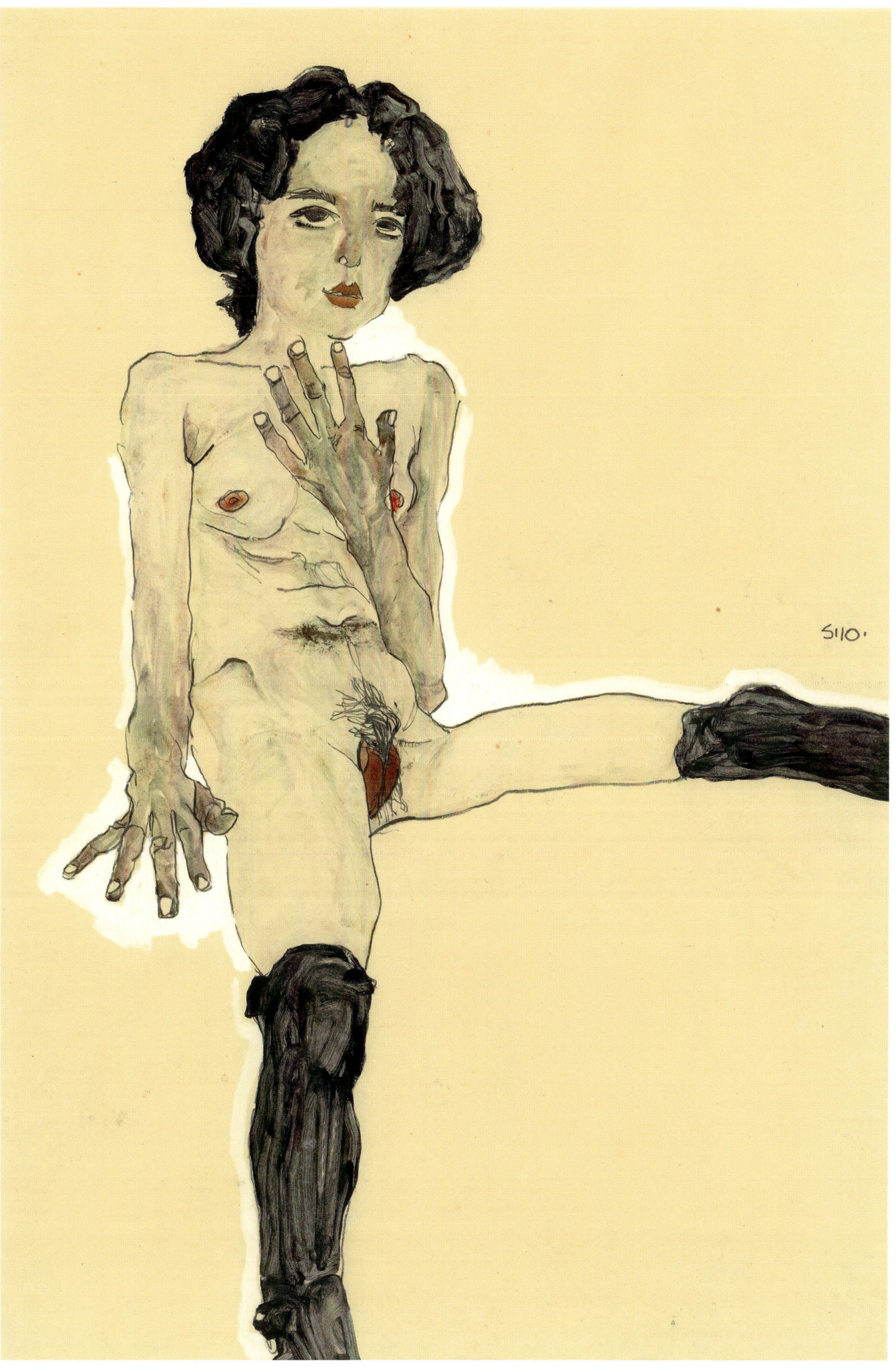
S10.

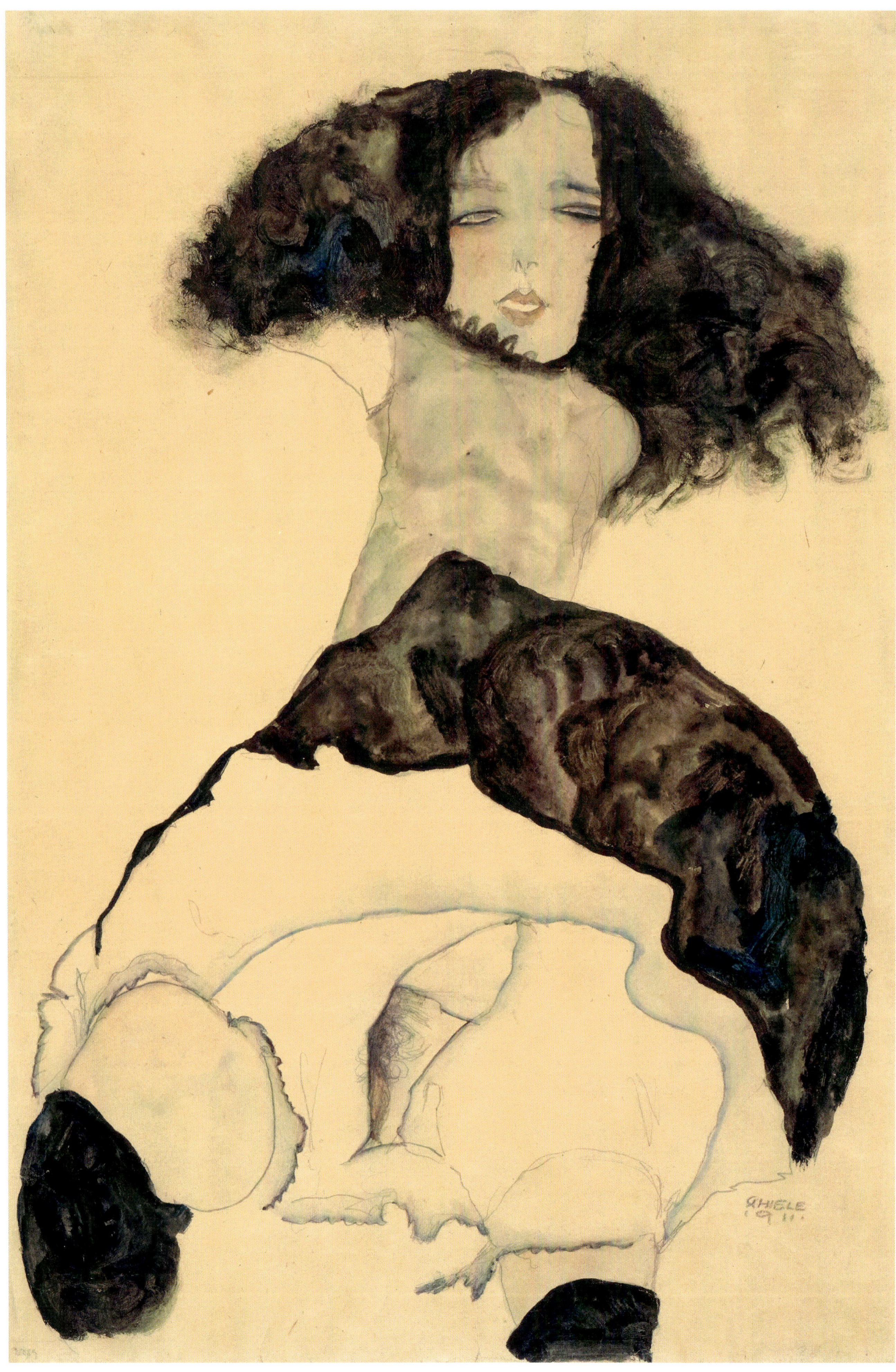
SCHIELE
1911

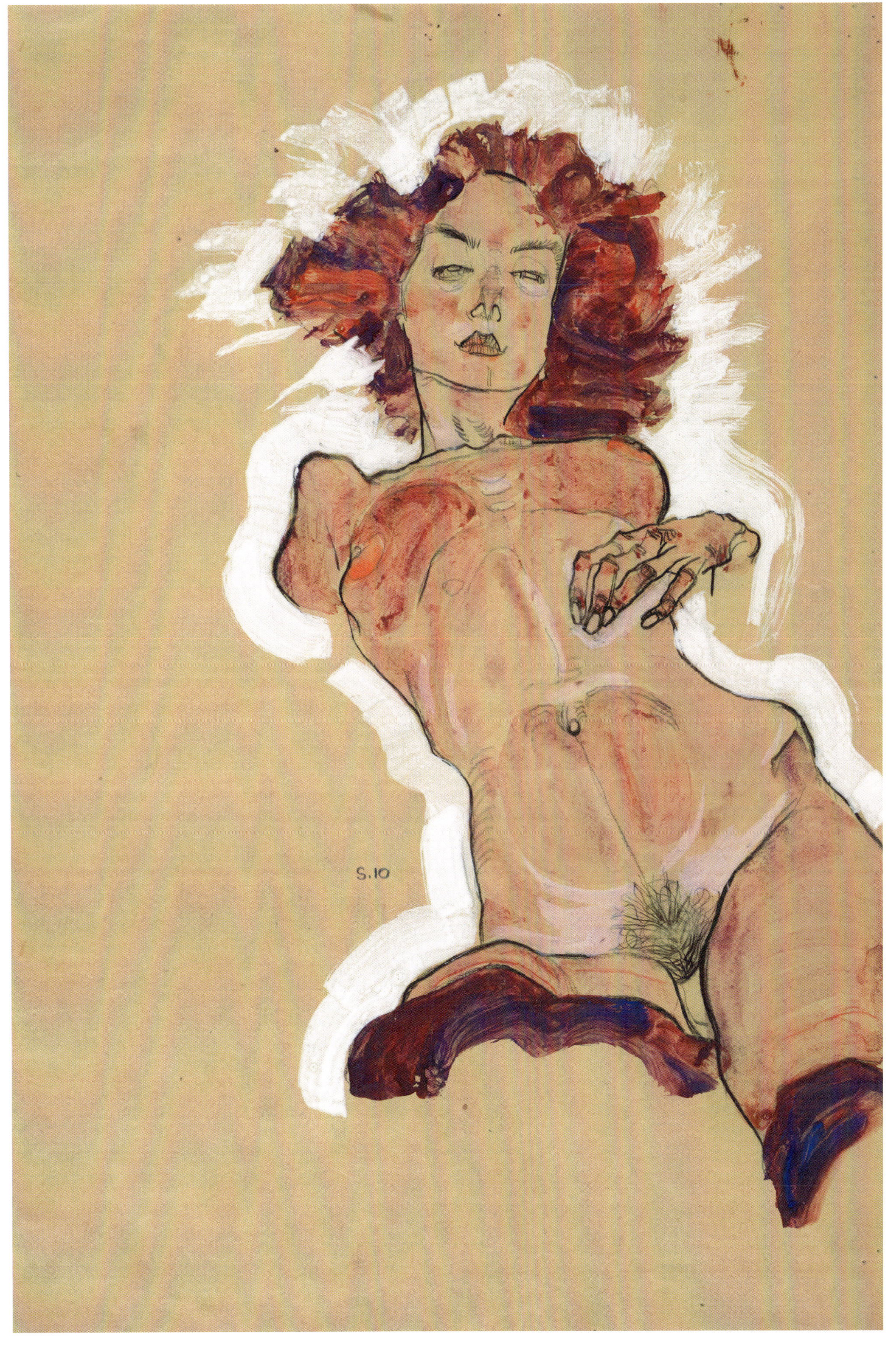
S. 10

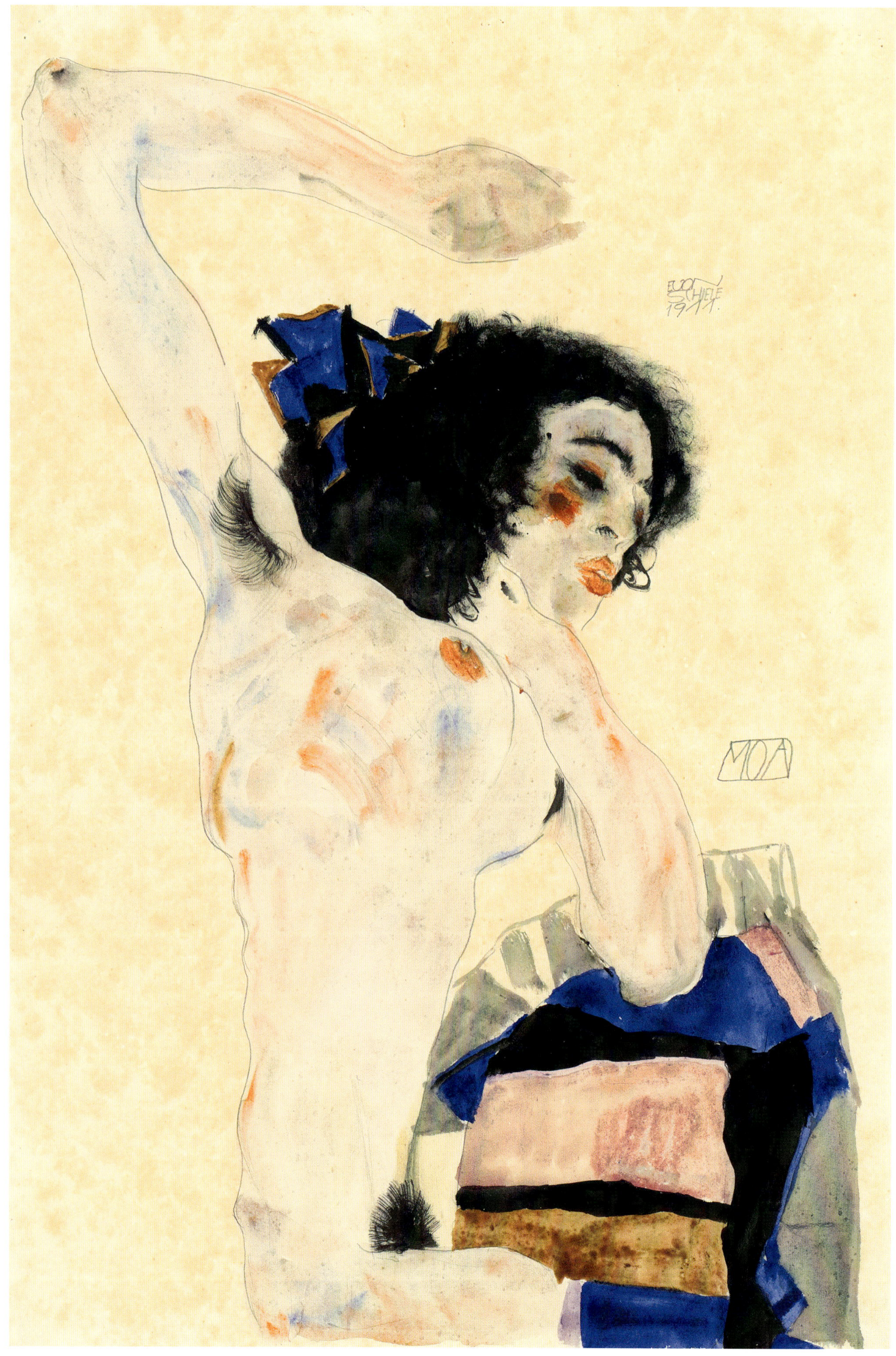

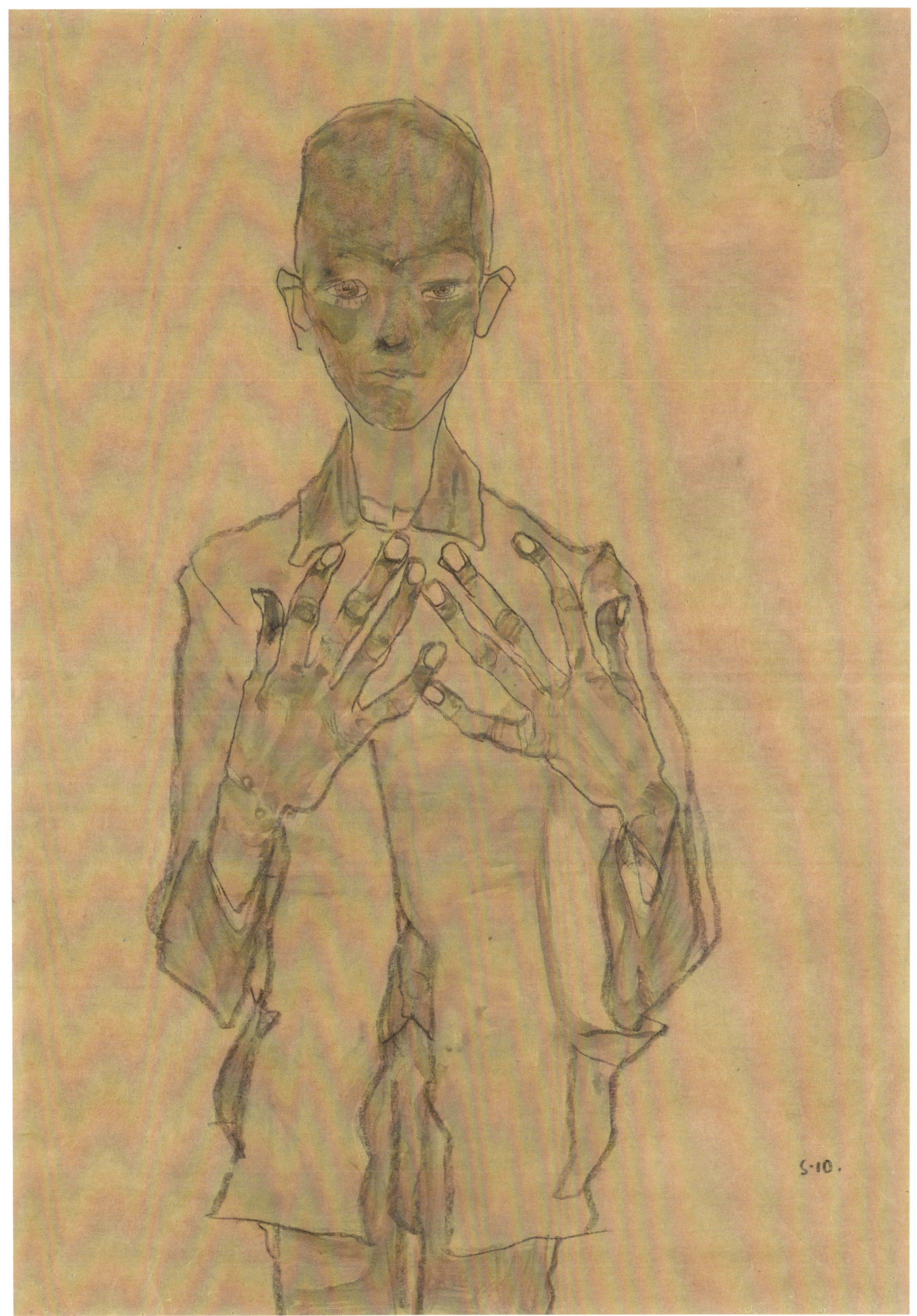
S·10·

In his letter to Schiele, Graff also sent his regards to the painter Erwin Osen (1891–1970),[44] who at the time was staying with Schiele and former fellow student and future brother-in-law, Anton Peschka (1885–1940), in Krumau (now Český Krumlov), Bohemia, where Schiele's mother was born. Graff had presumably met Osen at Schiele's studio. Osen and his girlfriend, the mysterious dancer Moa Mandu [Fig. 24], made a very strong impression on Schiele.

It is surely possible that Schiele visited Amon in the hospital, even though he was already in Krumau days before Graff admitted her to the clinic.[45] Schiele was back in Vienna in June[46] and again in Krumau in July.[47] In early August, Schiele announced he would be returning to Vienna on August 9,[48] which turned out to be the day when Amon gave birth to a girl. The known drawings of newborns are all boys, and therefore cannot have been Amon's daughter, with one exception: Schiele drew one baby in a top view from behind, so that its genitals are not visible. On August 25 at the latest, Schiele was back in Krumau, as Peschka reported to Schiele's sister Gerti.[49]

In the summer of 1910, Schiele began to draw children in Krumau as well, above all peasant children whose unaffected character and openness he appreciated. *Standing Boy with Hands on Chest* [Fig. 25] is an excellent example and clearly shows Schiele's nascent interest in hands as a way of expressing emotions. The boy holds his oversized hands in front of his chest with his fingers spread. It is a gesture of protection from the outside world. His facial expression is introverted and shy.

On August 30, 1910, Graff sent Schiele a postcard from Lignano, Italy, to Krumau. Amon is already not mentioned [Fig. 26]:

> *30 August 1910.*
> *Lignano. D[ear] Sch[iele]! Because of the*
> *cholera we abandoned our plan*
> *to travel to Venice and are here until*
> *ca. Sept[ember] 20, staying in an albergo*
> *that is as primitive as it is cheap and*
> *proudly bears the name Hotel Central.*
> *Letters and visits reach us*
> *best via Latisana, a train station*
> *on the Trieste–Venice line.*
> *The seaside is very beautiful and*
> *apart from us almost deserted.*
> *Come! Yours Graff.*

By this juncture their interaction was already so familiar that Graff asked Schiele to travel to Lignano to vacation with him and his wife, Olga.

On August 9, 1910, Amon gave birth to a daughter who was named Marie Liliana. There is no entry on the father, which was usually the case with births out of wedlock. The child was initially brought to a children's home in Vienna.[50]

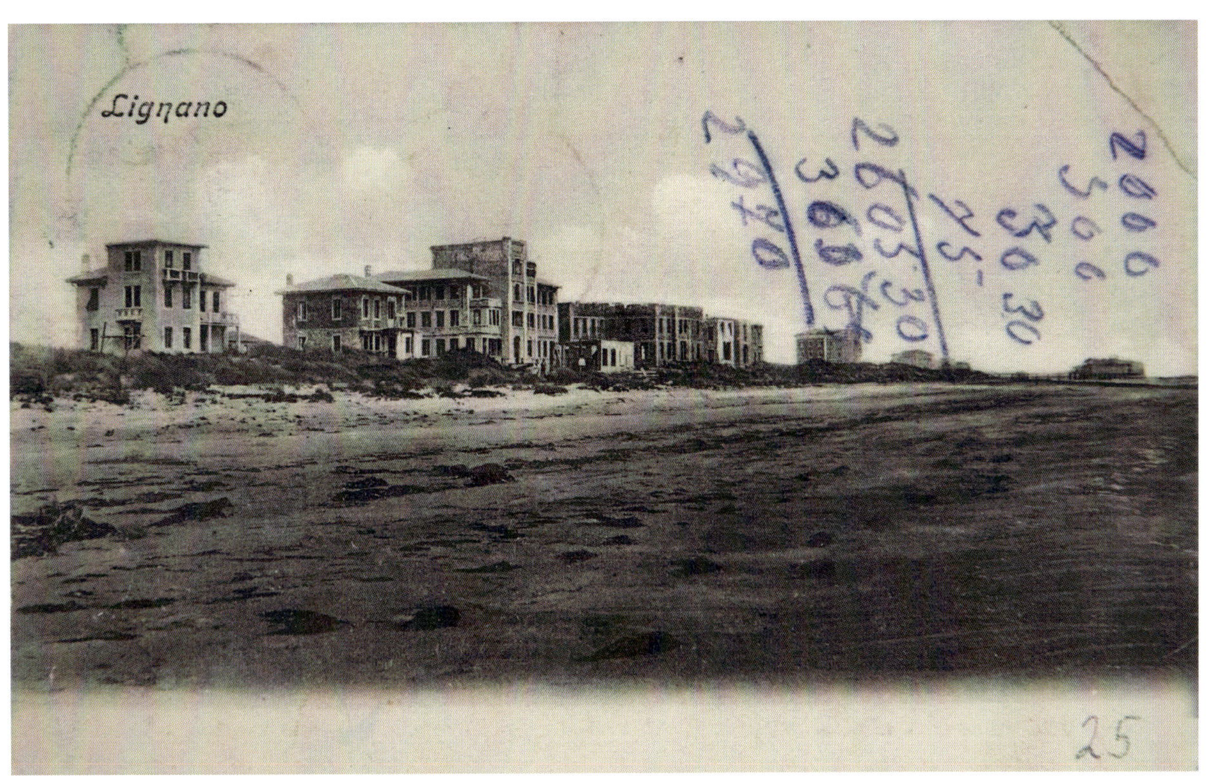
Lignano

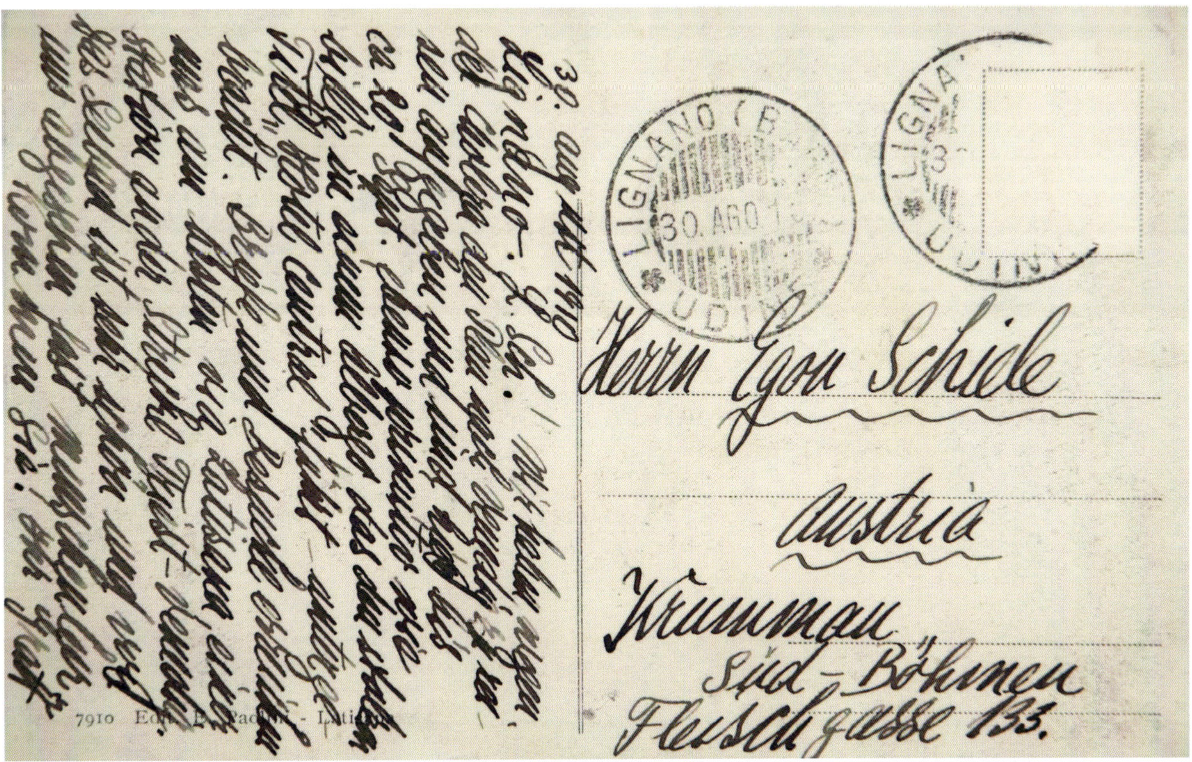
Herrn Egon Schiele
Austria
Krumman
Süd-Böhmen
Fleischgasse 133.

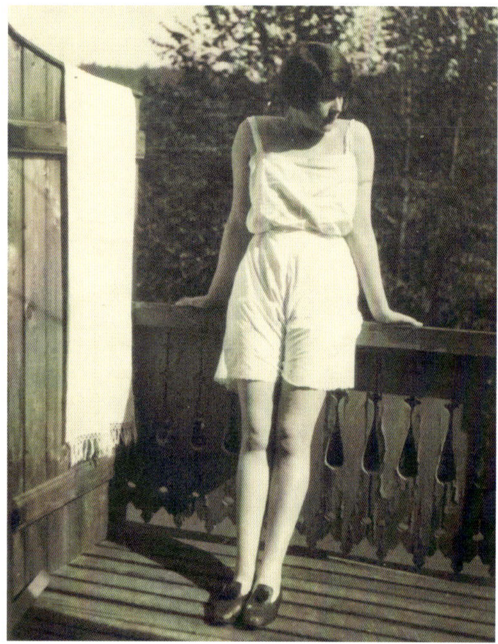

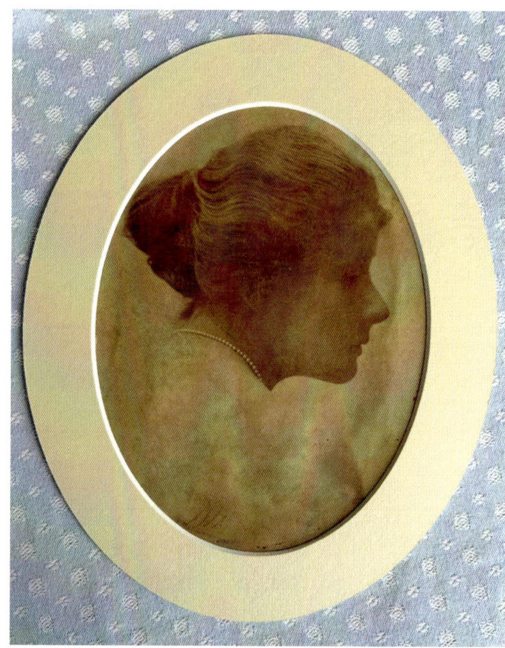

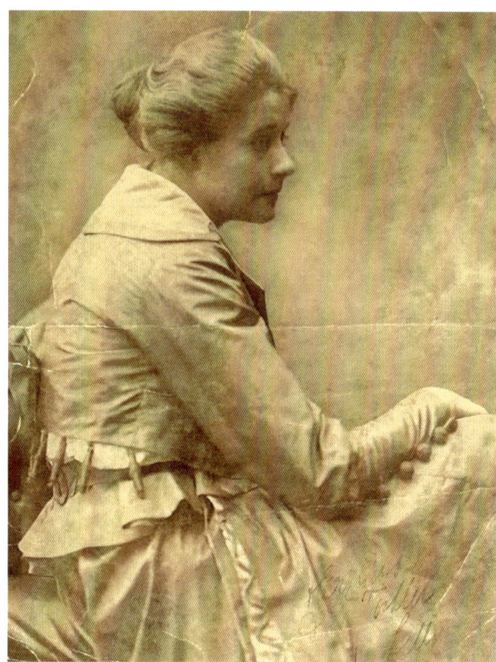

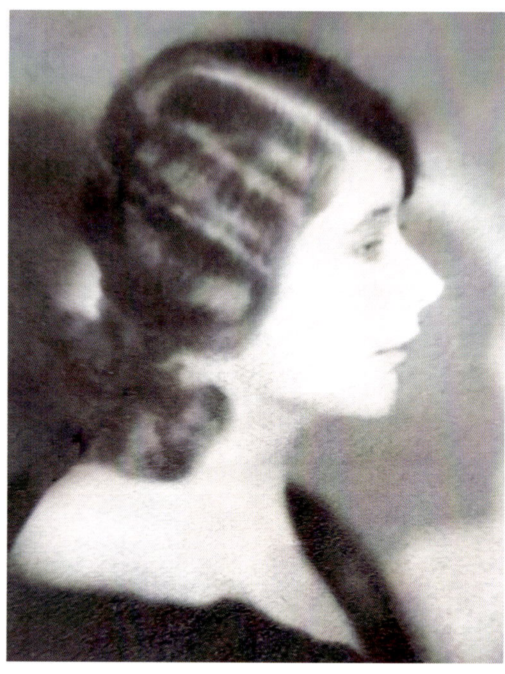

A few years after her love affair with Schiele, Amon became an integral fixture of the Viennese coffee house and literary scene [Figs. 27–30]. She often frequented Franz Blei's regular table of writers and artists at the Café Herrenhof, was immortalized in literature by Robert Musil[51] and Franz Werfel,[52] and was engaged to Anton Kuh, a famous Austrian journalist and essayist. She probably never saw her daughter again. Amon became an actress, moved to Berlin, and married the actor Eberhard Leithoff

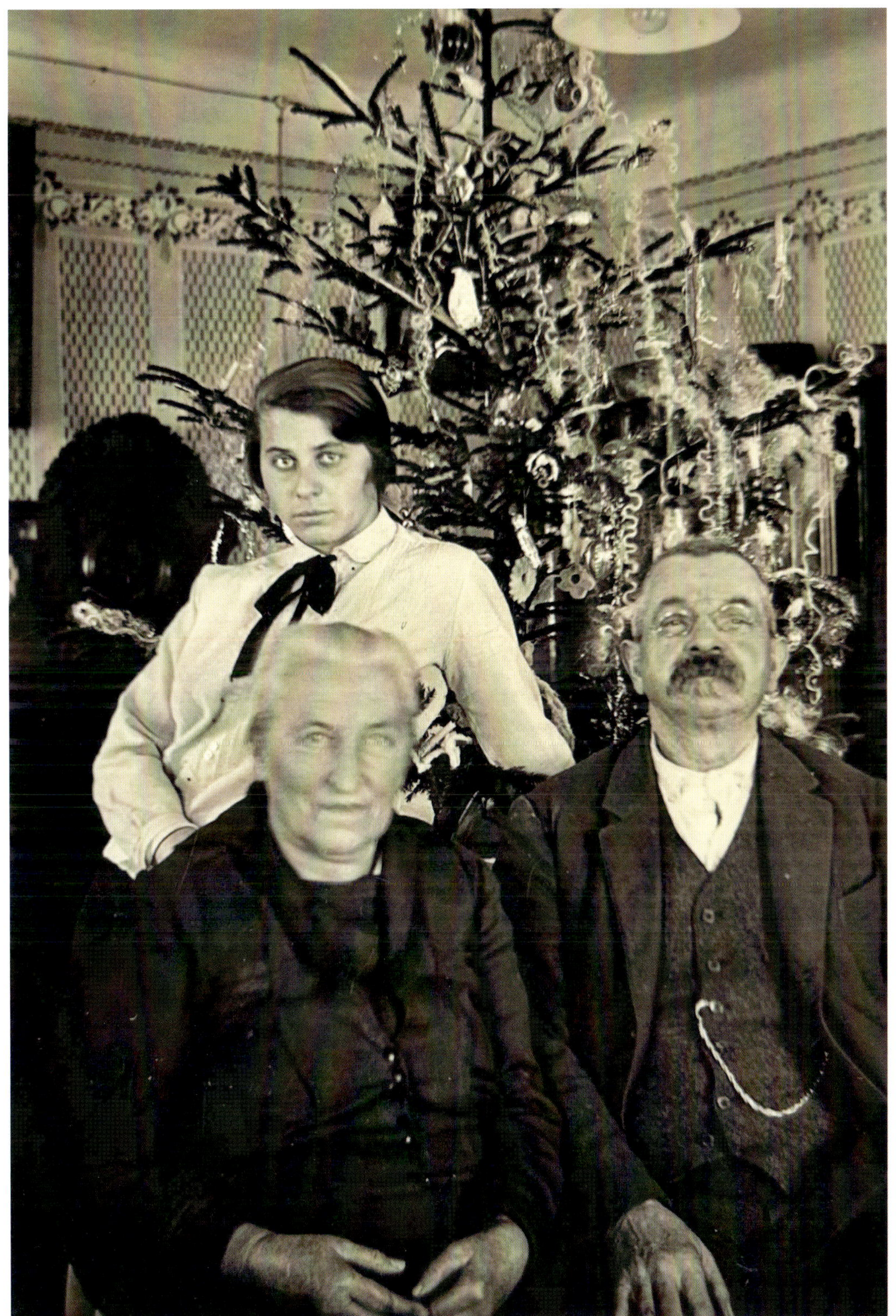

31. Marie Liliana at the age of fifteen
with her foster parents Böhm, 1925.
Private Collection

in 1924. The marriage failed and in 1929 she married the Jewish businessman Hans Ludwig Schwab. Schwab was a victim of the Holocaust in Poland in 1942. Amon emigrated to Paris, where she wrote her autobiographical roman à clef and died on February 1, 1966.

According to family stories, the illegitimate father was supposedly a "Count Salm," who had walked out on Amon after having spent a night together. Marie Liliana remained in a children's home in Vienna until she was three. Then she was sent to a so-called *Engelmacherin* (literally, "angel maker," a woman who performs illegal abortions) in Freistadt, Upper Austria, who took in the child in exchange for payment. These were traumatic years, because the girl received hardly anything to eat and had to find food in the garbage. The woman was later sentenced for abortions she had performed. Marie Liliana was then dispatched to a convent school in Hacking, part of the Vienna's thirteenth district. It must have been a convent of Dominican nuns that still exists today. At fifteen, Marie Liliana was sent to a foster family named Böhm [Fig. 31] in Kemmelbach, near Ybbs, about sixty-two miles west of Vienna. Even though her foster parents were old enough to be her grandparents, it was the first time in her life that the girl felt welcome and happy. When she turned eighteen, the family of her biological father wanted to bring her to their castle in Persenbeug, but the girl rejected this; she wanted no more changes and uncertainty. She married in 1938 and had three children: two sons and a daughter, Liliane [Figs. 32–33], who died in an accident at nineteen. Marie Liliana and her husband founded the Café Lilly in Strobl am Wolfgangsee in the Salzkammergut, and she was a loving mother and grandmother. But her traumatic childhood left traces that stayed with her all her life. She died in 1992.[53]

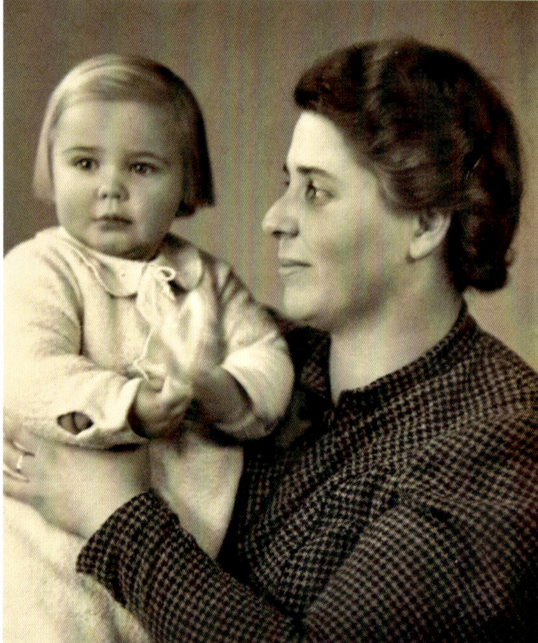

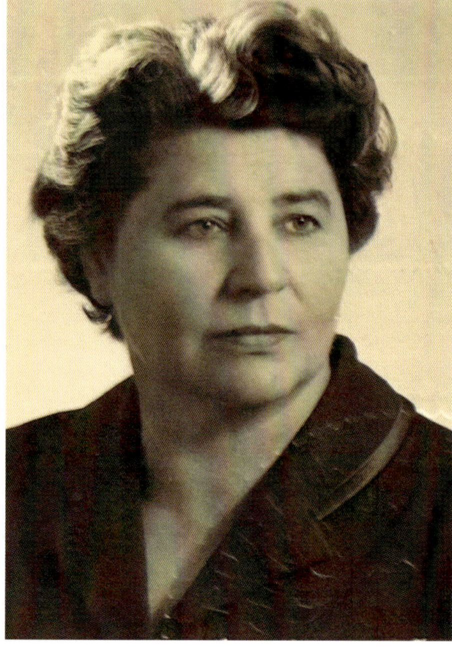

32. Marie Liliana with her daughter Liliane, 1939. Private Collection

33. Marie Liliana, ca. 1955. Private Collection

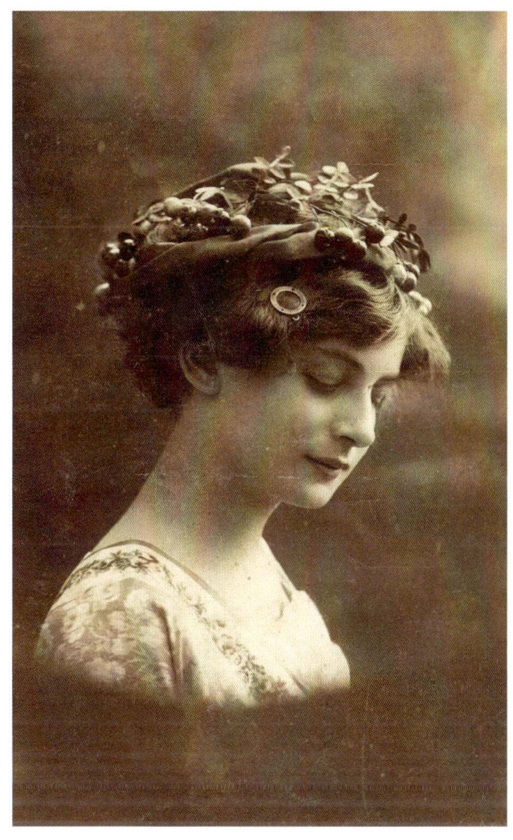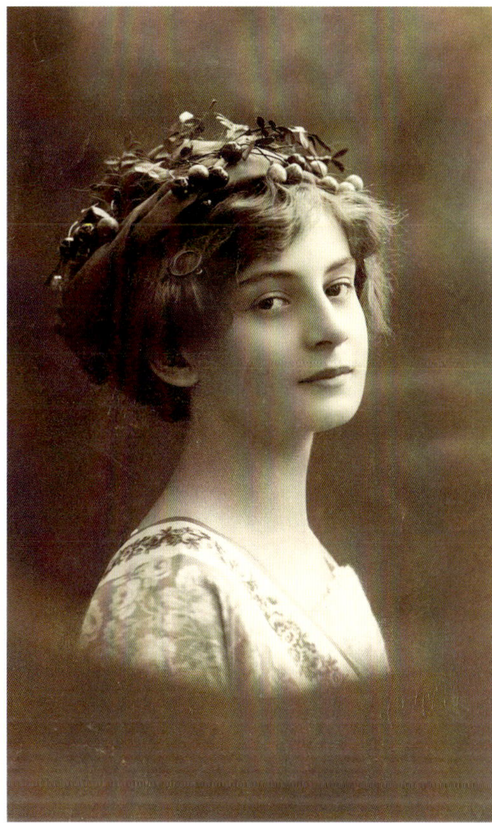

Erwin von Graff and Gerti Schiele

Schiele's sister Gertrude (Gerti) Schiele (1894–1981) [Fig. 34], who was particularly close to him and his favorite model for a time, began a relationship with her brother's friend Peschka and became pregnant in 1913. Schiele's mother wanted a quick marriage; already on November 14, 1913, just a few days before the birth, she wrote Egon[54] that the wedding would be announced three times in the coming days.[55] She also noted that Dr. von Graff had already been informed. On November 23, 1913, another letter from Marie Schiele to Egon followed.[56] Marie Schiele reported that Gerti had complained about suspicious stomach pains the previous day, and she had been brought by car to the clinic. In the evening, she drove to the hospital and wanted to ask about her daughter's condition. The hospital personnel had been very unfriendly, and she did not receive proper information. She immediately went to Dr. von Graff, who was on duty, and asked him to call the clinic, which he obligingly did. It was indeed the case that Gerti was about to give birth, but not that night. The following day, Peschka drove to the hospital, where Gerti had already given birth to a daughter. On the day she was admitted to the clinic, her wedding dress had been delivered. The newborn girl was baptized Gertrude,[57] and the nuptials were postponed for a year. The wedding was held precisely one year later, on November 24, 1914, when Gerti was already pregnant with their son Anton, nicknamed Toni. Schiele painted Gerti and her children many times, including a watercolor showing Toni as a baby lying on his stomach, wrapped in a decorative blanket [Fig. 35] and a charming painting of Toni when he was around three years old [Fig. 36].

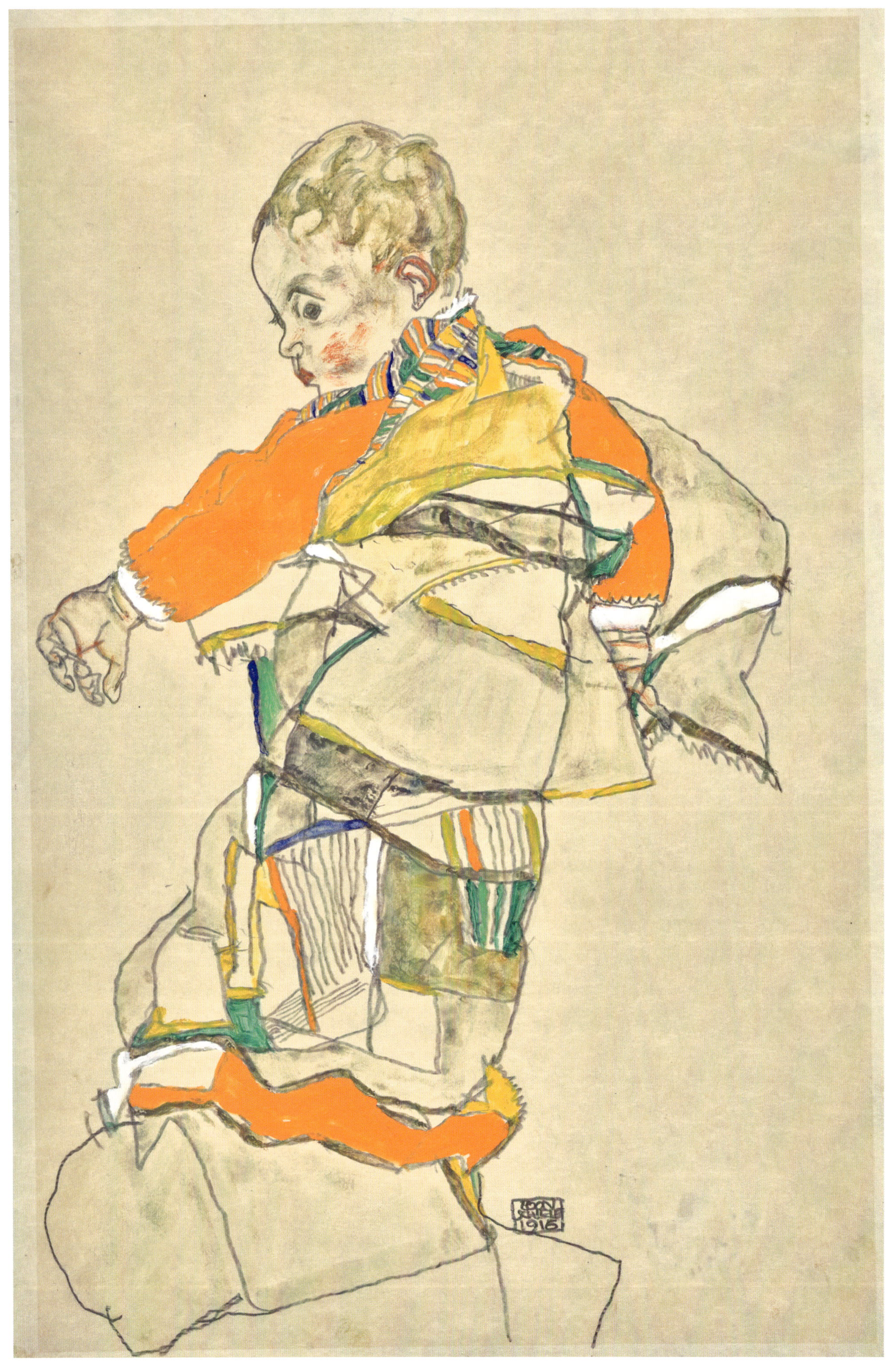

EGON
SCHIELE
1916

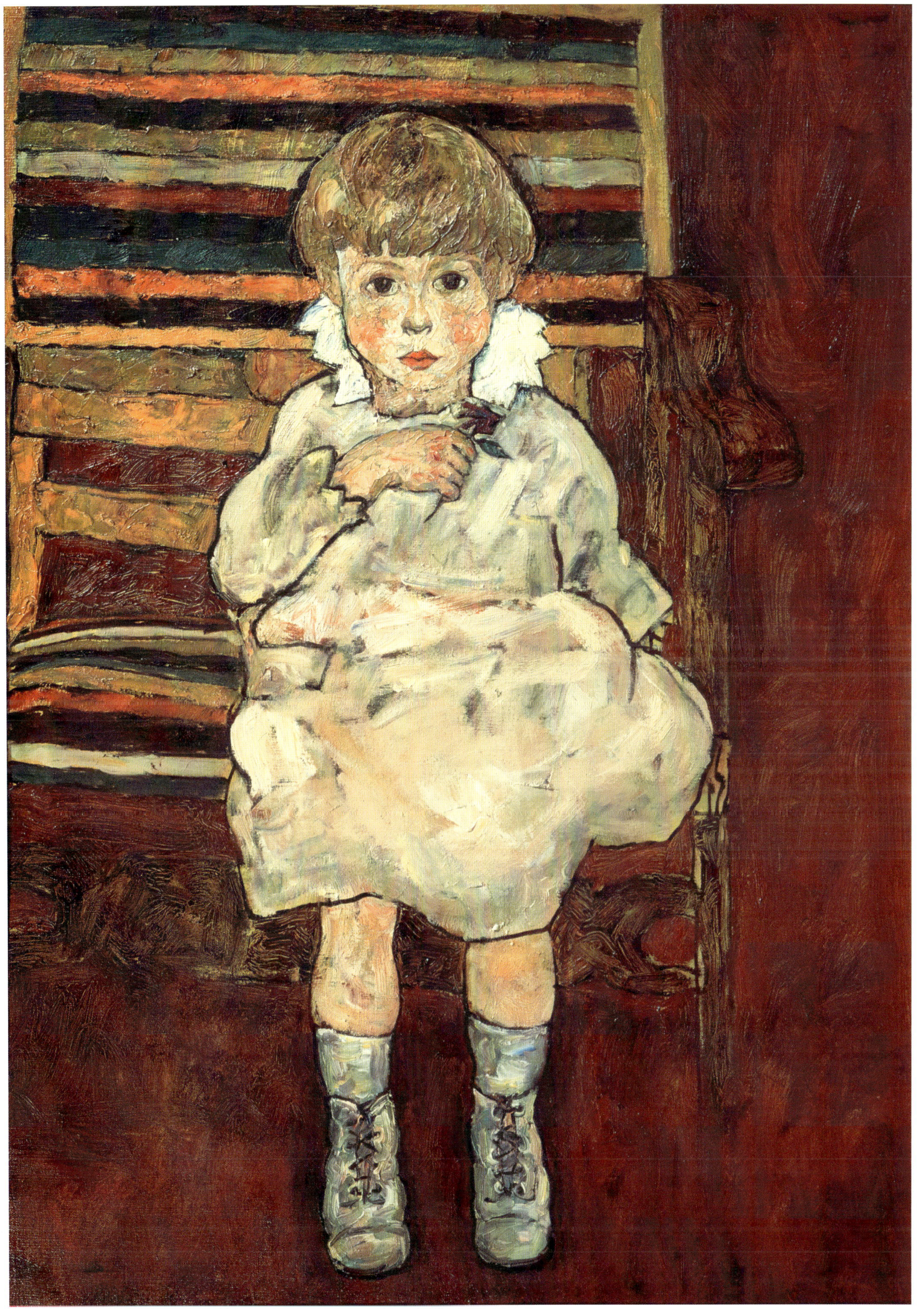

Erwin von Graff at Egon Schiele's Deathbed

In the year before he died, Schiele finally began to receive more recognition for his art. An exhibition at the Vienna Secession dedicated to him was very successful and led to the purchase of a portrait of Edith Schiele, Egon's wife, by the Moderne Galerie in Vienna (now the Belvedere). Edith Harms, whom Schiele had married on June 17, 1915, became an important model for the artist and posed for oil portraits as well as numerous watercolors and drawings such as *Portrait of the Artist's Wife Seated, Holding Her Right Leg* [Fig. 37].

Since the spring of 1918, a devastating global influenza pandemic had been spreading rapidly. The second wave in the autumn of 1918 was especially deadly and affected people between the ages of twenty and forty in particular.[58] Edith Schiele was in the sixth month of pregnancy when she fell ill in October 1918. On October 24, Graff noted in his diary: "At Schiele's in the evening, whose wife has the flu. He is living in a large —unfortunately, damp—home and studio in Hietzing."[59] Schiele had asked his friend the doctor to see his wife, who had already been bedridden for several days, had contracted pneumonia, and was having difficulty breathing. Just four days later, on October 28, 1918, she succumbed to the flu after infecting her husband.

Schiele's home in Hietzing was the former sculpture studio of Othmar Schimkowitz (1862–1947) at Wattmanngasse 6, which was located in the garden of the house. Schiele was planning to use the large studio, with more than a thousand square feet and nearly thirty-three feet tall, for large-format paintings. On the upper floor, above a side room, was a small living room where the drama of Edith lying ill and dying had transpired. Now Schiele was sick and was brought to his mother-in-law's apartment at Hietzinger Hauptstrasse 114 so she could care for him. Once again, Graff hurried to the deathbed and noted in his diary on November 10, 1918 [Fig. 38]:[60]

In the last 14 days, many dreadful things have happened. […]

Egon Schiele did not live to see it all. On Thursday the 31st, at 1:12 in the morning, he followed his wife who had died three days earlier.

My final act of love was an injection that relieved his difficulty breathing, giving him hope that he might recover so that he died without any struggle, having fallen asleep 2 1/2 hours earlier. A shame about this divinely gifted artist who took so much with him as a human being and master. As bitter as my sorrow is for him, I feel it is a consolation that he passed in supreme happiness as a person and as an artist: The Staatsgalerie purchased two portraits from his final Secession exhibition, and now he wanted to occupy Klimt's sanctuary and live and work closed off with his wife and child from the noise and plight of daily life.

By "Klimt's sanctuary," Graff meant the studio of the artist Gustav Klimt, who had died on February 6, 1918, at Feldmühlgasse 11 in Hietzing. Schiele worked for months, even shortly before his death, to be able to take over the studio, even though he had only recently moved into Othmar Schimkowitz's in July 1918.

Comini pointed out already in 1974 that Graff had treated Egon Schiele on his deathbed. She had received this information from Mell.[61] Nebehay rejected this as an error, because it had been discovered

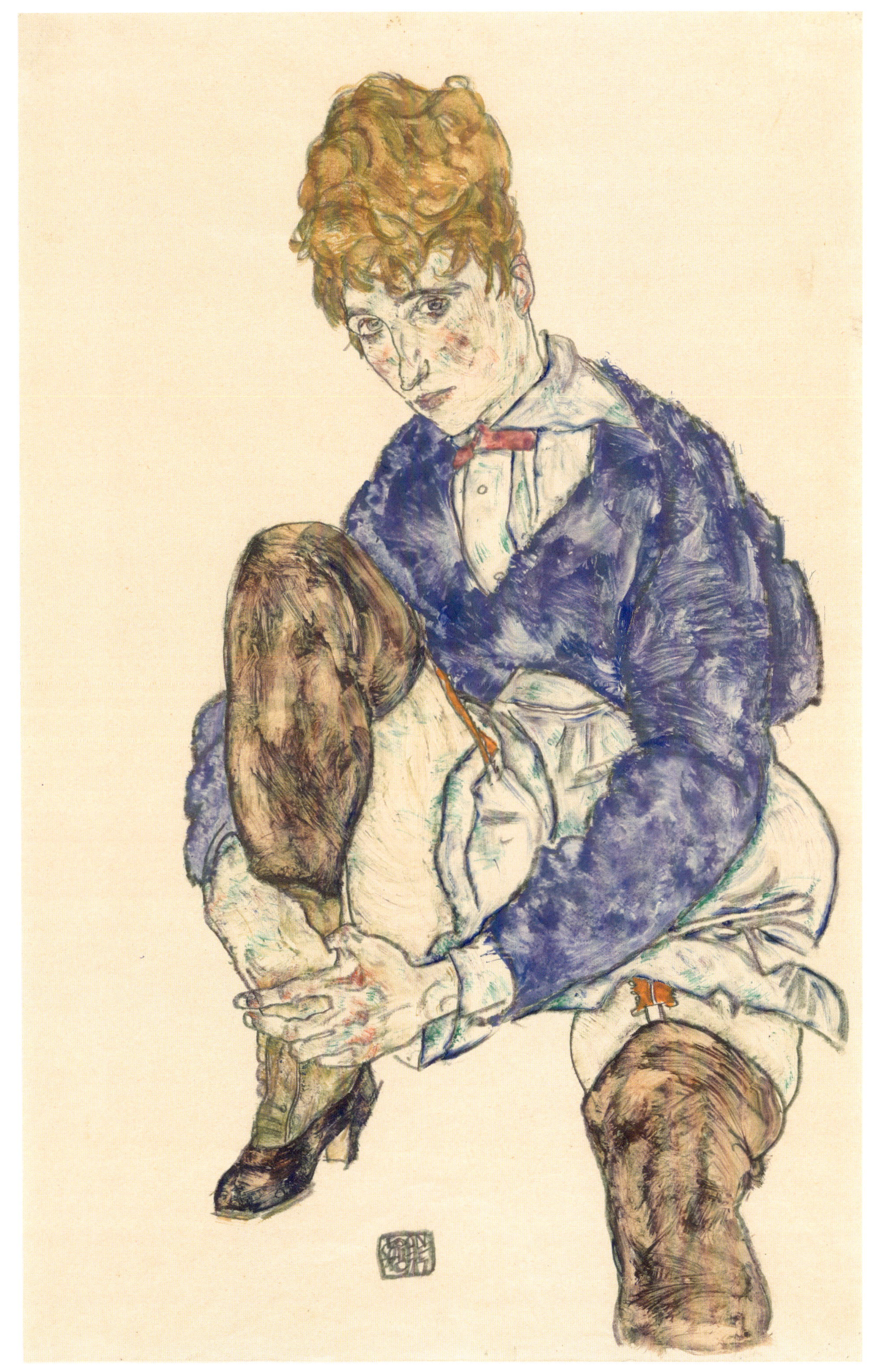

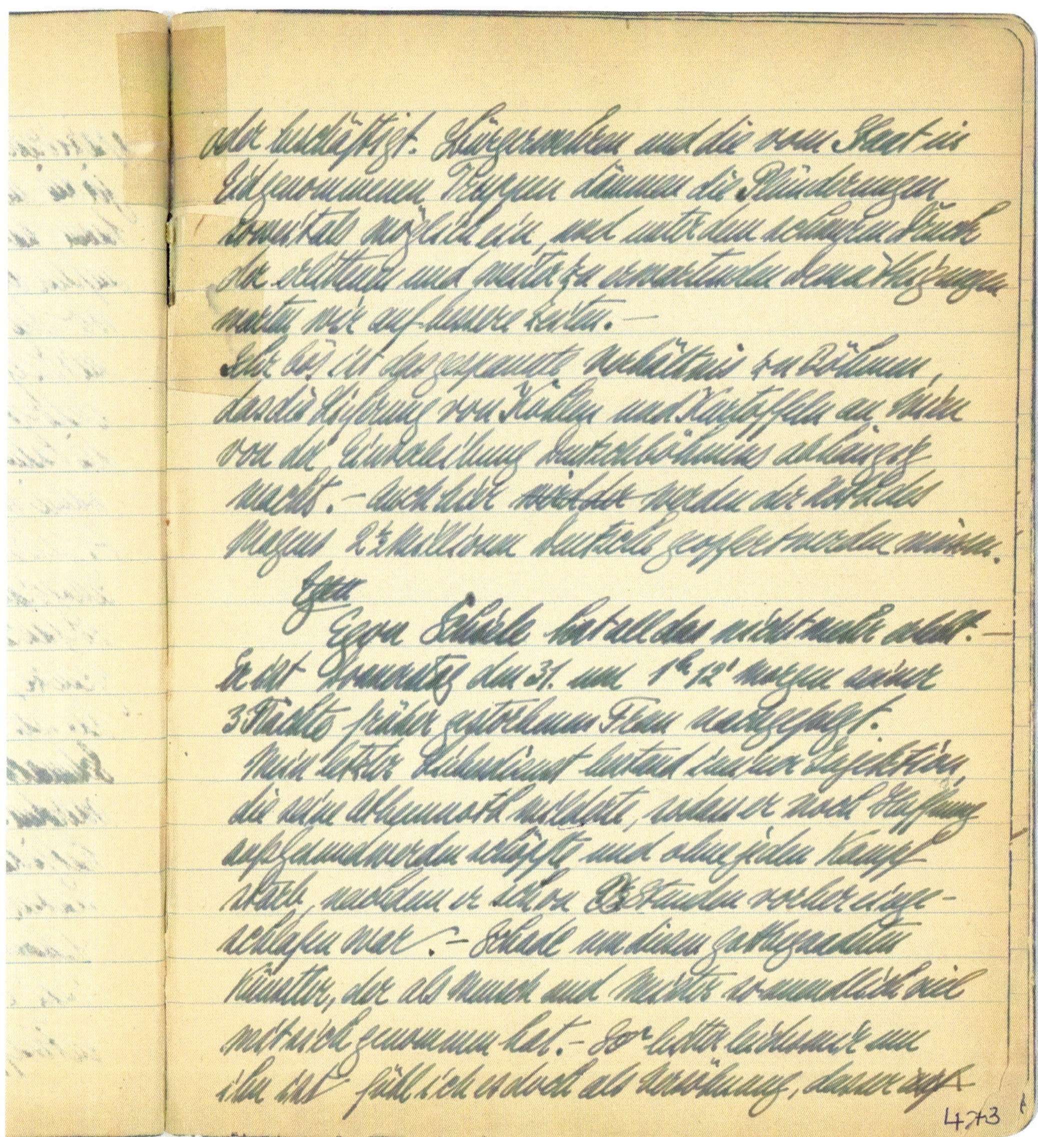

in the file of Schiele's estate that Dr. Franz Haldenwang, who had a practice in Hietzing, was the attending physician.[62] Graff's diary confirms, however, what Mell told Comini. Graff was indeed at Schiele's deathbed, not as the official attending physician but as a friend who wanted to be at his side.

We can only speculate about what injection Graff administered. It could have been morphine to mute the subjective component of his troubled breathing: Morphine represses the "perceived hunger for air"—the tormenting difficulty breathing. This therapy is no longer considered truly beneficial, because it also compromises respiratory rate and thus oxygen supply to the organs (including the brain). The patient, however, subjectively experiences it as an improvement.[63] Possible alternatives in those days would have included scopolamine, caffeine, adrenaline, procaine, or strophanthin.[64]

The precise nature of the injection administered by Graff can no longer be established with certainty and therefore remains a matter of conjecture. The most plausible assumption is that morphine was used. At the time, this opioid was well established for sedation and for mitigating the subjective sensation of "air hunger" accompanying severe dyspnea. Pharmacologically, morphine alleviated the

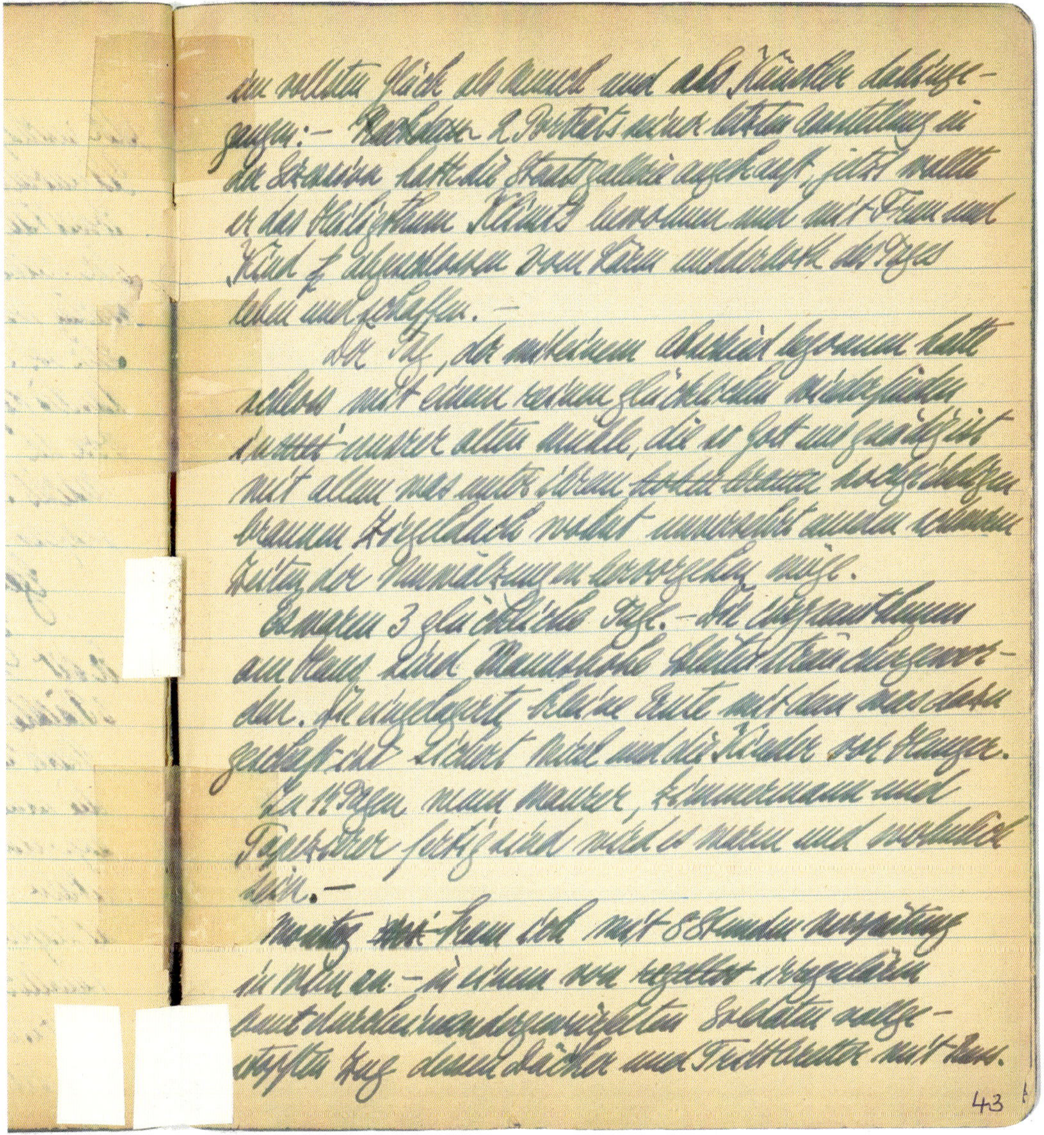

distressing perception of breathlessness but simultaneously induced respiratory depression, thereby reducing ventilation and oxygen delivery to the body. Such an intervention may have eased the dying process, yet it likely also accelerated death. In early twentieth-century medical practice, however, the physician's foremost concern was the patient's subjective comfort rather than the prolongation of life.[65]

Other agents in contemporary use might also be considered. Scopolamine was administered for its sedative and antisecretory effects, caffeine and adrenaline functioned as central and peripheral stimulants of circulation and respiration; procaine was occasionally explored for systemic therapeutic applications, and strophanthin, a cardiac glycoside, was employed for its positive inotropic action in heart failure. The range of these substances reflects the therapeutic repertoire of the period, which was characterized less by causal treatment than by empirically guided symptomatic relief.[66]

Graff, who was convinced of Schiele's genius as early as 1910, remained connected to him until his death and to the end regarded him as a divinely gifted artist who had also revealed special qualities as a human being.

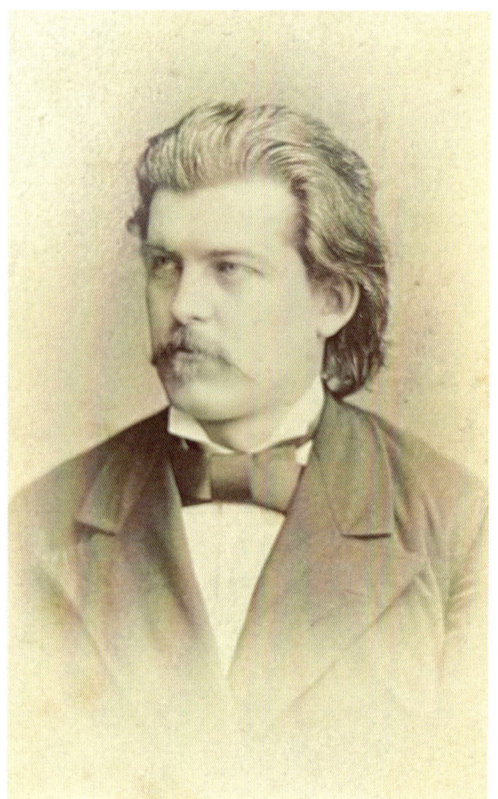
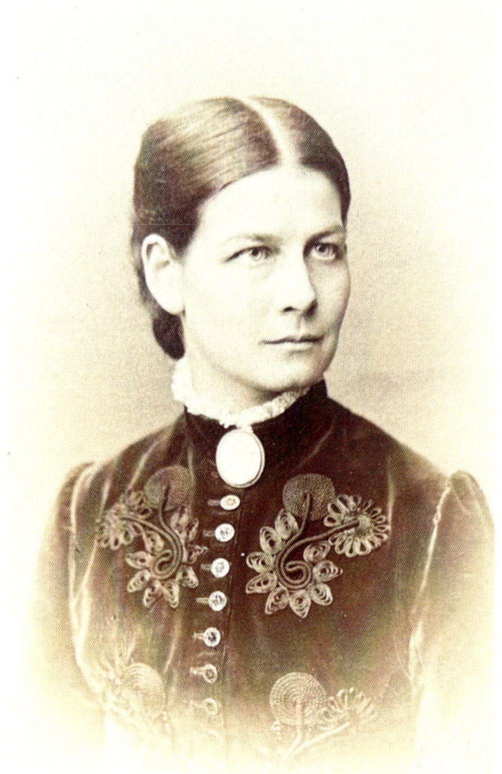

III. BIOGRAPHY OF DR. ERWIN VON GRAFF

Origins and Youth

The origins of the Graff family lie in the towns of Höbersbrunn and Poysdorf in Lower Austria—a region known for its outstanding white wines. It is said that the family immigrated there from Württemberg, but there is no evidence to support this. In 1786, one of their forebears crossed the Danube on a raft to the Torontál County, which had been incorporated into the Military Frontier in 1767, as one of the last waves of German colonization in the Banat of Temeswar under Emperor Joseph II and settled as a master carpenter in Pancsova, a small town in the Banat region of Austria-Hungary (now Pančevo, Serbia).[67] Graff's great-grandfather Bartholomäus Graff founded an apothecary there; his son Wilhelm Hermann established the Volksbank (People's Bank) of Pancsova and became mayor. One of his sons, Erwin von Graff's father, Ludwig, became a zoologist against his father's will.[68] Ludwig Graff was born in Pancsova on January 2, 1851. He studied medicine in Vienna and zoology in Graz and then went to Munich as assistant to Carl von Siebold (1804–1885). In 1876, Ludwig Graff was appointed professor at the Königlich Bayerische Forstlehranstalt (Royal Bavarian Forestry Institute) in Aschaffenburg, where he taught until 1884, and where his son Erwin was born. In 1881, Ludwig Graff was raised to the Hungarian nobility and from then on could call himself Graff de Pancsova. In 1884, Ludwig Graff de Pancsova was awarded a chair at the renowned Karl-Franzens-Universität in Graz, founded in 1586. He was a highly

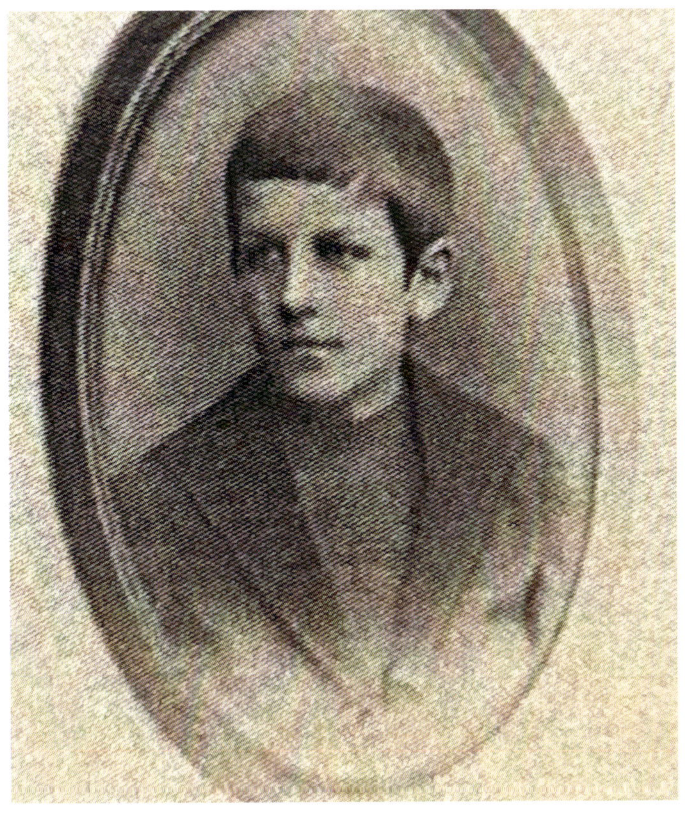

41. Erwin von Graff at the age of eleven, 1889. Private Collection

regarded zoologist who became rector of the university, made numerous study trips to Norway, Ceylon, Java, and North America and more, and left behind a considerable oeuvre of scholarship.[69]

Erwin's mother, Jenny Schorisch, was from an industrialist's family: her father Robert August Schorisch was a sugar manufacturer. She was born in Szentmiklós, Hungary (now Ischynadijowo, Ukraine) and married Ludwig Graff in 1874 in Lundenburg, Moravia (now Břeclav), where her father had since built a refinery.

Johannes Erwin Graff de Pancsova—his correct name (Erwin von Graff is merely an abbreviation of his title of nobility)—was born on September 23, 1878, on Frohsinnstrasse in Aschaffenburg in Bavaria as the third child of Ludwig Bartholomäus Graff [Fig. 39] and Eugénie (Jenny) Pauline Karoline Emilie Schorisch [Fig. 40] and baptized Protestant.[70] Erwin von Graff was raised in these upper-middle-class surroundings. He spent his early years with his parents and two sisters, Friederike and Dorothea (his brother, Erich, only lived for nine months) in Aschaffenburg and at age six [Fig. 41] moved with the family to Graz into the home of Jenny's parents at Heinrichstrasse 48. Later the family seat of Graff de Pancsova was the Villa Benedek at Beethovenstrasse 6. Erwin attended primary school and then the k.u.k. II. Staatsgymnasium (Second Imperial and Royal State High School), from which he graduated on July 4, 1896. During the summer, the family usually traveled to Pancsova [Figs. 42–43].

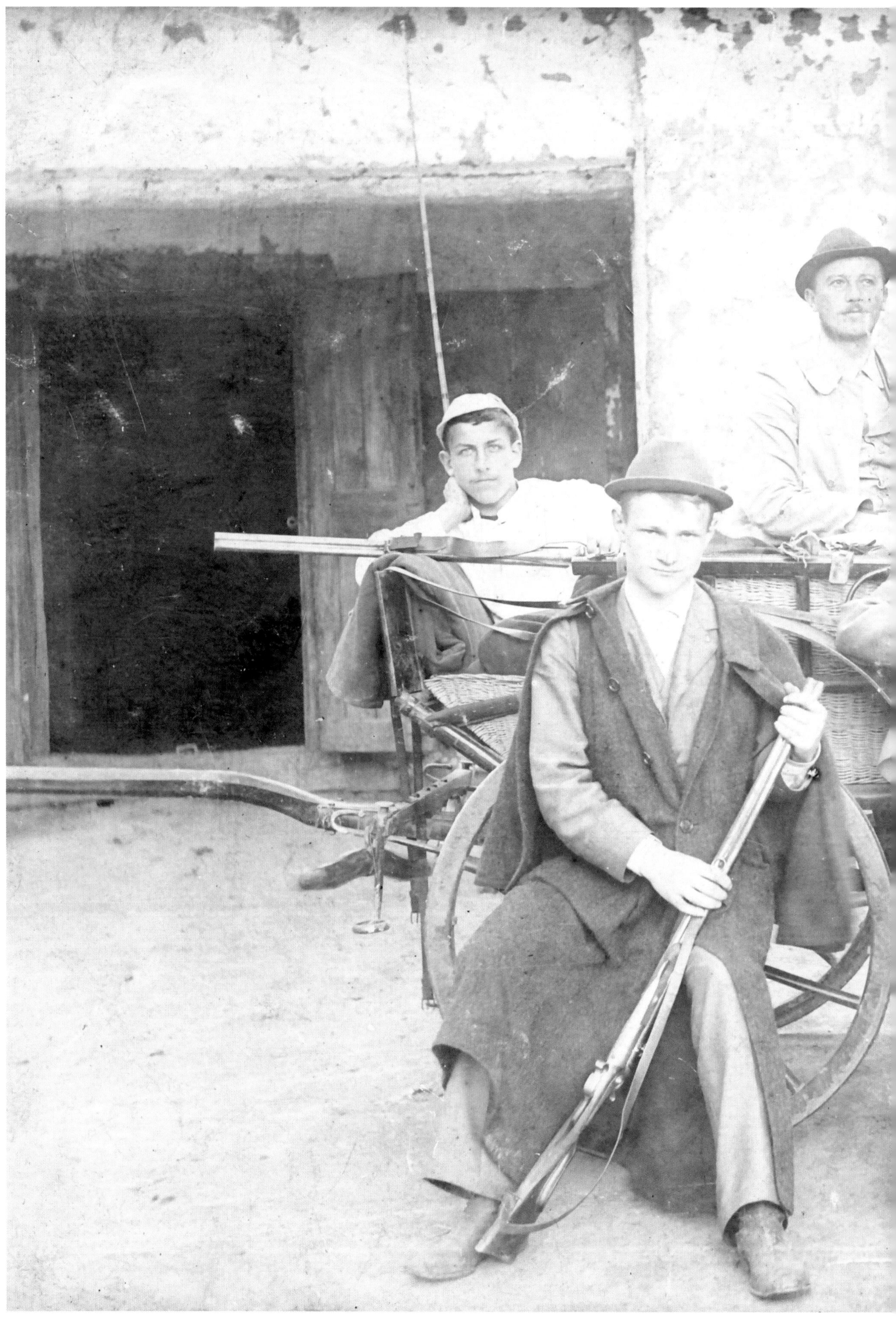

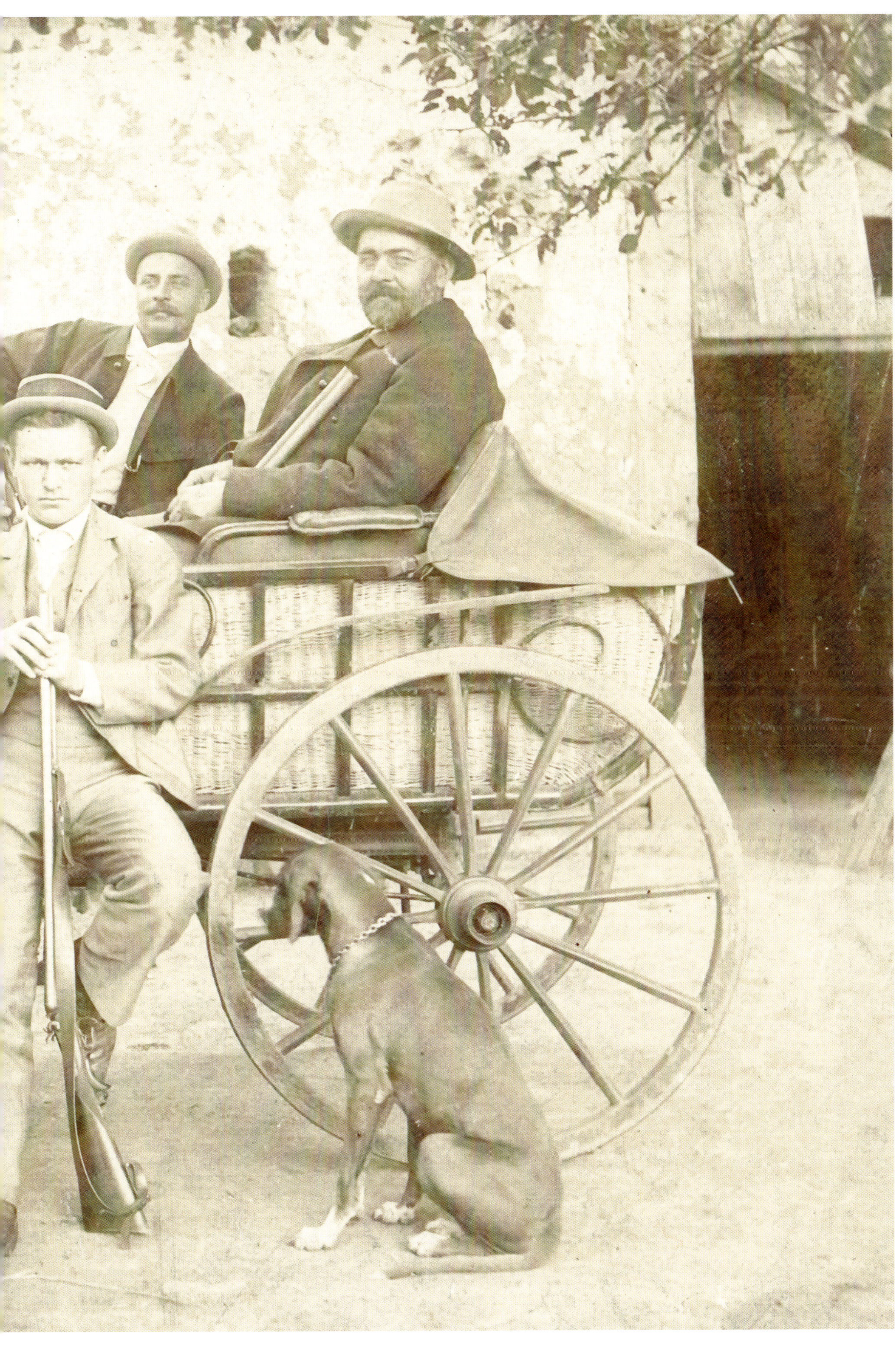

42. Erwin von Graff (left seated in carriage) at the age of sixteen, with a hunting party group, summer 1894. Private Collection

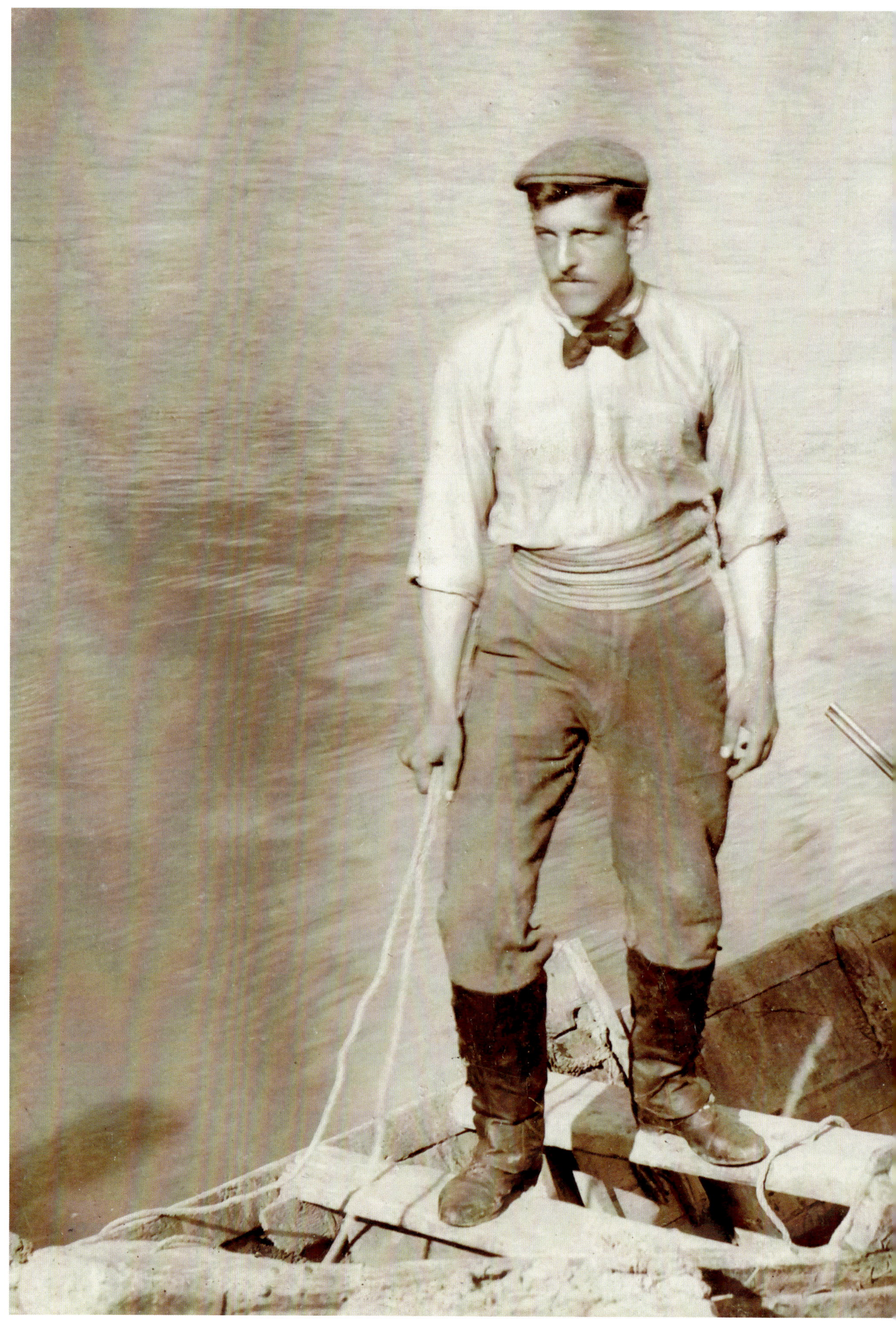

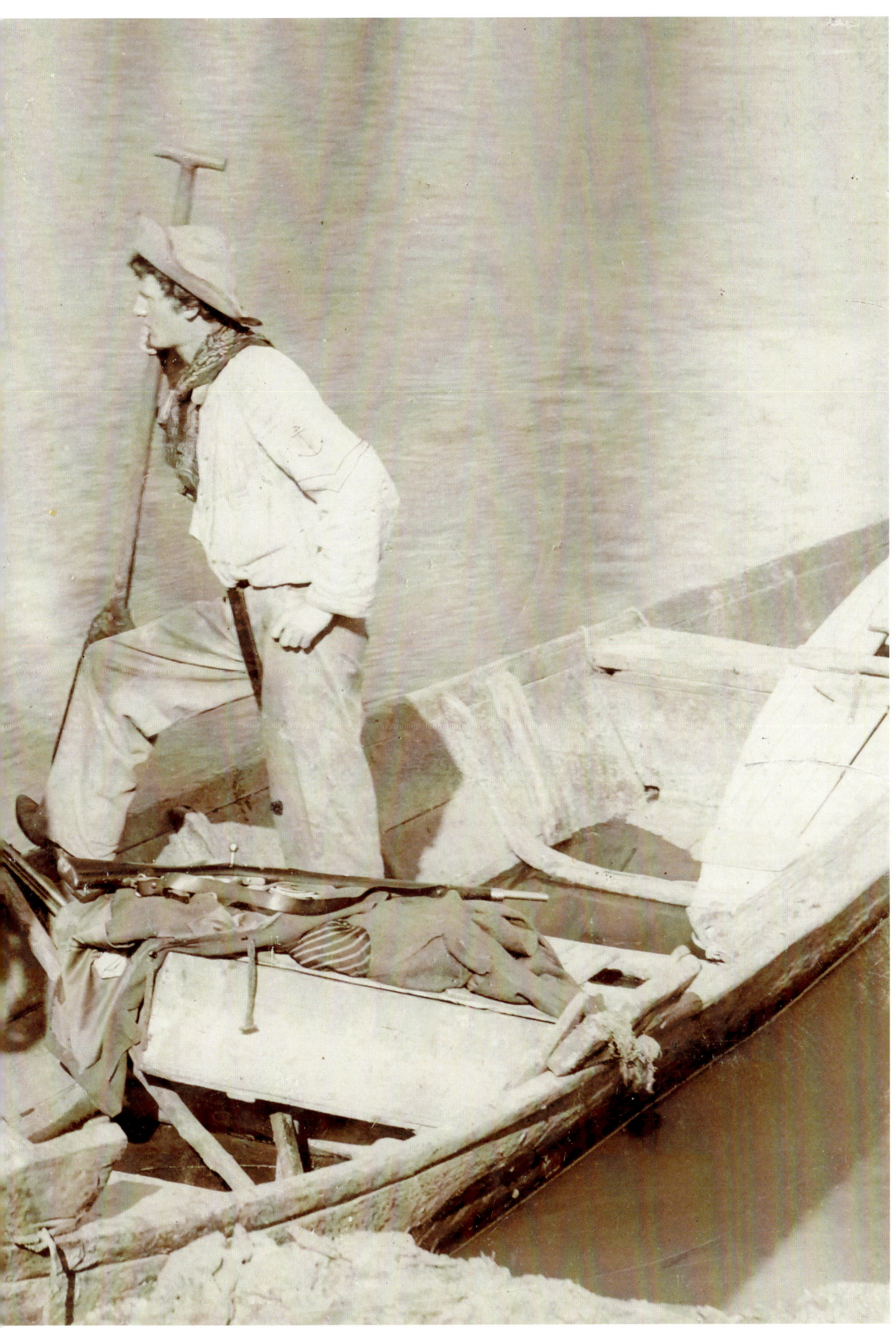

43. Erwin von Graff (left)
in Pancsova (now Pančevo,
Serbia), August 1899.
Private Collection

Nr. *202 / 41.*

Herr Graff von Pancsova Erwin

geboren zu *Aschaffenburg*

in *Baiern* · am *23. September 1878.*

wurde am *9. Mai 1902* zum

Doctor der gesammten Heilkunde

promoviert.

dz. Rector.

dz. Decan.

Promotor.

Dr Erwin v Graff

Studies of Medicine and Assistant Position in Graz

In October 1896, Graff began studying medicine at the Karl-Franzens-Universität in Graz. His first-year lecture courses covered human anatomy, anatomical dissection exercises, experimental chemistry, experimental physics, systematical botany, general zoology (the subject taught by his father), mineralogy, zoological and botanical anatomical practice, but also, interestingly, Greek art with Prof. Dr. Wilhelm Gurlitt, a half-brother of the architect and art historian Cornelius Gustav Gurlitt. He completed the two semesters of the academic year 1899–1900 in Munich.

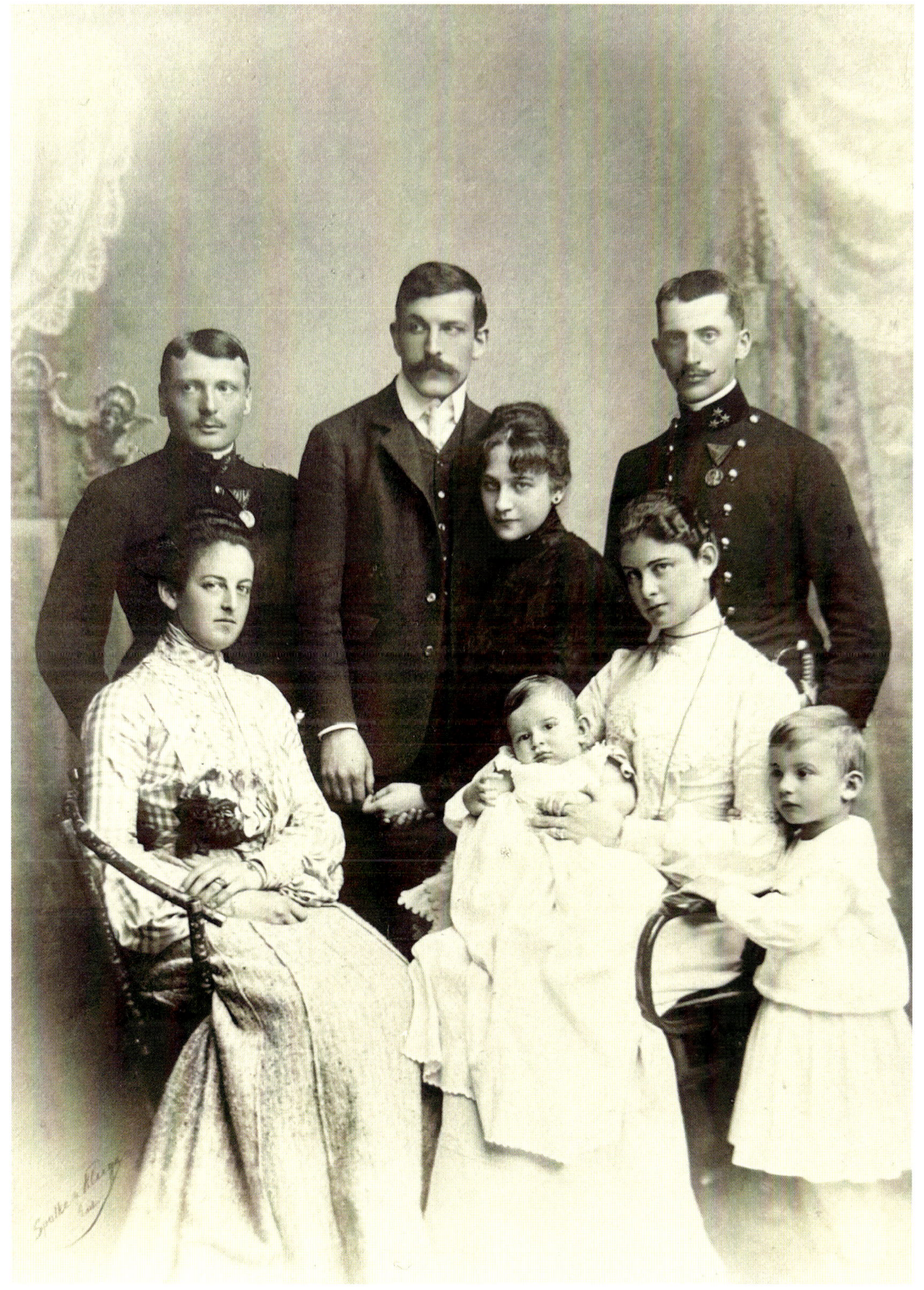

45. Erwin von Graff with his wife Olga (standing in the middle) and his sisters Dorothea and Friederike with their husbands and children, 1903. Private Collection

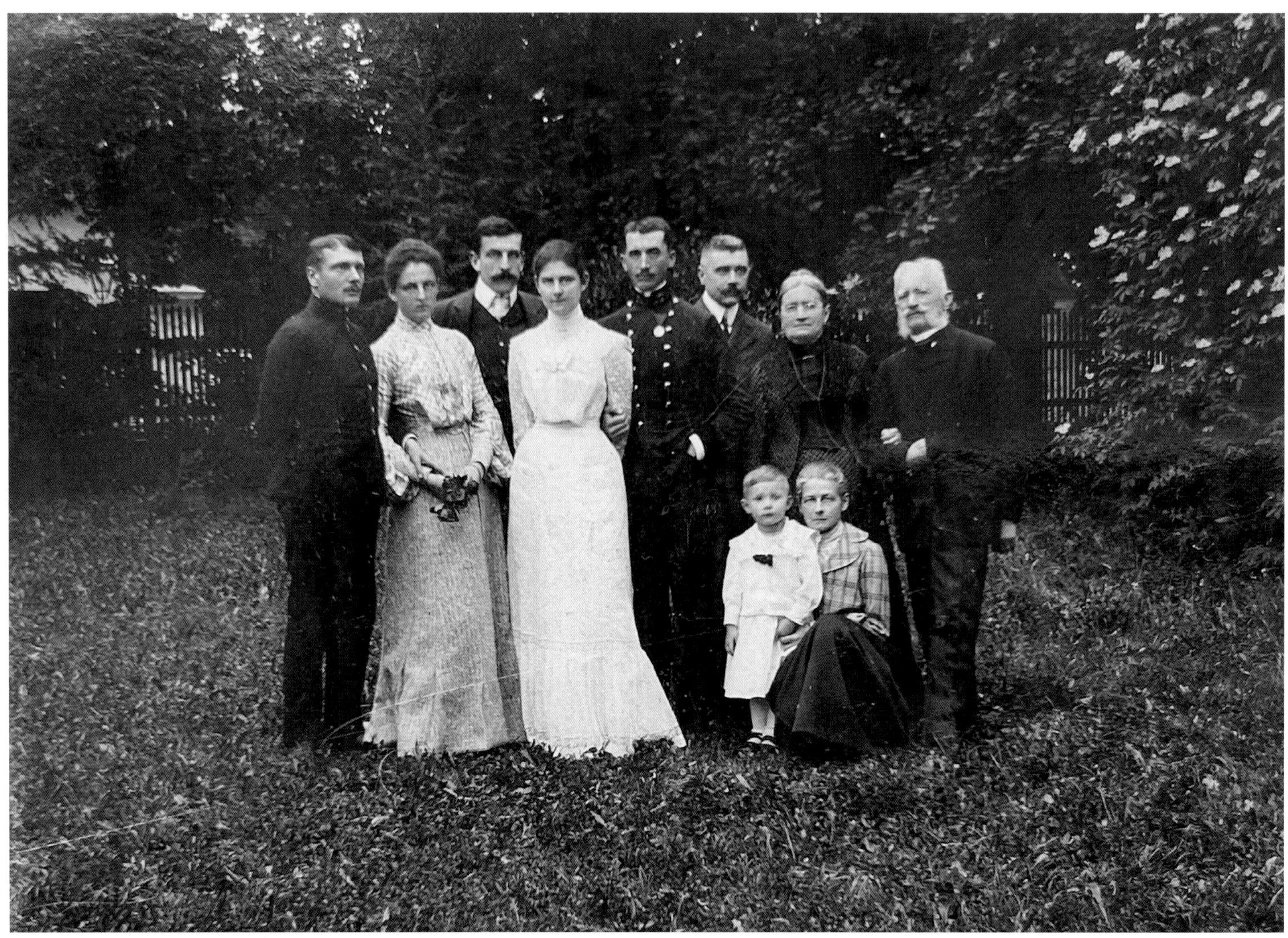

46. Erwin von Graff (third from left) standing between his sisters Dorothea and Friederike and along with their families. His mother is crouching in the foreground alongside her grandson Fritz, 1903. Private Collection

During his studies, Graff enjoyed being active athletically. He was a member of the Akademisch-technischer Radfahr-Verein (Academic and Technical Cycling Club) in Graz and was elected to its board on November 11, 1896.[71] He was also an enthusiastic alpinist and joined the social club with the humorous name Gilde zum groben Kletterschuh (Guild of the Crude Climbing Shoe) of Dr. Wolf von Glanvell, an important alpinist and law professor. During school vacations, his father paid for his travels, for example, in 1900 when he let him choose between a trip on the Rhine or a trip to Italy.[72] Jenny Graff wrote to her daughter Dorothea:

> Erwin studies diligently and is my faithful companion; he always spends evenings with me, much more than papa, who is usually out of the house twice a week for certain.[73]

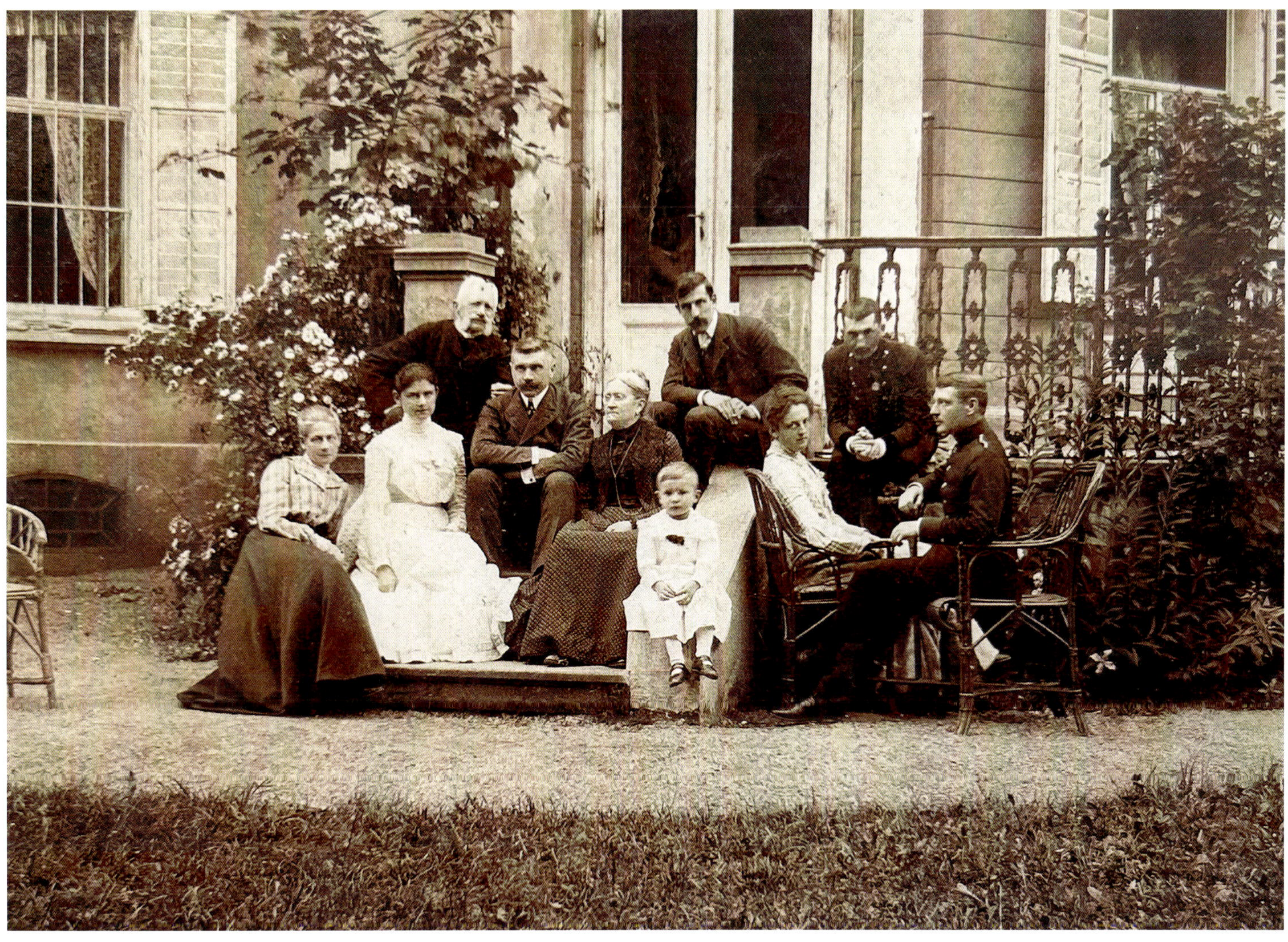

Graff completed his studies successfully and on May 9, 1902, received his doctorate in general medi-cine [Fig. 44]. Just three days later, the council of professors of the faculty of medicine decided to hire him as an assistant to the famous Professor Eppinger at the teaching chair for pathological anatomy at the Universität Graz for the period from April 1, 1902 (i.e., retroactively) to March 31, 1904. This haste and the sudden resignation of the previous assistant, Dr. Hermann Möschl, convey the impression that they wished to do his famous father and their university colleague a favor.

In March 1903, after completing his selective service as a one-year volunteer in the Austrian Army, Graff was appointed by Emperor Franz Joseph I to deputy assistant physician in Feldjäger Battalion no. 31 (part of the Infantry troops).[74] That same year, several family photographs were taken in the studio and the garden of the family's Villa Benedek in Graz [Figs. 45–47].

47. Jenny Graff (seated at far left) and Erwin von Graff (seated at top near the middle), surrounded by his sisters and their family members, 1903. Private Collection

Despite their geographical separation, Graff often hiked in the Alps with three climbing companions: Günther von Saar, a fellow student in Graz (later surgeon and alpinist) [Fig. 48], Karl Doménigg of Bozen (Bolzano) (later president of the Österreichischer Gebirgsverein [Austrian Mountain Club], and the engineer Othmar Sehrig from Innsbruck (pioneer of alpine skiing in Austria and editor of the first skiing guide for Tyrol).[75] During the Christmas holidays in 1900, they planned to escape their daily routines and venture the first climb of Grossvenediger Mountain with skis. With an altitude of nearly 12,000 feet (in 1900 it was 12,050 feet), Grossvenediger is the tallest mountain in Salzburg and one of the highest peaks in the Austrian Alps. With effort, they reached the summit in an eleven-hour ascent. They could only enjoy the grand view for a few minutes because they had to begin their descent quickly. Skis and bindings were still very primitive at the time, and they lacked knowledge of the technique of a sport that had only been introduced to Austria ten years earlier. It is therefore unsurprising that the descent took seven hours.[76] Their tour caused a great sensation in the media.[77] Reports even reached the United States.[78] Grossvenediger was the highest peak in the eastern Alps to have been reached on skis by that time. In Graz, Graff gave a lecture at the Deutscher und Österreichischer Alpenverein (German and Austrian Alpine Association) on January 21, 1901, titled "Eine Ersteigung des Grossvenedigers auf norwegischen Schneeschuhen" (First Climb of Grossvenediger on Norwegian Snowshoes, an old expression for skis).[79]

48. Fellow students Erwin von Graff,
Günther von Saar, and Edwin Rossival
(who did not participate in the ski tour),
ca. 1900. Private Collection

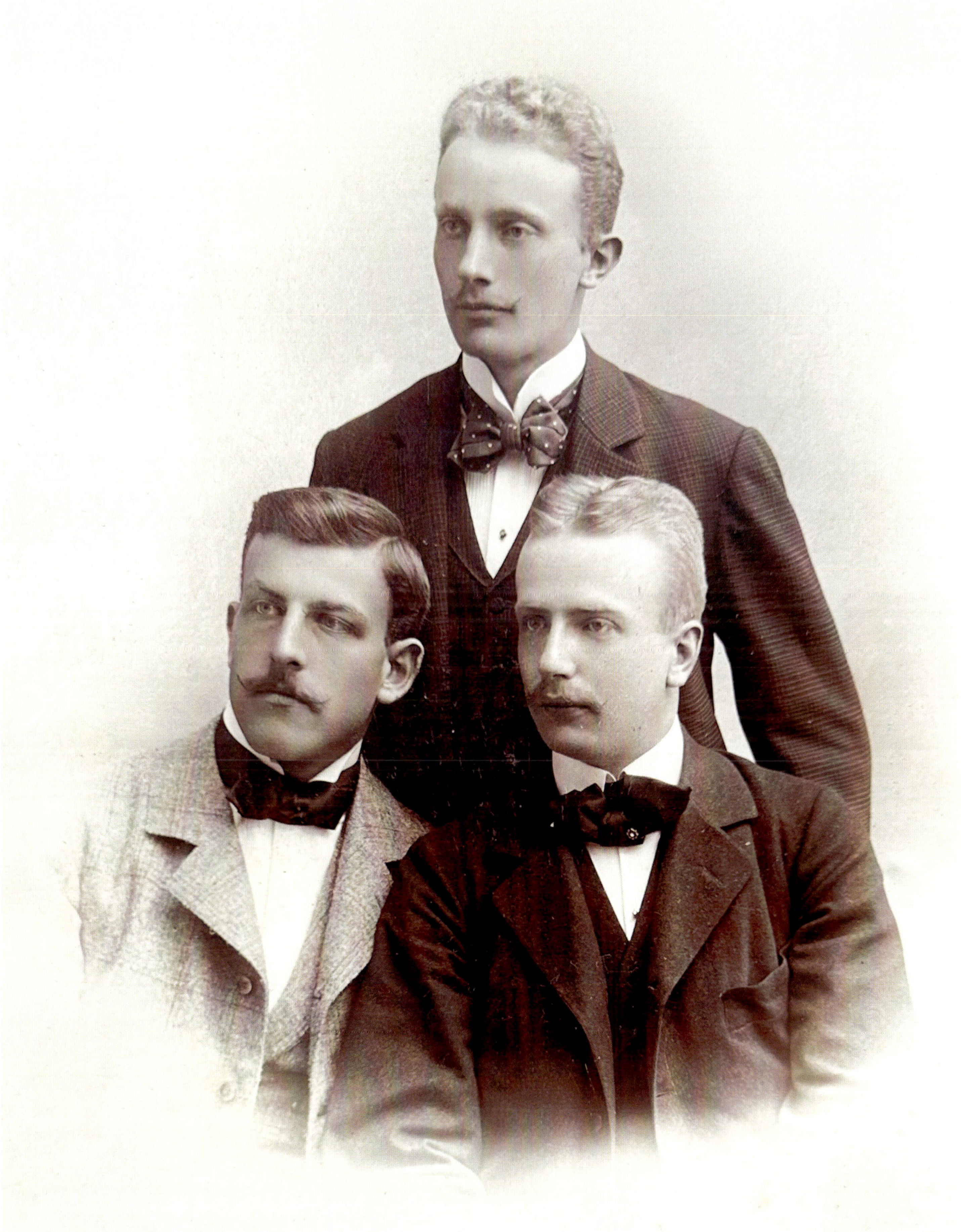

On April 1, 1904, Graff took a position as surgery pupil at the Chirurgische Klinik Eiselsberg (Surgical Clinic Eiselsberg) in Vienna. That was the name of the I. Surgical Clinic at the General Hospital in Vienna under the directorship of Anton von Eiselsberg. Eiselsberg was a student of Robert Koch, the founder of modern bacteriology and himself played an important role in introducing aseptic procedures in surgery and established surgery as an autonomous field of study. Radiology became a special subject under his directorship in 1904, just at the time when Graff arrived at his clinic. Von Graff had thus landed at the center of the Viennese medical school where European medical history was being written, and the most progressive medical teaching and research was taking place.[80] Von Graff was living at Höfergasse 13 in Vienna's ninth district at the time. Graff stayed with Eiselsberg until September 30, 1905, and then went to Innsbruck as a surgical student and assistant from October 1, 1905, to September 30, 1908, for the Graz surgeon Dr. Hermann Schloffer, who was ten years older and had been a full (tenured) professor in the faculty of medicine at Universität Innsbruck since 1903. In Innsbruck, Graff resided at Schöpfstrasse 27 [Fig. 49]. In May 1908, the army appointed him to assistant physician on inactive duty with the First Landwehr-Ulanen-Regiment (Territorial Army Uhlan/Lancer Regiment).[81]

49. Erwin von Graff in a rare instance without a mustache, 1907. Private Collection

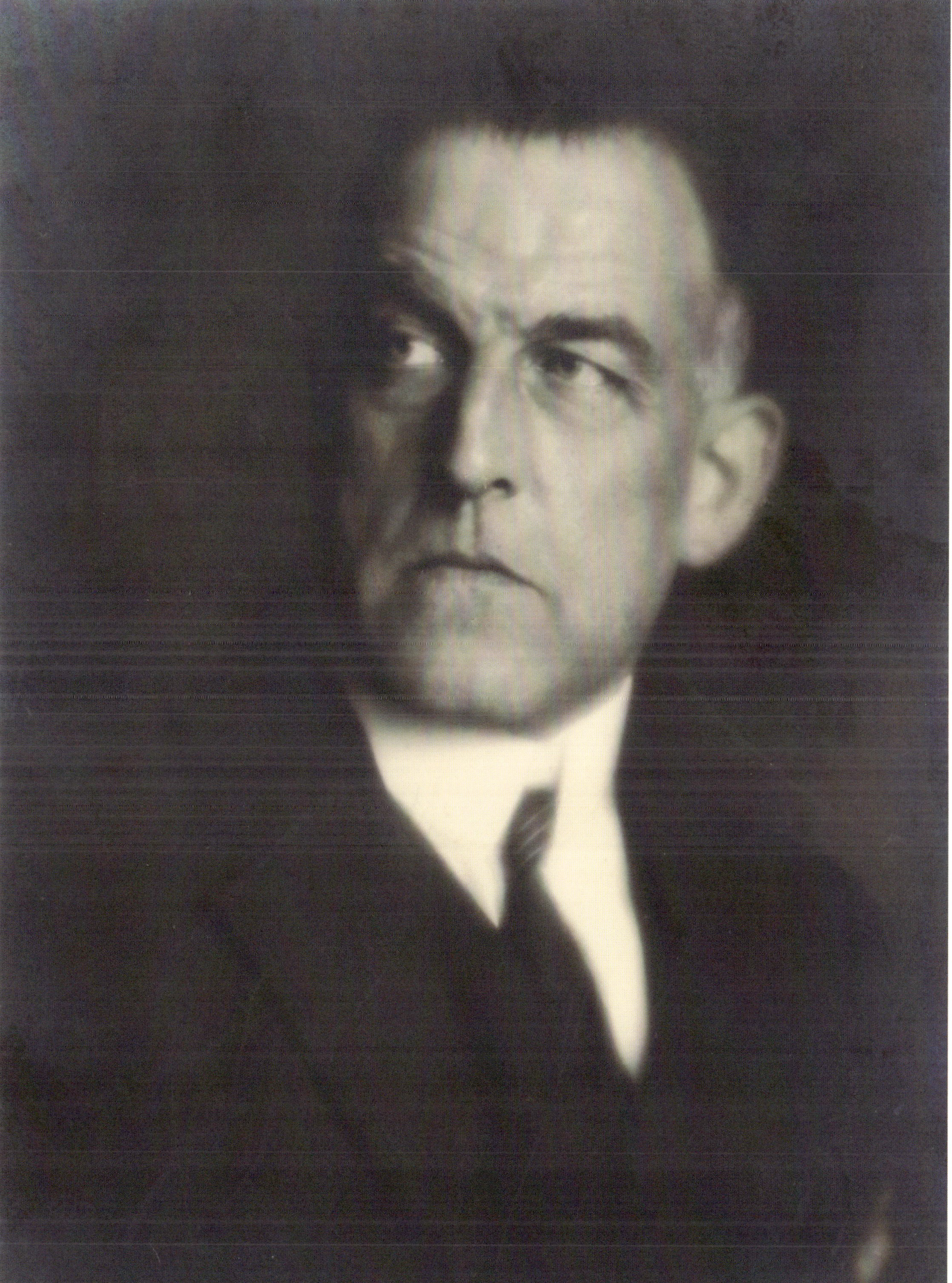

Universitäts-Frauenklinik II in Vienna

After his period in the surgical department in Innsbruck, Graff switched to the Second University Women's Hospital in Vienna as of October 1, 1908. At the same time, Professor Alfons von Rosthorn had been brought in from Heidelberg to take over as director of the recently founded clinic. Graff and Rosthorn knew each other from Graz, since Rosthorn was a full professor at the Universität Graz from 1898 to 1902, while Graff was a student there. Graff began working in the Second University Women's Hospital as an auxiliary doctor, until Prof. Dr. Wertheim proposed him for the approved fifth assistant position on October 1, 1911.[82] This position had to be reapplied for and approved annually and later biannually.

Prof. Dr. Rosthorn died unexpectedly in 1909. His successor at the Second University Women's Hospital was Ernst Wertheim, who had also studied medicine in Graz, and soon everyone was talking only about the Wertheim clinic [Fig. 50]. With an eye to the future, Wertheim pursued advances in X-ray deep therapy. This type of treatment was not well developed in the field of gynecology, however. He now championed especially an integration of radiotherapy into gynecology and already in 1910 arranged to acquire several pieces of modern equipment by circumventing the authorities.[83]

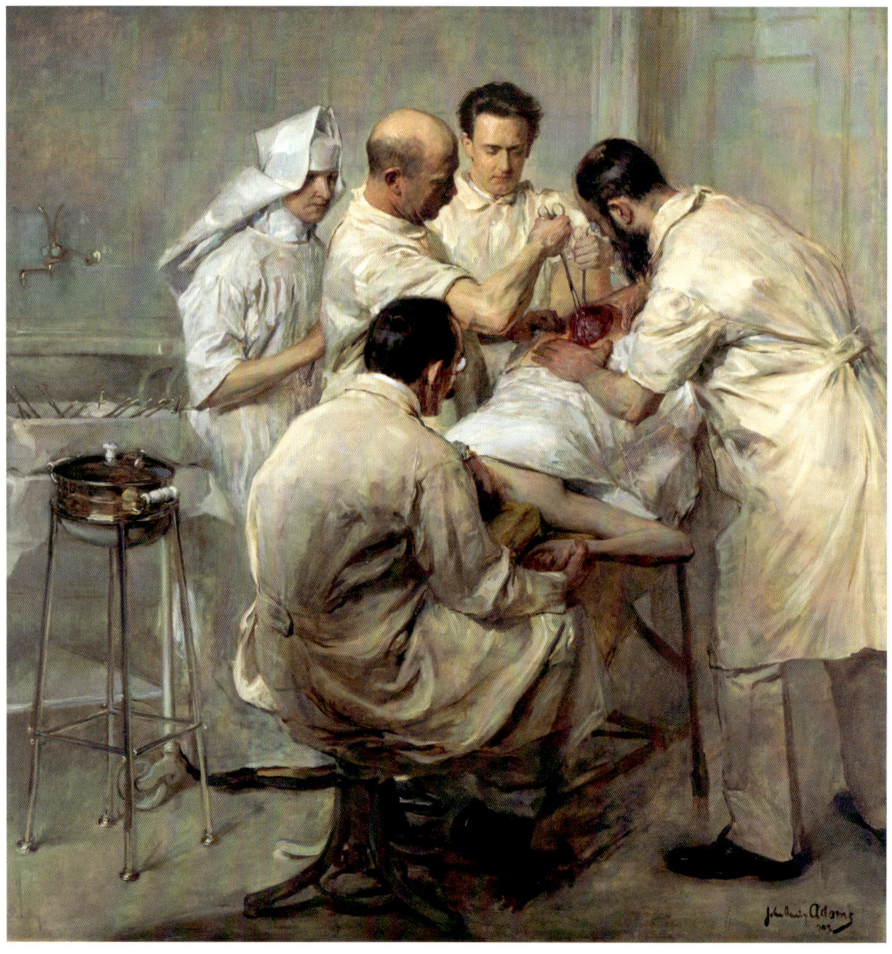

50. John Quincy Adams, *The Operation* (depicting Ernst Wertheim), 1909, oil on canvas, 200 x 200 cm (78 ³/₄ x 78 ³/₄ in.). Josephinum – Medical University of Vienna, inv. no. MUW-GE-006036. Photo Credit: Bene Croy

Graff lived for a year at Laudongasse 42 before finding an apartment very close to the clinic at Höfergasse 18 [Fig. 51].

Graff already had several years of surgical experience and had dedicated himself to cancer research specialized in radiation therapy under Wertheim. He neither studied nor published on the clinical picture of so-called hysteria. The Second University Women's Hospital focused on obstetrics and surgical interventions and did not admit any patients diagnosed with hysteria. In the spring of 1911, deep therapy—as the use of X-rays was called—began to be applied in the clinic. Graff explained in a lecture in 1913 that at the time there were two quite different treatment methods: one with a lower dose of radiation, the other with a higher one, though "nearly every gynecologist using radiation therapy has his own working method," influenced "by failures, on the one hand, and by the effort to shorten treatment time, on the other, prompting them to increase the amount of X-rays."[84] Graff also described daily life in the clinic with radiation therapy: Whereas at first one could "treat several women in one day, juggling with other activity in the clinic," the use of improved equipment for deep therapy now resulted in a "series of sittings, requiring the constant presence of a nurse and a doctor, six to eight hours."[85] Graff does not discuss the extent to which the nurse and doctor were protected from radiation, but it seems very likely that lengthy daily sessions led to levels of radiation exposure that would be inconceivable today. This has been proffered as a reason for his infertility, but it could be attributed to other causes as well.

Later a therapy combining X-ray and radium was developed that many doctors believed would make surgery unnecessary. Graff did not and emphasized from the beginning that the only reliable treatment for cancer was early detection and surgery. X-rays and radium could support and stabilize healing but could not replace the scalpel.[86] "A chance to cut is a chance to cure."[87]

As an assistant physician, Graff was also involved in teaching activity at the Medizinische Universität (Medical University) and gave lectures on obstetric operations.

On April 22, 1914, Graff applied to be granted the *venia legendi* for obstetrics and gynecology—that is, the right to teach at universities. He submitted thirty-four scientific papers or publications, which were "very favorably reviewed" by the director of his clinic, Dr. Ernst Wertheim, as stated in the evaluation of January 12, 1916.[88] Wertheim described Graff as an extraordinarily diligent person who intensely studied the scientific works of every field in which he was active. Wertheim also credited Graff with important contributions to the design of the X-ray station at the Second University Women's Hospital and described him as a very skilled, alert surgeon who had known all the methods and had had previous special surgical training. Because Graff was in the battlefield of war at the time, the Professoren-Kollegium (Committee of Professors) decided on March 29, 1916, to exempt him from the trial colloquium and trial lecture and grant him the *venia legendi* for obstetrics and gynecology.[89] Graff thus became a *Privatdozent* (qualified to teach at a university but without a position).[90]

On October 30, 1926, Graff was appointed as an "*ausserordentlich*" professor of obstetrics and gynecology.[91] At this time, the Faculty of Medicine was still part of the Universität Wien (University of Vienna) and not an independent university as it is today. It was remarked that Graff not only liked to teach but was a born pedagogue. He trained numerous Austrian and American physicians who had come to Vienna for that reason.[92]

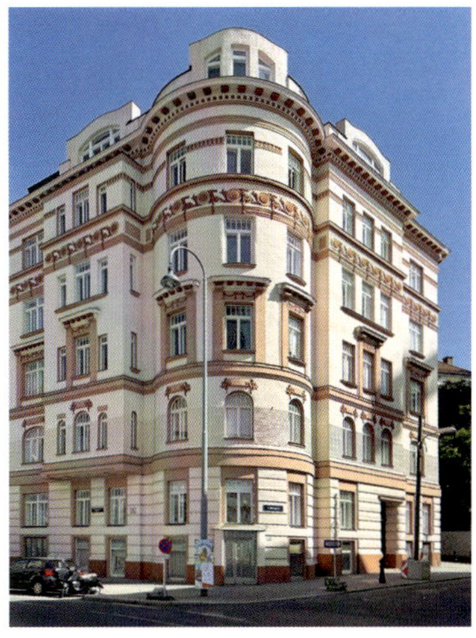

51. The building at Höfergasse 18 in the ninth district of Vienna, where Erwin von Graff lived from 1910 to 1915. Photo Credit: Elisabeth Dutz, 2025

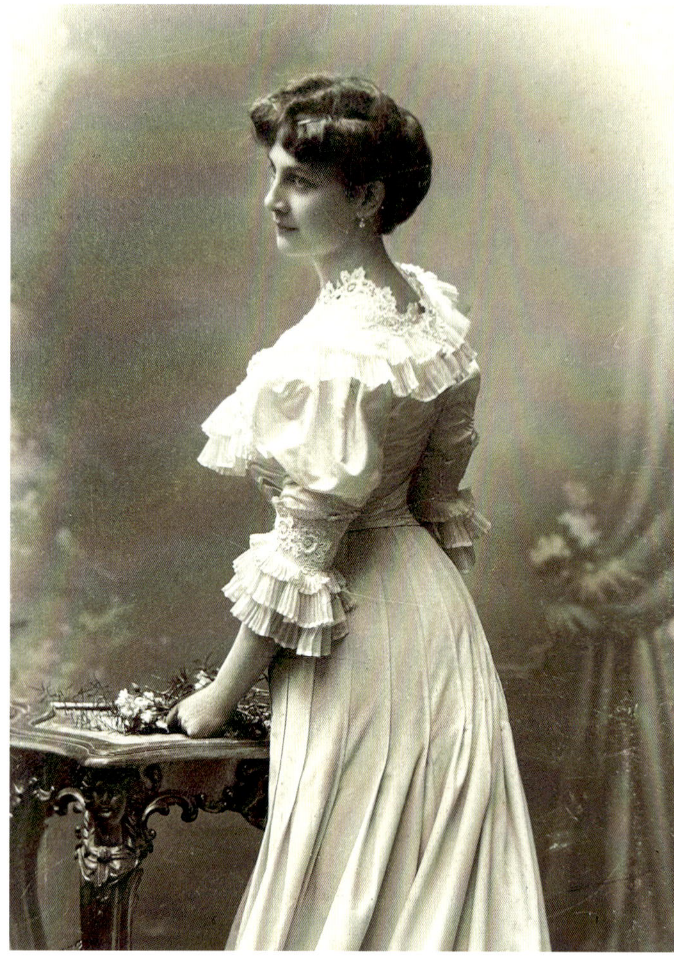

Marriage to Olga Fayenz

In Graz, Graff met Herta Olga Fayenz [Fig. 52], muse of his friend, the famous and aforementioned Austrian poet Max Mell. Olga had been born on November 5, 1880, in Fiume, Austria-Hungary (now Rijeka, Croatia), the daughter of Heinrich Fayenz, a naval officer from Trieste, and his wife. After Heinrich Fayenz retired, the family lived in Graz. Olga became a close friend of Graff's sister Dorothea and fell in love with him. The two married on October 4, 1902, in the Protestant parish church in Graz, a few months after he had received his doctorate [Fig. 53]. The young couple moved to Vienna in 1904 when Graff started his position with Professor Eiselsberg. He worked a great deal, and his wife was often alone and she never became accustomed to Vienna.[93] They later relocated to Innsbruck when Graff worked for Dr. Schloffer. Olga regularly wrote letters to her sister-in-law and friend Dorothea and reported on their social life. In 1910, the couple joined the Alpen-Skiverein (Alpine Skiing Club).[94]

The marriage remained childless and was dissolved on June 7, 1915, at Landesgericht IV (Provincial Court IV) in Vienna. Decades later, Olga wrote to Dorothea:

And then everything collapsed, the war came; Erwin, who was everything to me, left me, and the struggle for survival began; the best part was over.[95]

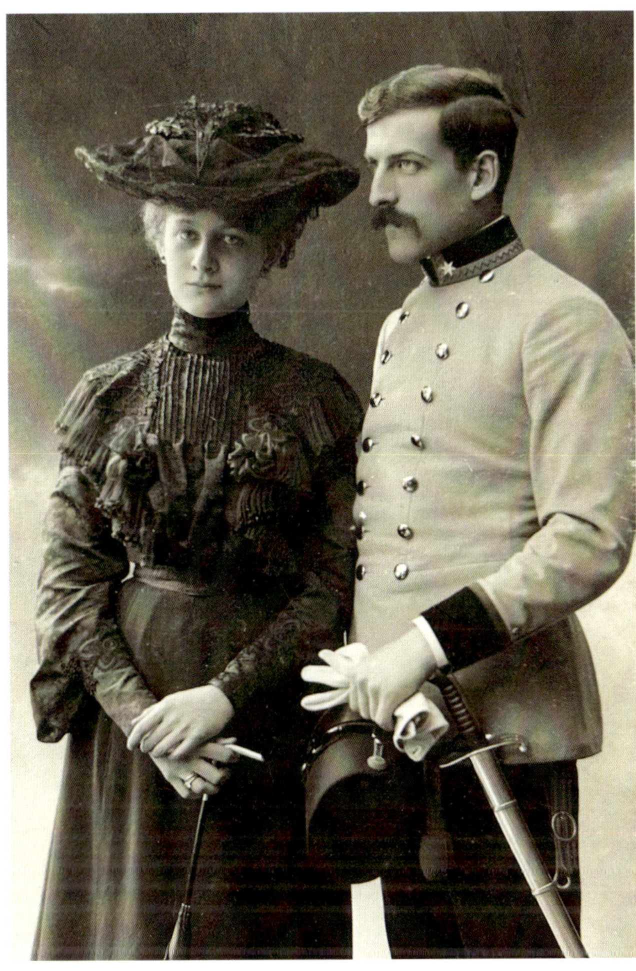

But Graff continued to feel responsible for her and mentioned her often in his diary of 1918–19:

> *Discussed everything with Olga because of the move. The poor woman is suffering doubly because of the war since it chains her to the cheerless and depressing company of her sister Irene.*[96] *Olgerl came yesterday—pale and slim. Vienna in the bright sunshine made her heart ache. The charming room at the Weisser Hahn is a great comfort. Today it is pouring, and after a day of hard work, we were at dinner with Max Mell. Olga will find her home and her peace. But her hour has not arrived yet—and I know that I can do a great deal to help with that.*[97]

Graff also thought about the reasons for their divorce:

> *Today I often understand so well that Olga had to let me go at the time because of my own immaturity, and I was neither strong nor free enough to transfer to her my idea of life's core: I had too much work to do on myself and could scarcely manage that. So, again and again, it is my fault—for the predisposition that kept her from finding the right path to me can never be considered her fault.*[98] *My heart is heavy with Olga and our lovely time together.*[99]

Olga kept the name von Graff after they divorced, lived in Berlin from 1929 to 1934, and then returned to Graz, where she died on October 17, 1971.

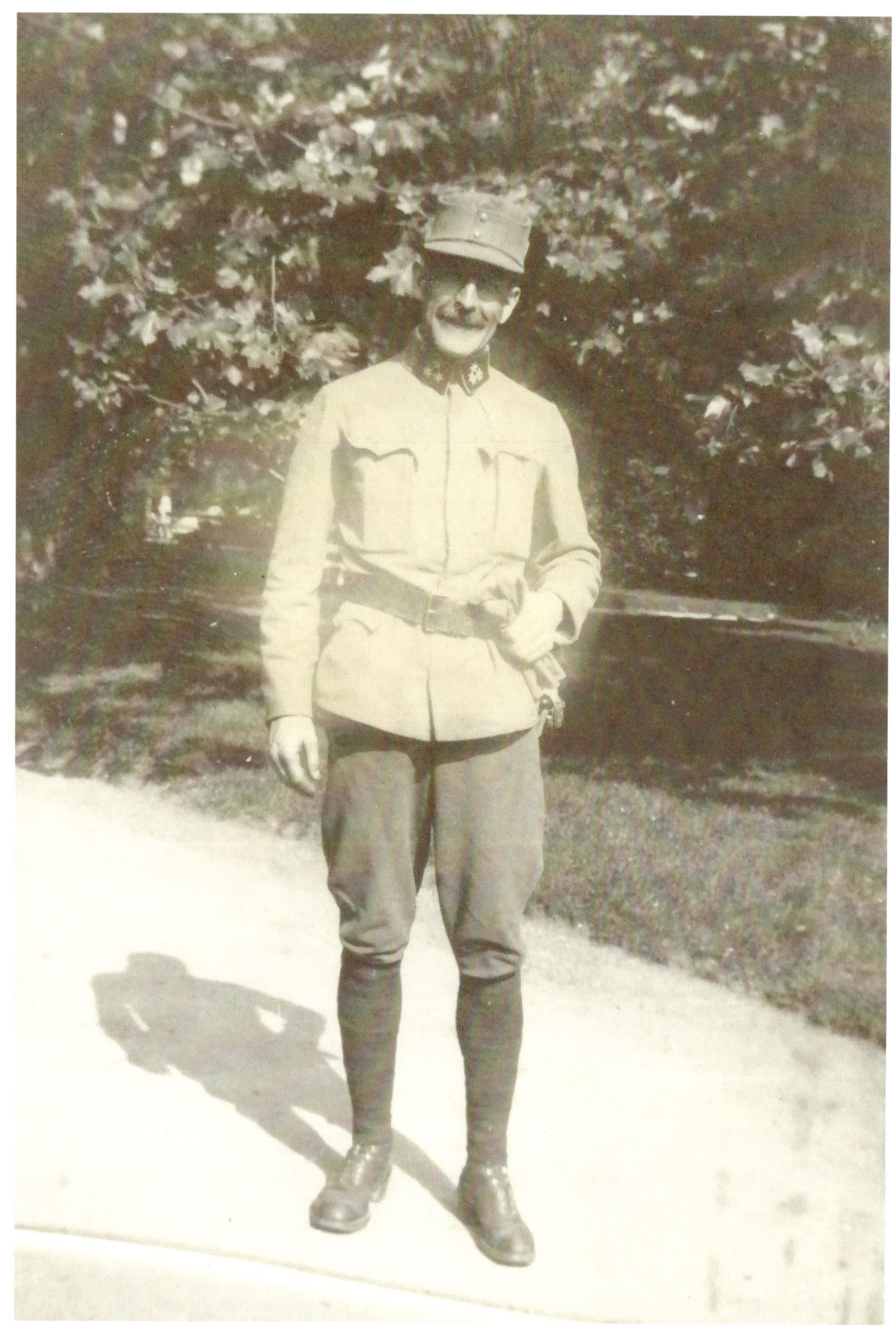

54. Erwin von Graff in his
military uniform, 1918, photo
from his diary from 1918–19.
Private Collection

Opposite:

55. Erwin von Graff's passport
1920. Private Collection

War Years, 1914–18

From the outset of the war, Graff served in the field as a senior physician;[100] in active service, he was sent to Krainburg (now Kranj, Slovenia), where he headed the department of surgery in the military hospital, which had been set up in the local secondary school [Figs. 54–55]. There he met Adele Fedrigoni von Etschthal [Figs. 56–57], who was born on August 1, 1891, in Bruck an der Mur in Styria and from the old patrician families Fedrigoni of Rovereto, Italy, and Ghetaldi-Gondola of Ragusa (now Dubrovnik, Croatia). In May 1915, she had to flee Görz (now Gorizia, Italy) to Krainburg because after entering the war against Austria-Hungary, Italy had declared as its goal to advance to the Isonzo River. Before the war, she had been living in Görz with her husband, the officer Konrad Saxl, and their three sons, but her husband had been reported as missing since October 1914. Adele and her sons Peter, Kurt, and Coloman found refuge with a friend in the Schlösschen Schrottenthurn in Krainburg. Because Adele had both a cook and a nanny, she decided to provide urgently needed assistance at the hospital along with several other women.

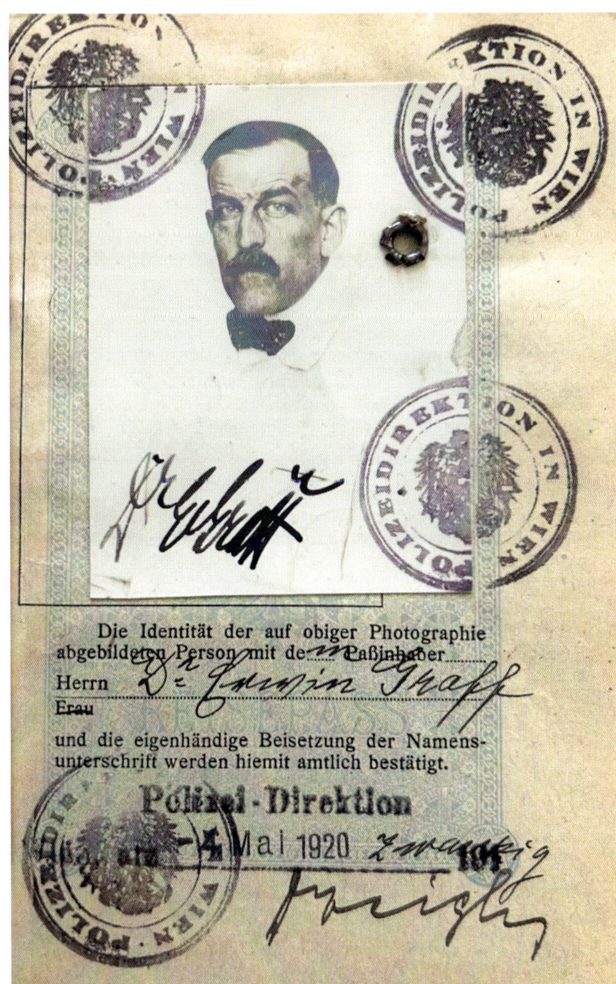

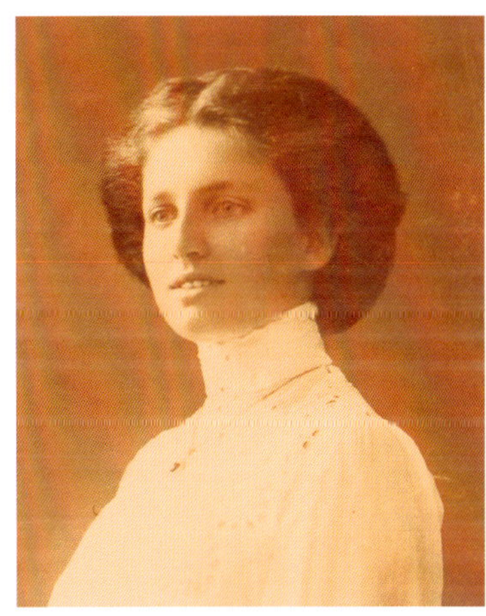

56. Adele Fedrigoni von Etschthal, 1910. Private Collection

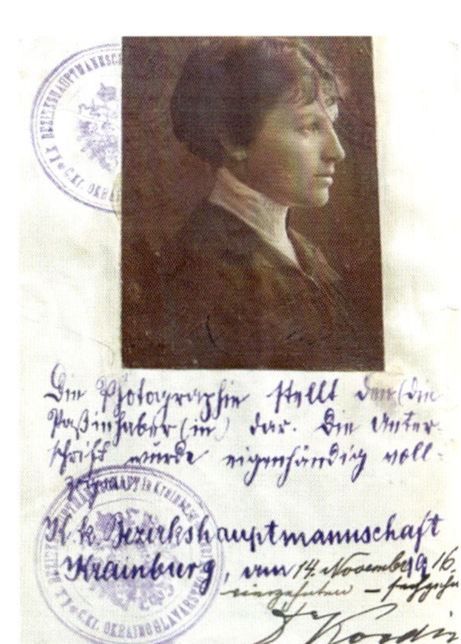

57. Adele Saxl, née Fedrigoni von Etschthal's passport 1916. Private Collection

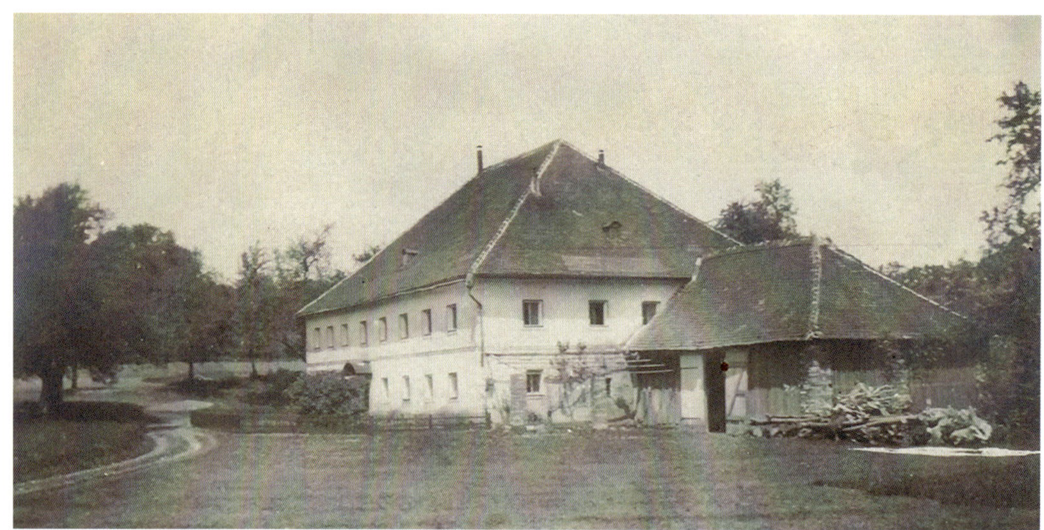

Graff proposed marriage to Adele shortly after they met. But years passed before the wedding could take place because they had to wait for the official declaration of Saxl's death. In the meantime, Graff and Adele lived with her children in a small house in Naklas (now Naklo, Slovenia) not far from Krainburg. Shortly thereafter, the reserve hospital was moved southward to the front in South Tyrol, and Graff decamped with it. Adele and her three young sons remained alone in the house, and soon they had to clear the ground floor when a sickbay for soldiers was set up there. Access to food grew worse, and it became increasingly difficult to quell her sons' hunger. In 1917, she obtained a loan to purchase the Ledertaschelmühle (Leather Bag mill) in Lower Austria [Fig. 58]. Von Graff had come across the property in an advertisement, and they were confident that it would be easier to survive the war in the countryside. The purchase of the mill was somewhat rushed, because Adele wanted to escape quickly from the terrible conditions in Naklas. As a result, when moving into the mill she was confronted by a large number of local residents who were being housed there. She convinced them to depart only very slowly, usually by compensating them for leaving.

Life was hard; there was no firewood and little to eat; rats were running around everywhere. Graff described the situation in his diary of 1918–19:

> The food is becoming ever more scarce and worse, and for ten days I was so down that I thought I was facing a serious illness.[101]

He tried to improve the provision of food by encouraging Adele to plant various vegetables and fruits and to raise animals [Fig. 59]:

> The carrots sown amid the barley are already sprouting, which represents great support, and our burgundy beets are doing well. Unfortunately, far too few of them. […] Yesterday, as the result of the first brooding experiment, eight splendid chicks hatched from the eighteen fertile eggs. Five developed well until the sixteenth day and fell victim only after being transferred from our laboratory to the hatching machine, which made me very sorry because it reduced the yield by nearly fifty percent.[102]

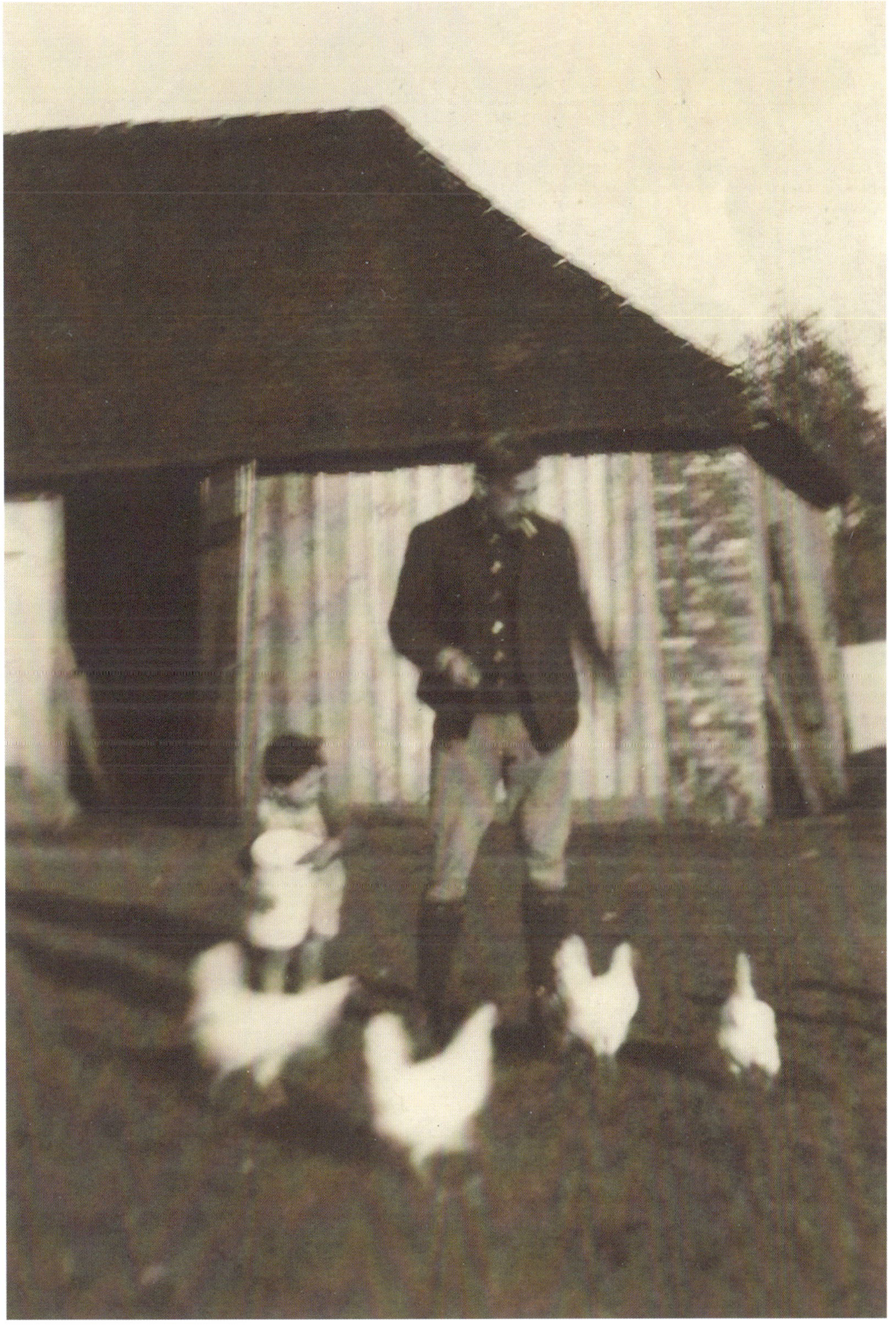

58. Mill in Lower Austria, where Graff visited Adele and her sons, 1918, photo from his diary of 1918–19. Private Collection

59. Erwin von Graff with one of Adele's sons on the mill grounds in Lower Austria, 1918, photo from his diary of 1918–19. Private Collection

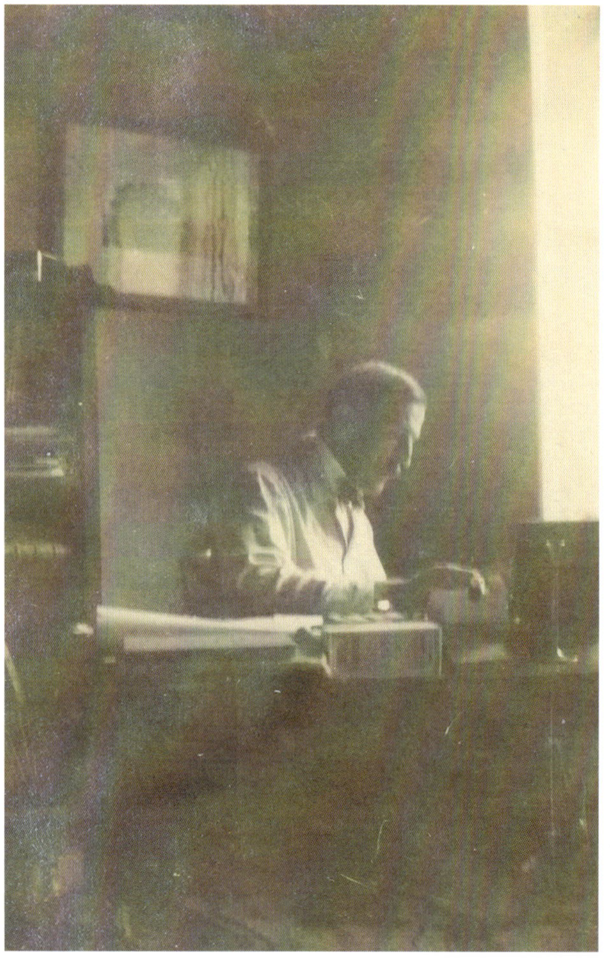
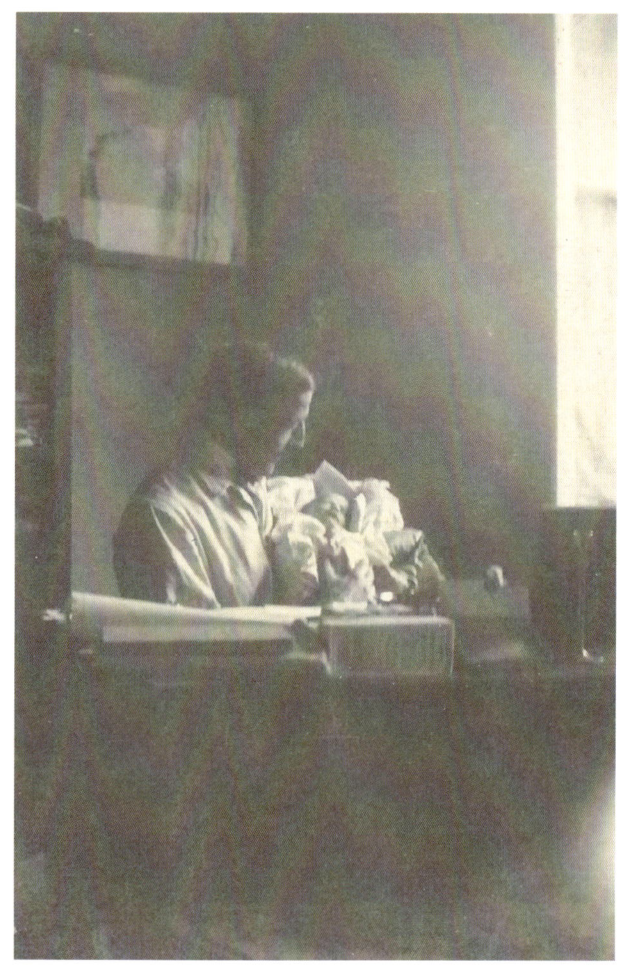

On October 10, 1916, Emperor Franz Joseph I awarded Graff the Ritterkreuz (Knight's Cross) of the Imperial Austrian Order of Francis Joseph with War Decoration.[103] Graff also received other decorations: the Goldenes Verdienstkreuz mit der Krone K.D. (Golden Cross of Merit with the Crown [and] War Decoration), Jubiläumserinnerungsmedaille (Jubilee Commemorative Medal), Jubiläumserinnerungskreuz (Jubilee Commemorative Cross) and Ehrenzeichen des Roten Kreuzes (Red Cross Decoration) with War Decoration. He was a member of the Gesellschaft der Ärzte (Society of Physicians) in Vienna, the Deutsche Gesellschaft für Chirurgie (German Society for Surgery), the Deutsche Gesellschaft für Gynäkologie (German Society for Gynecology), and the Gesellschaft Deutscher Naturforscher und Ärzte (Society of German Natural Scientists and Physicians).

Graff served in the military from August 2, 1914, to September 10, 1917, and then resumed his work at the Second University Women's Hospital [Figs. 60–62], living first in the clinic before finding a small apartment at Lange Gasse 50 in 1918. He worked in Vienna on weekdays and on most weekends traveled to Adele at the mill in Lower Austria, which was around 95 miles away. Adele, whom he referred to in his diary in alternation as *Marquislein* (Marchioness), because of her aristocratic origins, and Silpelit, after an elf in Eduard Mörike's "Elfenlied" (Elf Song), sometimes visited him in Vienna as well. Graff wrote of the situation with private patients: "'Business' was quite slow, although I made progress over May in the number of individual visits from twenty-five to twenty-nine. But there was not a single surgery." But sometimes his patients provided him with food:

> *Was so well supplied these past days by patients, with bread (milk bread), a roasted goose by Frau Kotal with all sorts of culinary arts, in addition to a daily coffee too good for words in the afternoon, that I arrived at the mill with a full load.*

Graff's diary also mentions taking carriage rides in the Prater in Vienna—a park in Vienna's second district, around four-square miles with abundant natural meadow landscape—in which he indulged despite their high cost.

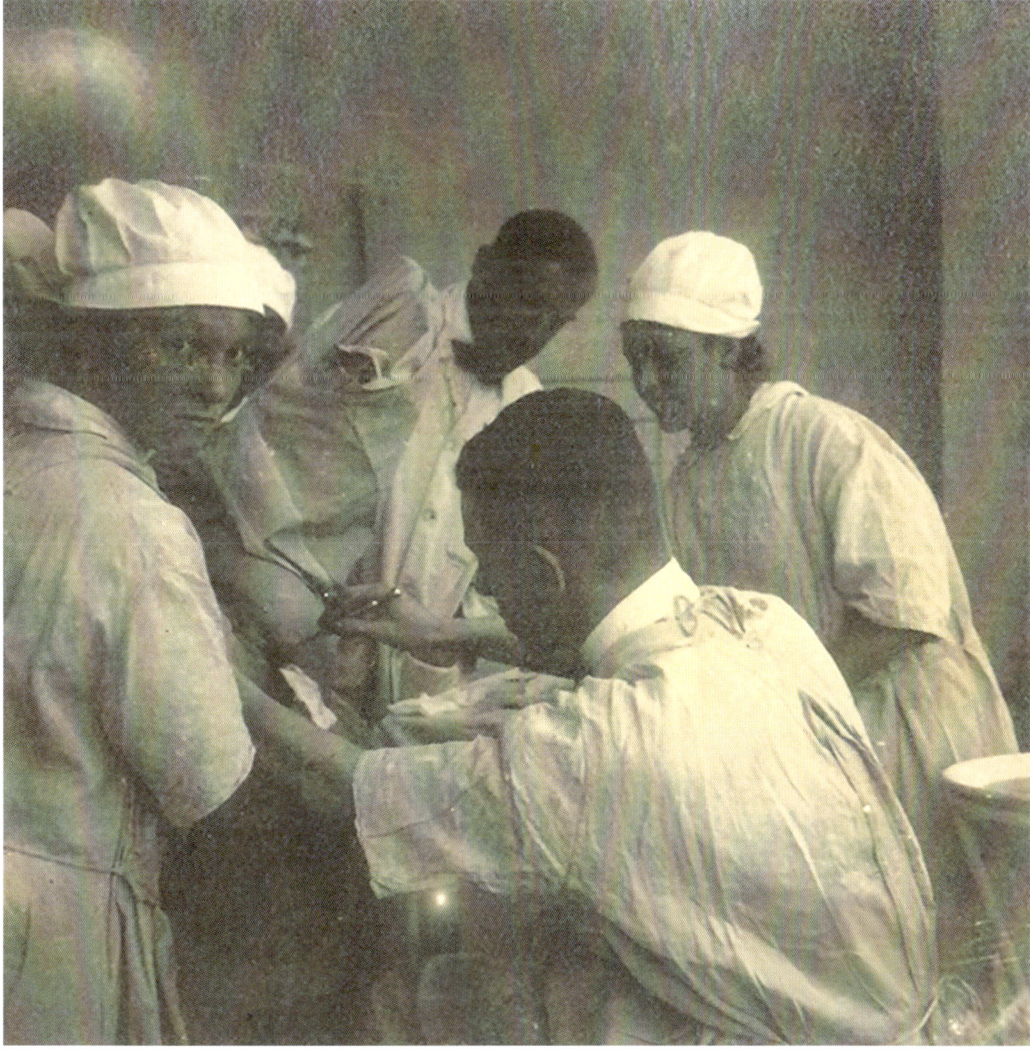

62. Erwin von Graff (standing at center in the back without a surgical cap) operating, 1918, photo from his diary of 1918–19. Private Collection

Repeatedly, Graff was overcome by melancholy about life before World War I:

> *The road through the old cemetery past [Gustav] Mahler's grave reminded me of the time long, long ago when we visited the tombstone and afterward placed a worthy memorial stone for Fritz Falk.[104] I often feel as if I must break all my chains and find my way back there at any cost. That is the torture and imperfection: believing that the yearning for the lost is unbearable—and yet one is alive after all, full of hope, and working on new happiness.*

Graff also found happy moments in music. He liked to play the cello and did so often, playing with Adele [Fig. 63]. "Sunday evening, tried for the first time a Brahms trio (B major after a sextet). Breathtakingly beautiful."[105] He was also interested in the visual arts. He reported on a visit to the memorial exhibition of Ernst Stöhr (1860–1917) at the Secession and of his friendship with the painter Oswald Roux (1880–1961), who was also a member of the Secession: "Oswald is serious and gaunt and since I last saw him a voice in the halls of the Secession, doggedly fighting against convention and for new talents."[106] "After a long time in the Alte Welt [an artists' club in Vienna], where I wanted to invite Roux to a Sunday at the mill. In the meantime, however, traveling has become such an uncertain undertaking that we prefer to postpone it."[107]

Graff wrote a great deal in his diary about the political developments of 1918–19 and very much longed for peace. When the war ended in November 1918, he noted:

> *Tuesday the 12th, the republic was proclaimed, but I cannot believe it will last given the monarchist mentality that runs in the blood of the Alpine countries and us Austrians. Above all, I am opposed to the much-vaunted annexation to the great Republic of Germany, which after all still means a Prussian system, and we Austrians are not suited to that. I am certainly a good German but much more decidedly an Austrian, and those are and will always be two distinct concepts.[108]*

63. Adele Saxl, née Fedrigoni von Etschthal, seated at a piano with Erwin von Graff's cello in the background, 1918, photo from his diary of 1918–19. Private Collection

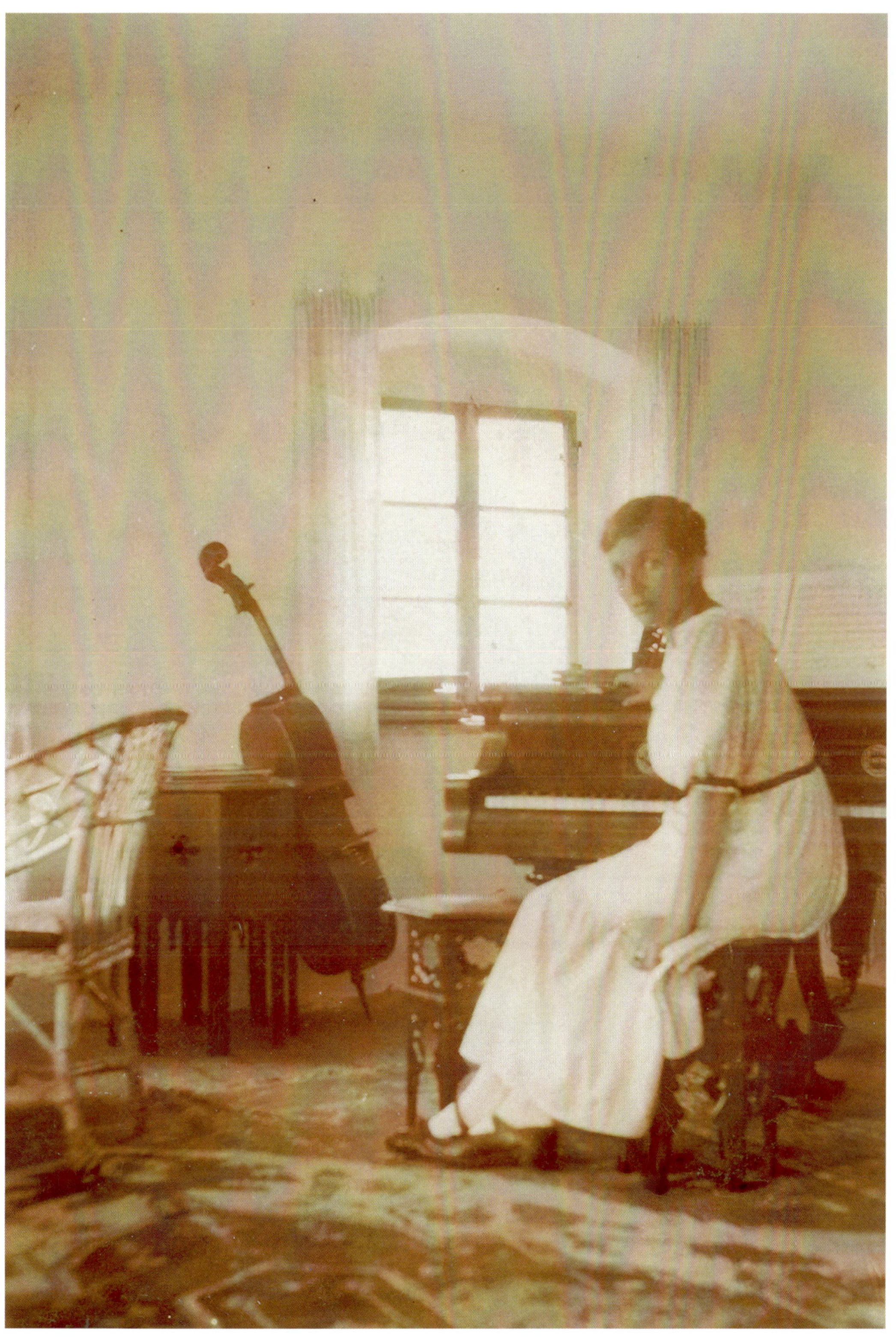

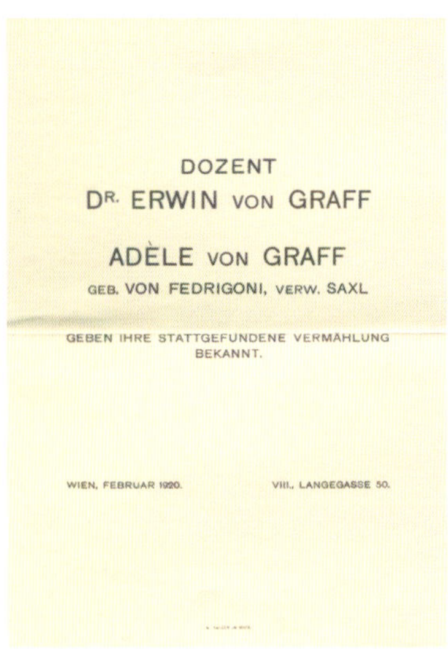

64. Marriage announcement
of Dr. Erwin von Graff and
Adele Fedrigoni von Etschthal,
1920, sent to Max Mell. Vienna
City Library, ZPH 891/8

Marriage to Adele Fedrigoni von Etschthal

At the beginning of 1920, Adele's missing husband was finally officially declared dead. Graff and Adele married on February 14, 1920, in the Lutherische Stadtkirche (Lutheran City Church) in Vienna [Fig. 64]. One of the witnesses was the painter Oswald Roux. Schiele had married Edith Harms in the same church on June 17, 1915. For Graff, the sons from Adele's first marriage were a very welcome bonus; he enjoyed the role of father and adopted them, so that they took the name Graff de Pancsova [Fig. 65]. The family lived at Grillparzerstrasse 5 in Vienna, directly behind the town hall and twenty minutes by foot to the Second University Women's Hospital, where Graff continued to work [Fig. 66]. In 1924, they moved to nearby Universitätsstrasse 8, even closer to the clinic. The marriage was not a happy one. Graff absolutely wanted children of his own and every month severely reproached his wife for failing to get pregnant. As early as 1918 he noted many times how much he wished to have a child:

Unfortunately, a large, silent, happy hope turned out to be futile, which weighed heavily on my mood.

Elsewhere he revealed:

Two things keep me going: work—clinically, through recognition from Wertheim, whose student I only now am truly becoming, and the slow but sure growing into scientific work—and then the happy hours with Silpelit, who comes in here frequently [i.e., travels to Vienna]. Once I even believed that my life's dream had come true—but unfortunately the joy did not last long.[109]

The problem was clearly with Graff: the large amount of radiation to which he was constantly exposed in the clinic could have caused his sterility. Only after many years of its use did doctors gradually realize the dangers of radiation. In 1927, the geneticist Hermann J. Muller emphasized its genetic effects.[110] It is no longer possible to identify the exact cause, but the subject of infertility preoccupied him as a gynecologist as well. It goes without saying that he saw it as a problem for women. In 1926, he wrote the book *Die Unfruchtbarkeit der Frau* (Female Infertility). But Adele Graff was, as she noted, subjected to terrible psychological suffering in her marriage and felt profound disappointment and despair.[111]

In her memories Adele summed up her marriage with Erwin von Graff:

This man, who was thirteen years older than me, had a huge influence on me. He was highly educated, cultured, musical, and gifted with knowledge of beauty and art, and had a refined taste. He was a true embodiment of the fin de siècle, somewhat decadent, and very handsome. He was far superior to me in experience and refinement. He was delighted by the fact that I had three healthy and magnificent little sons and promised to adopt them, which was done after our marriage.[112]

Through a mutual friend, the musician Gedeone Rosanelli, Adele met Wilhelm von Lička (1897–1971) in the early 1920s while skiing on the Turracher Höhe, located on the border between Carinthia and Styria in the Austrian Alps. Lička had served as a first lieutenant during World War I and participated in the daring September 1918 Battle of San Matteo operation to recapture Punta San Matteo in the Ortler Alps in northern Italy. As his family's fortune was lost during the war, Lička abandoned his dreams of studying chemistry and accepted a position with the Shell corporation, which offered a stable career. Over time, his friendship with Adele evolved into love, and they had two children together during her marriage with Graff, which was legally dissolved in 1929. In 1932 Adele married Lička and had another child with him. After the separation from Graff, Adele lived in Vienna with her children at Am Wasserturm 111–112, but following her wedding moved to Graz and had an extraordinarily happy marriage with Lička for the rest of her life.

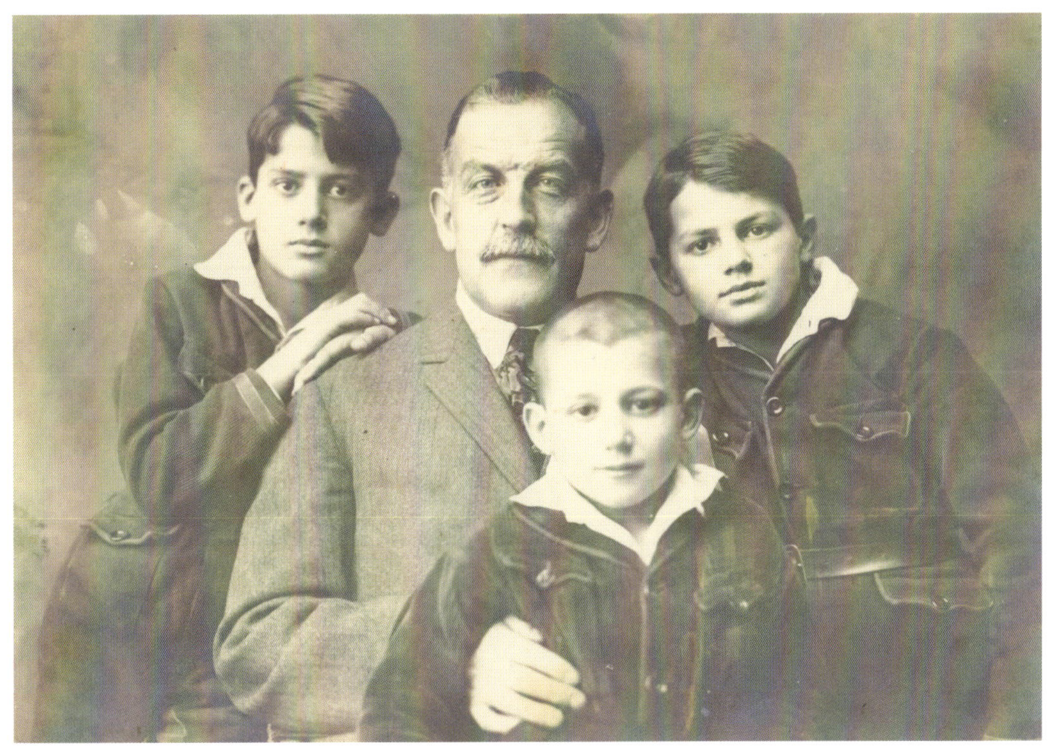

65. Erwin von Graff with his adopted sons Peter, Kurt and Coloman, 1920. Private Collection

66. Staff of the Second University Women's Clinic, Vienna. Erwin von Graff is seated on the far right and the clinic's director, Fritz Kermauner, is seated in the middle, 1925. Josephinum – Medical University of Vienna, inv. no. MUW-FO- 000670-0767

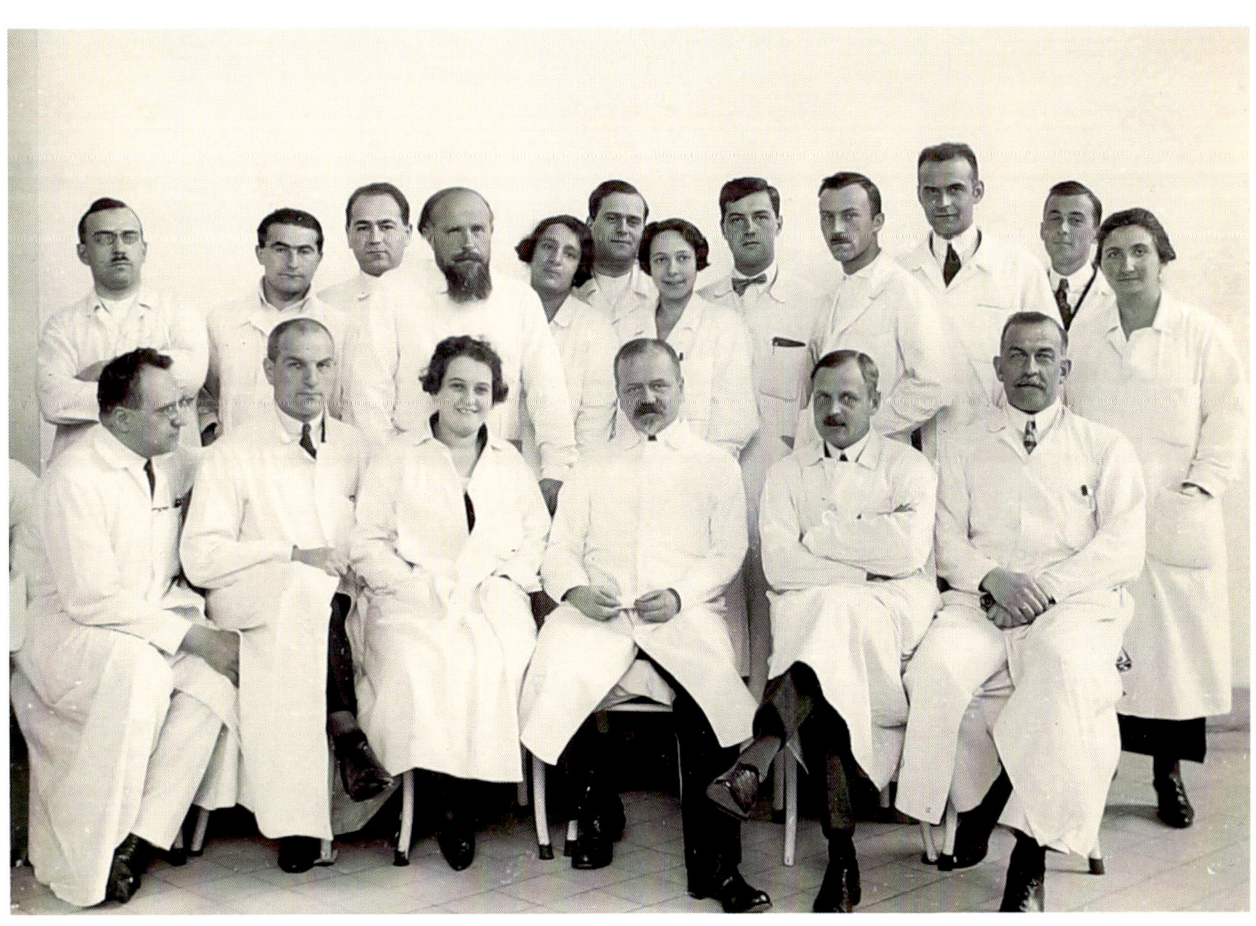

Graff [Fig. 67] worked with university lecturer Anton Werkgartner on the inheritance of red blood cell type in connection with paternity testing. They identified six so-called irregular cases that could be explained by the fact that the child had been fathered by someone other than the man named by the mother.[113]

Another publication was "*Behandlung der Sterilität*" (Treatment of Sterility), in which Graff spoke out vehemently against abortion and lamented the moral decline of today's youth. At the same time, he noted an enormous increase in cases of sterility and directly connected the two.[114] In his lecture "*Die Fruchtbarkeit der Ehe*" (The Fertility of Marriage), Graff argued that children are the basis for the happiness of a marriage. He claimed that majority of unhappy marriages are the result of "the lack of a bond that has to be formed via the child."[115]

From 1928 to 1931, Graff gave lectures both as continuing education for physicians and for interested lay audiences. He continued to work at the Second University Women's Hospital.

Freemason

On October 28, 1928, Graff was admitted to the Gleichheit (Equality) freemason's lodge in Vienna. His code name was Bartholomäus, his father's middle name and the first name of his great-grandfather. On January 14, 1930, Graff was promoted to journeyman, and on December 27, 1930, became a master. He was "*gedeckt*" (demitted) on December 9, 1936, which amounted to his leaving the lodge.[116] Because one did not normally leave a freemason lodge, the reason may have been that he had joined a lodge in New York, although this could not be verified.

University of Iowa

On January 4, 1931, Graff travelled from Vienna for a two-month lecture tour in the United States that took him to Los Angeles; Kansas City; San Francisco; Marshfield, Wisconsin; Chicago; and Honolulu, among other places, giving several lectures at each stop as well as clinical demonstrations. He participated in medical conferences and also spoke about the political and economic situation of Austria to a Rotary Club and a commercial club in Marshfield.[117] The tour was at the invitation of Dr. Monti L. Belot (1885–1963), who had studied with Graff in Vienna, and the Jackson County Medical Society.[118] In Los Angeles, Graff met other former students, Dr. A. Kincoln Dresser and Dr. Leon Tiber,[119] as well as Dr. Erich Wisiol in Stevens Point, Wisconsin.[120] Altogether, the media reported, two thousand leading pediatricians owed their postgraduate know-how to Graff.[121] In his lectures, Graff advocated some form of birth control, since "Every woman has the inherent right to regulate the size of her family."[122]

Graff gave several newspaper interviews and stated, among other things, that he considered it important to take a patient's personality into account as a factor when making a diagnosis. The human body cannot simply be taken apart like a machine and studied, he argued. Each body belongs to a personality of its own, which is often much more significant than a blueprint of the heart and lungs. He stated that the laboratories in America were incomparably equipped and that this leads to an overestimation of the value of laboratory results, leaving out the patient's personality. Given the same laboratory result, there are patients who will die and others who will recover. A good physician with precise knowledge of a patient's psychology is necessary to combat illness more effectively.[123]

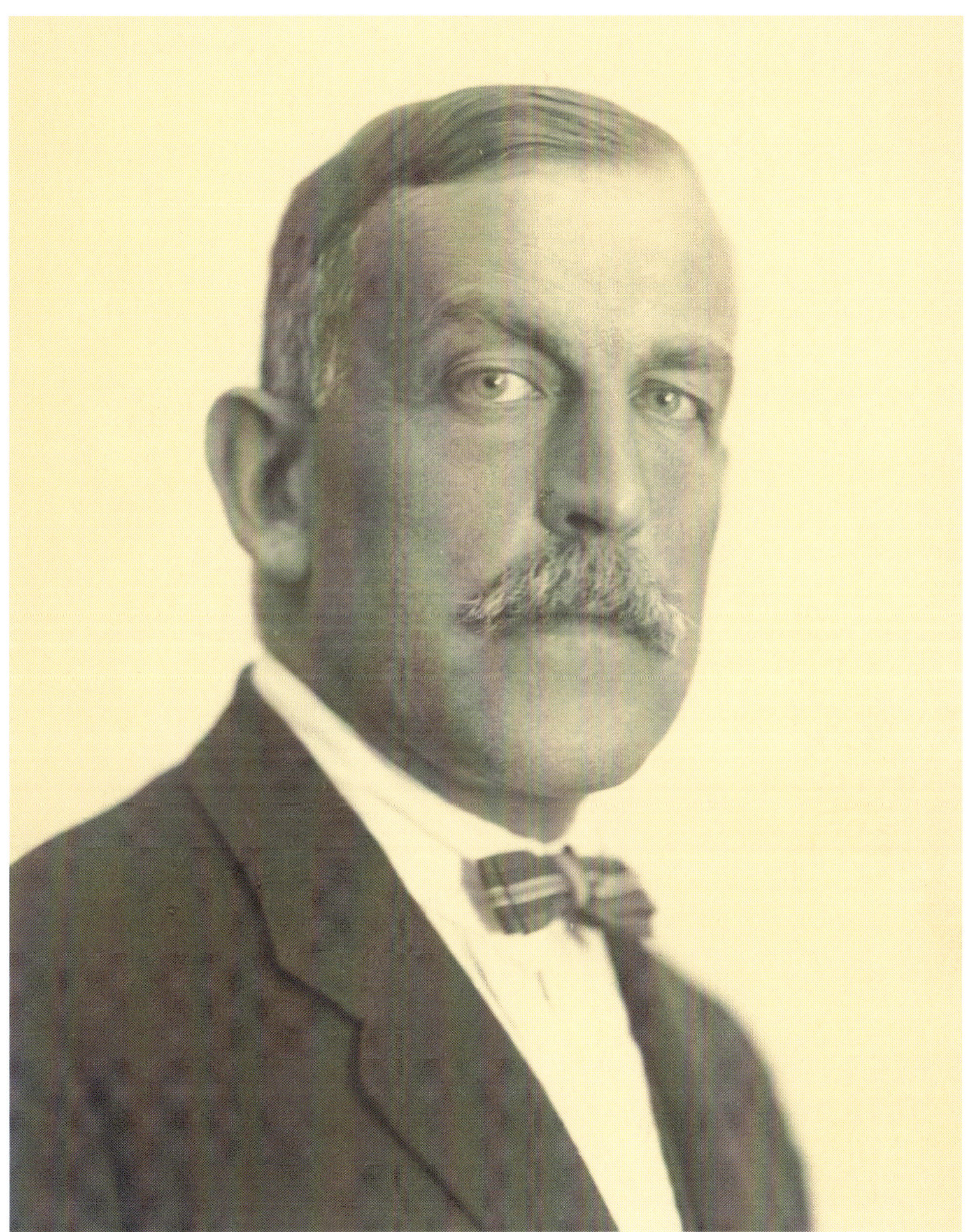

68. "Vienna Specialist Here,"
accompanied by a photo of
Dr. Erwin von Graff, *The Kansas
City Times*, April 30, 1931,
p. 2 www.newspapers.com/
image/655449085/ [Accessed
August 11, 2025]

The text reads:

*VIENNA SPECIALIST HERE
SERIES OF LECTURES BY
DR. ERWIN VON GRAFF,
GYNECOLOGIST.*

*He Also Is an International
Authority on Obstetrics—Guest
of Dr. M. L. Belot and Medical
Society.*

    *Dr. Erwin von Graff,
professor of gynecology at
the University of Vienna, and
an international authority on
gynecology and obstetrics, arrived
here last night to deliver fourteen
lectures to Kansas City physicians
and surgeons.*

    *Dr. von Graff is a guest
of Dr. Mont L. Belot and of the
Jackson County Medical Society.
His first lecture will be at 11
o'clock today, before obstetricians
and gynecologists, at the
assembly room in the Medical
Arts building.*

    *In addition, he will conduct
clinics at various hospitals in
the city for the specialists. Next
Tuesday night he will speak to
the Jackson County society at
the Medical Arts building, and
May 4 he will speak at the Alfred
Benjamin clinic.*

    *Dr. von Graff has been in
America two months. He came
to America at the behest of
numerous American surgeons
who were former pupils, among
whom is Dr. Belot. Dr. von Graff
came here from Los Angeles,
where he delivered a similar
series of lectures.*

Graff warned of alcohol and tobacco misuse, because it could have a negative influence on the fertility of men and women.[124] Prohibition in America was a "psychological mistake" that had led to people who had never drunk before suddenly feeling the desire to do so, causing many people to become habitual drinkers.[125]

In Kansas City, Graff drove a car for the first time in his life. He explained that he owned no car in Vienna because he would have had to pay taxes equivalent to $300 annually. Driving a car fascinated him, because you simply forget everything: work, office, whatever you are thinking about, and even your family.[126]

In the spring of 1931, he received an appointment at the University of Iowa [Fig. 68]. It was offered to him as a chair in the Department of Obstetrics and Gynecology. On June 20, 1931, he wrote to the dean of the Faculty of Medicine in Vienna:[127]

    Honored Dean!

    After more than twenty-five years as a clinical auxiliary physician, assistant, lecturer, and ausser-ordentlich professor under the aegis of the Faculty of Medicine of the University of Vienna, it is my pleasant duty to inform you, Honored Dean, as the representative of the committee, that during my lecture tour through the United States of America, I was offered the Chair of Obstetrics and Gynecology at the University of Iowa in Iowa City, Iowa, and after several discussions I have accepted this offer.

    At the same time, I express my sincere gratitude to the committee of professors for the support I have received during my career. To my great regret, it is impossible for me to do this personally, since I begin my teaching duties in Iowa on July 1, 1931.

    With my sincere compliments,

    Dr. Graff

PLANE CRASHES WITH 10

FIVE ARE INJURED WHEN N. A. T. SHIP IS FORCED DOWN.

Sam Taylor, Pilot, Is in a Critical Condition After Ohio Accident —"Gorilla" Jones, Who Fought Here Tuesday, a Passenger.

(By the Associated Press.)

ELYRIA, O., April 29.—Three passengers and two pilots were injured, the latter severely, when a National Air Transport tri-motored passenger and mail plane from Chicago to Cleveland, crashed in making a forced landing about five miles north of here late today. Five passengers escaped injury. The plane was damaged badly.

Sam Taylor, widely known mail and passenger pilot, received a possible skull fracture and a fractured left ankle and his co-pilot, Allen McDiarmid, also of Cleveland, received possible fractured ribs and internal injuries.

The three passengers, all of whom were treated for minor injuries, were P. O. Gadebusch and W. Weber, both of New York, and Harry J. Flaber of Cleveland.

"GORILLA" JONES A PASSENGER.

"Gorilla" Jones, Akron Negro welterweight boxer, and his manager, Suey Welsh, were among the passengers who escaped injury. Others were Miss Zola Taylor of New York, Lynn Jordan and Raymond Bjorkbohm, both of Cleveland. Bjorkbohm is an employee of N. A. T., but was riding as a passenger.

Passengers and witnesses agreed that the forced landing was caused by two motors going dead. The passengers said Taylor warned them to fasten their safety belts when motor trouble developed, and made sure they were fixed before he started to set the plane down.

The left wing of the plane slipped off the top of a small tree, the impact turning the craft around and sending it careening through telephone wires beside a road. It landed partly on its nose and left side against a barn in a farmyard.

CONTINUE THE JOURNEY.

The New Yorkers continued to their destination in a special plane tonight.

Jones was scheduled to box Madison Dix of San Francisco in a 6-round main bout in Cleveland tonight. The program was postponed.

Taylor has figured in two previous events which brought him widespread attention. February 25, 1929, all three motors of his plane went dead over the center of Cleveland, but he landed in a small lot on the East Side. Although the plane crashed through several fences, only one of his thirteen passengers was slightly hurt.

Taylor became the center of a controversy with Col. Charles A. Lindbergh at the national air races in Cleveland September 1, 1929. Flying a passenger plane into the port, Taylor charged that Lindbergh prevented him from landing by stunting around the transport ship. Lindbergh in turn complained that Taylor interfered with his scheduled aerial acrobatics, a part of the air show program.

"Gorilla" Jones, Negro welterweight, won a 10-round fight over Ham Jenkins of Denver, here Tuesday night over Ham Jenkins of Denver. He and his manager, Suey Welsh, left here on the eastbound N. A. T. plane yesterday morning.

STROKE KILLS AN EDUCATOR.

Dr. Edwin A. Alderman, Virginia U. President, Dead.

(By the Associated Press.)

CHARLOTTESVILLE, Va., April 29.—Dr. Edwin A. Alderman, 69, president of the University of Virginia, died late tonight at Connellsville, Pa. Mrs. Alderman was advised by a hospital there.

Dr. Alderman, long recognized as one of the leading educators of the South, was stricken with apoplexy while on the way from Charlottesville to Urbana, Ill., where he was to deliver an address Friday.

Mrs. Alderman was advised that he was taken off the train when it reached Connellsville and died in a hospital there.

Dr. Alderman would have completed his twenty-seventh year as president of the University of Virginia in June.

Pembroke Band Places Second.

EMPORIA, Kas., April 29.—Pembroke school's 30-piece band tied for second place in Class C in the Kansas state-wide contest today.

INSTANT CONTACT

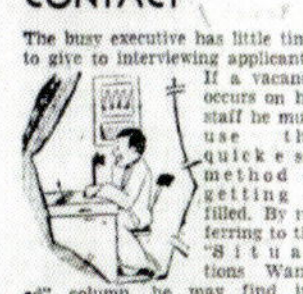

The busy executive has little time to give to interviewing applicants. If a vacancy occurs on his staff he must use the quickest method of getting it filled. By referring to the "Situations Wanted" column, he may find instantly the type of man he is looking for. For example, an advertising man, experienced in life insurance, building and loan and financial advertising is immediately available. Instant contact may be established for he gives his telephone number.

UNDER COVER

A car that stands outside all the time, exposed to all sorts of weather, depreciates much more rapidly than one which has good care. The finish can not last, the nickel plating be bituous any length of time, and the paint wears off with such treatment. A car that is worth driving is worth taking care of. Give the car a break and also add to the value of your property by having a garage built. See "Contracting and Building" for reliable contractor.

A SEVERE RAINSTORM GIVES PRESIDENT HOOVER A SOAKING, BUT THE CHIEF EXECUTIVE TAKES IT AS ONE OF "THOSE THINGS."

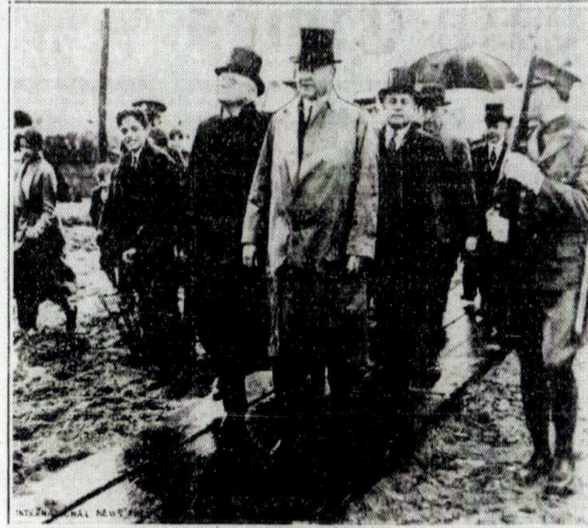

While attending the recent ceremony marking the 324th anniversary of the landing of English colonists at Cape Henry, Va., President Hoover and his party were caught in a violent rainstorm that drove everyone to cover. Taking refuge in a railroad depot a quarter of a mile away, the chief executive joked about the incident, although dripping with rain water. The above photograph shows President Hoover and Governor Pollard of Virginia on their way to shelter. Governor Pollard said later that he intended to see if there wasn't some state fund that could be used to purchase new silk toppers for himself and the President to replace those ruined by the rain.

BANDITS KIDNAP A GIRL

BUT SHE IS RETURNED TO HER HOME UNHARMED EARLY TODAY.

Posing as Officers, Two Men Take Miss Evelyn Mitchell, 20, From Car and Order J. A. Reed to Go to Police Station.

A young woman was kidnaped early today on a country road near Turner, Kas., by two bandits, annoyed because they found nothing of value when they searched her man companion. They returned her to her home about 2 o'clock this morning, unharmed.

The woman, Miss Evelyn Mitchell, 20 years old, 529 South Eleventh street, Kansas City, Kansas, and Jake A. Reed, a 30-year-old painter living at 625 South Eighth street, were parked in Reed's motor car near the town, which is seven miles west of Kansas City, Kansas, on Kansas highway No. 32.

Two men drove up in a Ford sedan. They said they were officers, and ordered Reed out of his car. Their dark suits resembled uniforms, Reed said. He obeyed them.

The men searched Reed. Failing to find anything of value, they told Miss Mitchell to get into their car. Then they told Reed to drive to his 2 police station in Armourdale. They drove west.

Although convinced by that time the men were not officers, Reed obeyed and returned to the station. Neither of the men displayed a weapon or a police badge, Reed said.

A HOLDUP BY "OFFICERS."

Dr. H. F. Sheldon and a Woman Are Robbed Near Odessa.

Dr. H. F. Sheldon, a chiropodist living at the Park Central hotel, early this morning reported to the police that he and a woman companion were held up last night on U. S. highway No. 40, three miles west of Odessa, and robbed of $3.

Dr. Sheldon said he was driving toward Kansas City when a large sedan which had been following him for several miles, crowded him off the highway, one of the bandits ordering him to stop as they were officers. Dr. Sheldon said he believed they might be officers because of the speed at which he had been driving.

When he got out of his car, the four in the other car also got out, one of them leveling a revolver. After they had searched him, Dr. Sheldon said he saw another car coming down the road. With his hands up, he walked in the light from the other machine to his own car, entered and drove away. Two or three shots were fired, he said.

BIG PROFITS FOR BROOM

(Continued from First Page.)

ernment and compel him to testify as to the validity of Broom's signature on another government exhibit. Coen objected on the ground that McQueen was Broom's lawyer and that his relationship with his client, was confidential. The objection was sustained.

Koyes then placed George Powell, cashier of the Baltimore Bank, formerly the Twelfth Street Bank, on the stand. Powell identified ledger sheets and deposit slips for accounts in Broom's name and also listed under C. E. Gill, for 1925, 1926, 1927 and 1928. The deposits in this period exceeded $162,000. One month's deposits totaled $62,000, another $48,000 and another $52,600.

The court recessed at 5 o'clock and resumed at 4:30 last night. Judge Otis warned the jury to refrain from reading about the case in the newspapers.

J. T. Estes, an internal revenue agent, who investigated Broom's bank accounts, calculated his 1926 income tax for the benefit of the jury last night at $22,000, on the basis of the bootlegger's earnings for that year.

He told of a conversation he had with Broom about his tax in which the latter admitted to him he was in the alcohol business, but assured government agents he was not making as much money as his position indicated.

"Broom would not admit that the C. E. Gill account was his," Estes said, "but did tell me that the reason he would not talk was because he was then under indictment for conspiracy to violate the prohibition act. He told me that he was not making much money because he was losing about one out of every four carloads of alcohol."

An effort to have the testimony of Estes ruled out by Mr. Coen was overruled by Judge Otis.

The Ray Broom Jury.

Charles W. Beip, store manager, Kansas City.

Ed Sullins, farmer, Centerview, Johnson County.

Albert Roy King, miner, Camden, Ray County.

Fred Richardson, grocer, Kansas City.

Elmer H. Perry, bus owner, Oak Grove.

Edwin F. Borgman, lumberman, Levasy.

Jack Detert, lumberman, Kansas City.

J. O. Coburn, farmer, Tina, Carroll County.

Harry E. Seekatz, barber, Kansas City.

Henry Schwartz, farmer, Nashua, Clay County.

Walter E. Botts, telephone employee, Independence.

Wesley F. Rohn, farmer, Grand Pass, Saline County.

HOOVER'S HEART TO A BOY

(Continued from First Page.)

He occupied an inconspicuous place in the room during the concert and seemed to have difficulty trying to listen and look at the same time.

Bryan arrived in Washington at 8:40 o'clock this morning. William H. Davenport, head of the United States secret service office in Kansas City, accompanied him on the trip across the continent. At the station a White House limousine, with a chauffeur in the familiar livery of the President, was awaiting. Within twenty minutes Bryan was crossing the threshold of the White House.

After Bryan had been shown to his room, a luxuriously furnished apartment with a private bath and a closet as large as the average-sized modern room, he was escorted over the house by Mrs. Hoover. Then President Hoover, who had been busily engaged in his office, sent for him.

The meeting of the President and this youngster was indeed impressive. As the boy entered the office Bryan walked to the President, who had arisen and was standing near his desk, with his hand outstretched. The President's kindly smile and low voice put him at ease.

"I am glad to meet a boy like you Bryan," the President said to him as he pointed to a chair.

Bryan's spirit seeing today included a visit to the Washington monument, the capitol and the supreme court. At the monument Bryan went to the top and the boy was amazed at the sight of the city from that high point. He also visited Ford's theater, where President Lincoln was assassinated, and the building across the street in which Lincoln died. Tomorrow Bryan will be taken to Mount Vernon, Arlington and other places.

When the matter of sight seeing and Bryan's entertainment was discussed this afternoon President Hoover is said to have remarked:

"I want that boy to see everything in Washington any boy of his age would want to see and I want him to stay at the White House until he has seen everything."

Bryan will remain the President's guest probably for three days.

DR. WARREN H. TOULE WEDS.

Miss Helen Scholler the Bride— Supper at Aladdin Club.

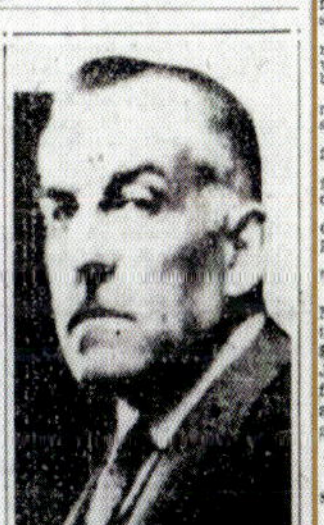

Miss Helen Scholler, daughter of Mr. and Mrs. W. T. Scholler, 464 Westover road, and Dr. Warren H. Toule, 2 East Thirty-ninth street, were married last night at the home of the bride.

The announcement of their wedding came as a surprise to a small group of intimate friends, who made up the wedding supper party at the Aladdin Supper Club.

The bride's father is foreign buyer for Emery, Bird, Thayer Dry Goods Company. The bride is a former student at Christian college, Columbia, Mo., and at the University of Kansas. The bridegroom is a native of Winfield, Kas. He came to Kansas City three years ago to begin his practice.

The couple will spend their honeymoon in Chicago. They will be at home at the Valentine-on-Broadway hotel after May 13.

A BANDIT GETS LIFE TERM.

Ross Castel, Sentenced in a Joseph, Is Wanted in Several States.

St. JOSEPH, Mo., April 29.—Ross Castel, 26, bandit wanted in several states, was sentenced to life imprisonment today when he pleaded guilty to robbery in the first degree before Judge J. V. Gaddy in circuit court.

NOTICE OF A POLICE SUIT

ACTION WILL BE TAKEN NEXT WEEK IF FUND IS NOT INCREASED.

Commissioners Will Confer With a Council Committee Tuesday Morning in Effort to Reach Pay Agreement.

The police commissioners announced last night they would give the city council official notice today that a mandamus suit would be filed in the supreme court next week to force the council to appropriate $1,442,000 for the operation of the department the next fiscal year unless an agreement is reached.

The commissioners said they would confer at 10:30 o'clock Tuesday morning with a council committee. The decision came after Mayor Bryce B. Smith failed to arrange an immediate conference between the police officials and the council committee, which is composed of A. N. Gossett, Ruby D. Garrett and Byron Spencer.

The committee was appointed Monday night by the mayor to confer with the commissioners in an effort to reach a compromise after the council had passed a police appropriation of $1,200,000, fixed by H. F. McElroy, city manager.

EARLIER MEETING IMPOSSIBLE.

Mr. Gossett told the mayor yesterday the committee would be unable to meet until Tuesday because Mr. Garrett would be unable to attend before then.

The commissioners, Russell Field and August F. Behrendt, said they would the notice of suit to avoid a repetition of a charge made by the city manager two years ago in a previous suit that the police had waited until other departments had spent their funds before acting.

"The same situation existed in the controversy two years ago," Mr. Field said.

The costs of the suit was approximately $27,883.71.

The city had to issue $313,934 in judgment bonds to pay the police. It had spent the money which the city manager had refused to appropriate to the police department.

BONDS DRAW INTEREST.

The judgment bonds, 10-year serials drawing 4½ per cent interest, were taken by the First National Bank, which paid the police. In the 10-year period, the taxpayers must not only pay off the bonds but must pay $49,-254.69 interest.

Mayor Smith and Mr. Gossett have opposed such expense.

Records show the following expenses in the litigation two years ago:

Sam C. Major, special commissioner of the supreme court, $6,000 fee, $539 for his expenses and $2,864.61 for stenographical hire.

James Luther Roberts, stenographer, received $612.50 from police for transcripts.

K. L. Mendenhall, received $1,091.25 for printing records of suit for police.

First National Bank received $887 for acting as trustee for members of department in the suit.

Filing fees and trips to Jefferson City by Frank Schlndly, attorney, for police board, $116.

Expense of Schlndly to go to Minneapolis, $750.

The city sent three attorneys to Minneapolis and to Cincinnati and their expenses have been estimated at $1,000 for the trip and for trips to Jefferson City. The cost to the city for stenographic records is estimated at $812.50 and its printing expenses at $500.

WARNED OF RABIES BY RADIO.

Science Reaches Out to Find Woman Who Was Bitten by Dog.

(By the Associated Press.)

GLENS FALLS, N. Y., April 29.—The radio today reached out to warn Mrs. Anna Smith in the Adirondack hamlet of Newcomb that the dog which bit her some time ago had developed rabies. The woman and her husband promptly started for the home of relatives in Mechanicville to begin the Pasteur treatment.

Mrs. Smith, who sells religious books and magazines, was bitten by the dog in Roper, N. C. Since then the dog has shown evidence of rabies and a warning was sent to Mrs. Smith at her home in Castleton, N. Y. However, she had gone on a sales tour to the mountainous region of Northern New York. It was then that an appeal was made to WGY, the General Electric Company's station at Schenectady, and the station broadcast a warning.

HIT BY A POLICE BULLET.

Stray Missile, Aimed at Men in Car, Strikes J. C. Christian.

J. C. Christian, 42 years old, 3406 Coleman road, last night suffered a flesh wound in his left leg when he was struck while standing at Eighteenth and Summit streets by a stray bullet from the revolver of Dudley Steele, city detective.

Steele and his partner, Harry Young, were pursuing two men in a motor car when, at Sixteenth and Broadway, Steele fired several shots. One of the bullets evidently ricocheted to hit Christian, who was standing on the northeast corner. He was awaiting friends before boarding a street car for his home. He had been to a church service at the Pentecostal Mission church.

CAR RUNS OVER NEGRO GIRL.

Young Woman Is Arrested After Accident in Front of 1912 Euclid.

May Wright, 4-year-old Negro, 1913 Euclid avenue, was struck by a motor car yesterday in front of her home. She had started to cross the street and then ran back into the path of the car.

She was taken to General hospital No. 2, where it was said her condition was dangerous. A wheel of the car is believed to have passed over her body.

Miss Chloe Thomas, 25 years old, 1308 Troost avenue, the driver, was arrested.

First Aid! When there's a room to rent or a house to sell or a job to find 'phone a Want Ad to HArrison 1200.

VIENNA SPECIALIST HERE

SERIES OF LECTURES BY DR. ERWIN VON GRAFF, GYNECOLOGIST.

He Also Is an International Authority on Obstetrics—Guest of Dr. M. L. Belot and Medical Society.

Dr. Erwin von Graff, professor of gynecology at the University of Vienna, and an international authority on gynecology and obstetrics, arrived here last night to deliver fourteen lectures to Kansas City physicians and surgeons.

Dr. Von Graff is a guest of Dr. Monti L. Belot and of the Jackson County Medical Society. His first

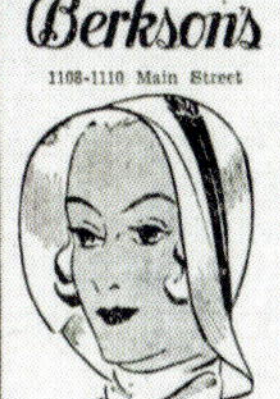

DR. ERWIN VON GRAFF.

lecture will be at 11 o'clock today, before obstetricians and gynecologists, at the assembly room in the Medical Arts building.

In addition, he will conduct clinics at various hospitals in the city for the specialists. Next Tuesday night he will speak to the Jackson County society at the Medical Arts building, and May 4 he will speak at the Alfred Benjamin clinic.

Dr. Von Graff has been in America two months. He came to America at the behest of numerous American surgeons who were former pupils of Dr. Belot. Dr. Von Graff came here from Los Angeles where he delivered a similar series of lectures.

A BERKSON EMPLOYEES' PARTY.

Store's Founding 25 Years Ago Celebrated at Dinner.

The employees of Berkson Brothers, Inc., last night had their part in the celebration of the twenty-fifth anniversary of the store's founding here at a party at the Hotel President. A 10-day sale period commemorating the anniversary will end Saturday.

The store was opened in April, 1906, by Sol Berkson and J. C. Berkson, at 1118 Main street. In the twenty-five years of business the first store had only one floor and the firm has grown from a company which started with three employees to one which now employs more than 150. The first store had only one floor and the firm now made the first sale after the store opened and also still an employee, were at the party. Carl Stephan, manager, was toastmaster. A short talk was made by Sol Berkson. A dinner was followed by dancing and bridge.

In September 1931, he began his position as full professor; his residence was at 3607 Ingersoll Avenue in Des Moines, a three-story apartment building constructed in 1920. In 1933, he participated in a Christmas party at the home of Mr. and Mrs. A. B. De Vilbiss dressed as an "Iowa Farmer" [Fig. 69].[128]

On December 27, 1933, Iowa physicians and gynecologists discussed whether twins could have different fathers. This followed a divorce ruling in South Dakota in favor of the plaintiff's husband. The husband, Mr. Ewald Peddie, had claimed that one of the twins to whom his wife had given birth was not his. They did not resemble each other and had been born several hours apart. His wife had also admitted her infidelity. The judge decided that the husband would get custody of the child whom he regarded as his, while the other child would remain with the mother. The physicians had different views on this; a genetic test was not yet possible at the time. Graff [Fig. 70] believed that the dual paternity of the twins could not be proven medically and scientifically. One could at best draw certain conclusions based on blood tests of all involved but only if they had different blood types. Moreover, twins can be born as much as twenty hours apart, and similarity of appearance was by no means a deciding factor, even if it was usually the case.[129]

The University of Iowa did not extend Graff's contract as professor in 1934,[130] and so his duties ended there on June 30, 1934.[131]

In 1935, Coloman von Graff, the youngest of Erwin's adopted children, who had apprenticed in the federal gardens in Schönbrunn, Austria, from 1930 onward, immigrated to the United States and settled in New Jersey, where he founded the company Von Graff Greenhouses in North Plainfield.[132] His hope that Graff would support him was disappointed. They were not in close contact.[133]

"FAVORITE PERSONS" FROLIC AT FANCY DRESS PARTY

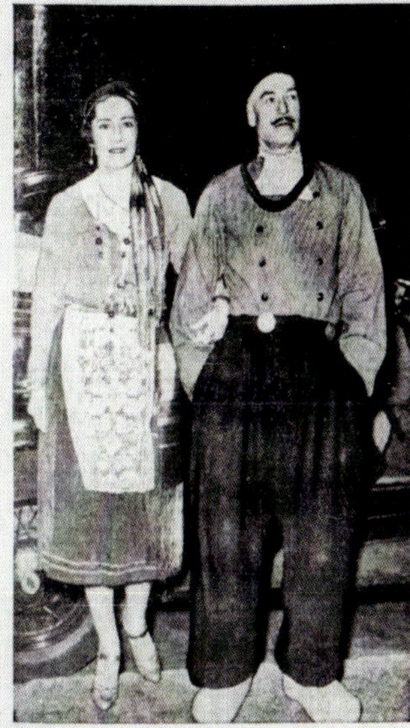

Portraying Their "Favorite Characters," Either Actually or ironically, guests attended the fancy dress party given Saturday night by Mr. and Mrs. Byron Ben Boyd in the former's studio at the Wallaces Homestead building. Above are Mr. and Mrs. Grover Hubbell as Hans and Gretel Brinker.

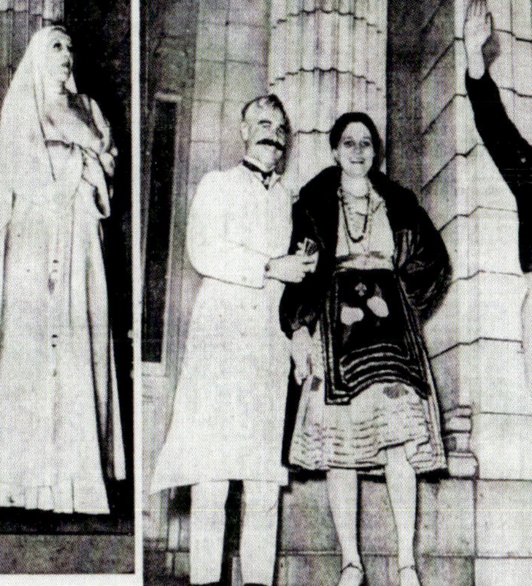

Mrs. Fred Bohen in Garb and pose portraying her favorite character for the evening, the "White Sister" of the film by that name.

Left to Right Are Charles S. Howard As "Charlie the Bartender," Mrs. C. A. Leland As Carmen and Maj. Harding Polk as Mussolini.

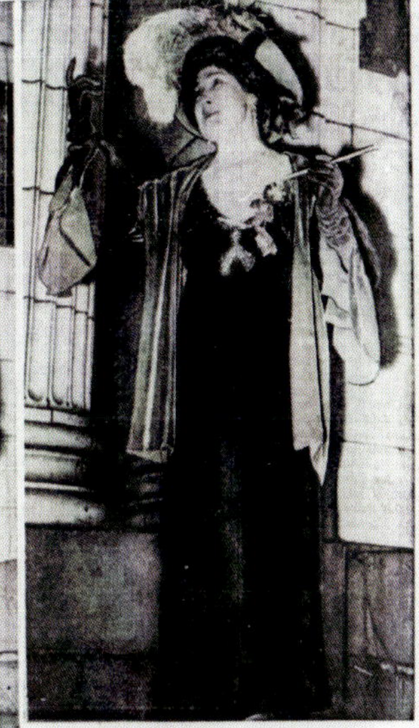

Mrs Dante Pierce Portrayed the Voluptuous Mae West.

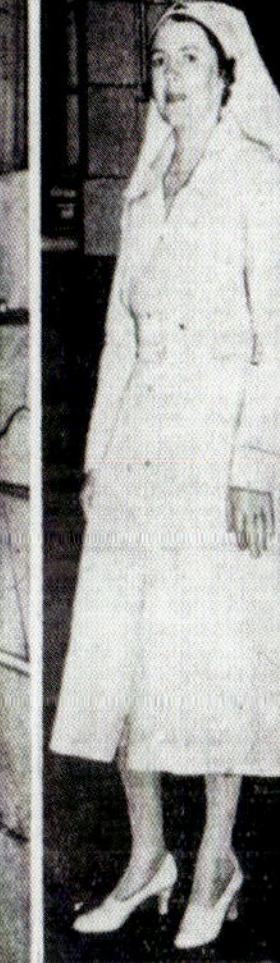

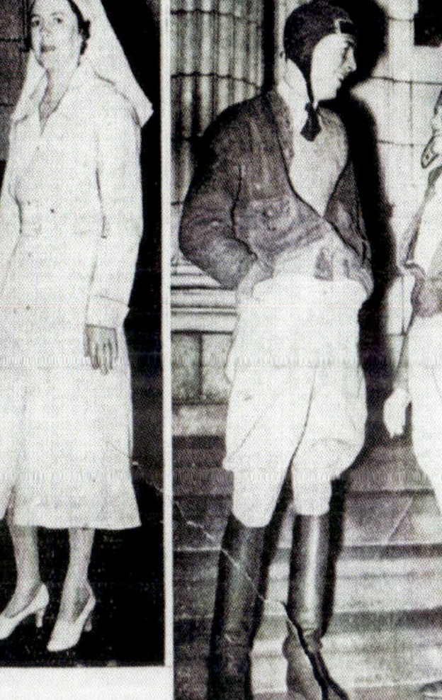

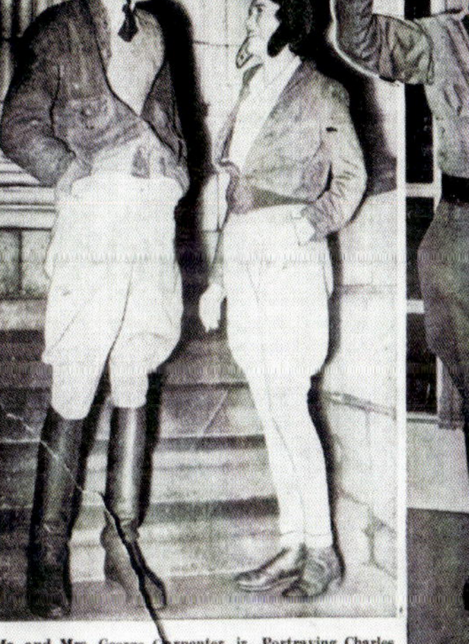

Mr. and Mrs. Albert Robertson As Cyrano De Bergerac and the "Lady on the Dollar."

Mrs. Vernon L. Clark As Edith Cavell.

Mr. and Mrs. George Carpenter, jr., Portraying Charles and Anne Lindbergh.

Allan Friedlich, In Heroic pose, as "his hero," Adolf Hitler.

Dr. Erwin Von Graff of Iowa City Attended the Party As "the Iowa Farmer."

De Vilbiss Family Hosts At Holiday House Party

MR. AND MRS. A. B. DE VILBISS and daughter, Helen, 2515 High st., are entertaining with a houseparty over Christmas. Those attending are Mrs. Carrie Mullins and son, William, jr., of New York City, John Masterson of Chicago, Mr. and Mrs. M. J. Bokirk of Panora, Mr. and Mrs. J. C. Masterson and daughter, Irma, of Boone and Mr. and Mrs. W. D. Roberts, Mr. and Mrs. P. W. Geiwicks and son, Paul, jr., Mrs. A. C. Brown, Miss Dora Mowry, Mrs. Alva Van Deventer and daughter, Donna. Miss Alice Paulson, Kermit Fitch and George Carlin all of Des Moines.

J. J. Bittle's Entertain

Mr. and Mrs. J. J. Bittle, 903 Thirty-first st., and Mr. and Mrs. H. R. Parker and family will have a Christmas dinner today at the Bittle home. Those who will attend are Harold, Merle and Virginia Bittle, Mr. and Mrs. Joe E. Bittle and Mr. and Mrs. K. Parker and son of Lenox.

Will Have Family Christmas Dinner

Mrs. L. C. Deets will entertain with a family Christmas dinner today at Hoyt Sherman place. Those who will attend are Mrs. S. C. Umpleby and daughter, Mr. and Mrs. Roy Umpleby, Will Umpleby and daughter, Phyllis, Mrs. Paul Marsden and children, Betty, John and Gloria, and Mr. and Mrs. W. A. Castle of Marshalltown.

Mr. and Mrs. C. W. Roth Will Entertain

Mr. and Mrs. C. W. Roth, 2107 Courtland drive, will entertain with a family Christmas dinner today at their home. Those who will attend are the Messrs. and Mesdames Ira M. Stevens and daughter, Mary, Karl E. Stevens and son, Lodoit, John L. Stevens and children, Jock and Betty, Ward A. Stevens and daughter, Juanita, F. Joe Stevens and G. E. Roth and sons, John and Richard, Tom E. Dotson and Billy, Maxine, Gene and Lois Mae Roth.

Mr. and Mrs. L. Lazarus, 1410 Thirty-second st., were entertained at a surprise dinner party in celebration of their twenty-fifth wedding anniversary on Christmas eve. Covers were laid for 40, after which bridge was played.

A. J. Gutheries Will Entertain

Mr. and Mrs. A. J. Gutherie will entertain with a Christmas dinner today at their home, 1503 Kent st. Those who will attend are Mr. and Mrs. L. C. Marquis and sons, Allen and Rodman, Mr. and Mrs. LaVerne Gutherie, Mr. and Mrs. Edwin Moore and son, Kenneth, and Mrs. Alena Gutherie and daughter, Barbara.

Phi Sigma Beta Holds Party

Members of Phi Sigma Beta sorority held their annual Christmas party recently. Those present were Martha Meyrat, Virginia Poepping, Marie Shepard, Margaret Ruvane, Robert Rauwolf, Margaret Nemmers, Mary Jean Raymond, Catherine Wehle, Mary Louise Avery, Eileen Howe, Lucille Burtch, Marie Carolan, Everill Hauge, Eleanor Connell, Mary Lucille Harkin and Mary Blount.

Entertain With Dinner Sunday

Mr. and Mrs. Quint Groves, 1360 E. Fourteenth st., entertained with a dinner Sunday. Those present were Miss Mary McDonell, Frank McDonell, Joe McDonell, Lewis McDonell, Elizabeth Groves, Paul Groves, Foster Groves, and Mr. and Mrs. Walter Barnard and son, Walter, jr., of Forest City. The party honored Miss McDonell who will be married Thursday to Paul Groves.

E. B. Fishers Entertain

Mr. and Mrs. E. B. Fisher, 1515 Hull st., entertained with a Christmas party Saturday evening. Bridge was played. Miss Helen Fisher was assisting hostess. Those present were Mr. and Mrs. Carl Mau, Mr. and Mrs. Paul Gustafson, Mr. and Mrs. George Tolvert, Miss Ruth Bayless, Peter Peterson and Harold Sorenson.

Will Have Xmas Party

Baldwin-Patterson American Legion Post and Auxiliary will hold their annual Christmas party today at 7:30 p. m. in the clubrooms in the Home Lodge building, E. Sixth and Locust streets. Children of post and auxiliary members will be guests and will provide the program.

The auxiliary committee includes the Mesdames James Bowen, Harvey Peterson and Joe Chocholka. Those on the committee from the post are Harry Baines, Orie V. Dawson and Joe Chocholka.

Have Party At George Peak Home

Friday the parents of the preschool children who attend the Kiner-Dell Nook of Learning had a party at the George Peak home. The children provided the program which included games, songs and an orchestra.

The C. E. Smiths Will Entertain

The home of Mr. and Mrs. C. E. Smith, 1329 Twenty-third st., will be the scene of another family reunion and dinner Monday.

Covers will be laid for Mr. and Mrs. H. W. King and daughter, Lois, of Ottumwa, Mr. and Mrs. C. A. Thompson of Ackworth, Miss Marie Conway and the Messrs. and Mesdames T. S. Weiss, G. W. Onthank, D. R. Smith and son, Richard, all of Des Moines.

Visitors Invited To Nolan Home

There will be a Christmas celebration at the home of Mr. and Mrs. T. Jeff Nolan, 637 Forty-first st., with H. J. McCarty and son, James of Lincoln, Neb., and Mr. and Mrs. Albert Carney of Maxwell as the out of town guests.

Des Moines persons invited to the dinner are Mr. and Mrs. John Ryan, Mr. and Mrs. James Walsh and son, James, Margaret McNerney, Mrs. M. M. McDermott, Owen, Edwin, Helen and Edna McDermott.

Loren Hartmans To Entertain

Mr. and Mrs. Loren E. Hartman, 818 E. Sixth st., will entertain with a Christmas dinner today at their home. Guests will be Mr. and Mrs. W. E. Carson and Mr. and Mrs. Harry G. Carson of St. Paul, Minn., Mrs. Catherine Carson, Mrs. Lillian Hartman, Mr. and Mrs. Frank Carson, Ruth Carson and Mr. and Mrs. Charles Burascott and son, Jack.

Maxine Gilmore Entertains

Maxine Gilmore entertained the members of Gamma Sigma Phi sorority Tuesday evening at her home. Prizes in the bunco games were won by Kay Dykstra and Bessie Koeppel. Plans also were made for a basket for a needy family. Members attending the party were the Mesdames William Yaggy, George Martin, Harry Staffen and Phil Wright and the Misses Myrtle Erickson, Grace Rorabaugh, Mary Lawton, Margaret Maison, Maxine Murray, Bessie Koeppel, Ann Neighbor, Wilma Zimmerli, Doris Noah, Garnet Henderson, Miriam Barrum, Helen Mitchell, Sigma Henderson, Amy Hurlbut, Edna Mendon, Hazel Clark, Kay Dykstra, Dorothy Miller and Louisa Grinnell.

Ledlie Family To Have Reunion

The annual Ledlie gathering will be held Christmas day at the J. C. Sawhill home, 3119 Fourth st. A Christmas dinner will be served. Those who will attend are J. D. Ledlie and family, J. A. Mitchell and family, T. A. Ledlie and son, all of Des Moines, J. V. Ellison and family of Carlisle, Dr. and Mrs. F. Mitchell of Evanston, Ill., Mrs. Peal Martins and daughter of Grinnell and Harold Sawhill of Winterset.

Miss Erbacher Is Honored

Miss Dorothy Rose Erbacher, who will be married Wednesday to Wallace Hainline, was honored Saturday with a luncheon at the Savery hotel given by Miss Helen Holehan. Those present were the Misses Mary Schiltz, Jean Frink, Lucille Robinson, Lonnie Ames, Grace and Gladys Ogden, Ruth Bailey, Ann Martin, Merl Patterson and Aimee Buchanan and the Mesdames C. A. Erbacher and A. P. Holehan.

Wednesday evening, the Misses Grace and Gladys Ogden, 1055 Twenty-ninth st., entertained for Miss Erbacher with a buffet supper and miscellaneous shower. Guests were Mrs. Erbacher, and the Misses Schiltz, Martin, Holehan and Buchanan.

Mrs. Erbacher, 1111 Polk blvd., complimented her daughter Thursday evening with a buffet supper and miscellaneous shower at their home. Those present were the Mesdames R. R. Morden, Ethel Nichols, B. B. Keeney, E. A. McClanahan, J. J. Dysart, Myrtle Goettel, Russell Carlson, Holehan and J. W. Hull and the Misses Holehan, Ethel Ash and Buchanan.

E. B. Seidels Honor Out of State Visitors

MR. AND MRS. E. B. SEIDEL, 133 Fifty-first st., have as their Christmas guests, Mr. and Mrs. R. O. Davis and daughter, Shirley Ann, of Yankton, S. D., and Mrs. Davis' mother, Mrs. George Agee of Kansas City, Mo. New Year's guests at the Seidel home will be Mr. and Mrs. Knowles McReynolds and Mr. and Mrs. Frank Latz of Kansas City.

Dr. John H. Matheson of Iowa City and George Marshall Matheson of Chicago, Ill., are spending the holidays with their parents, Dr. and Mrs. George A. Matheson, 1710 Twenty-third st.

Alice Cave of Cedar Rapids arrived Saturday to spend the holidays with her parents, Mr. and Mrs. Eugene W. Cave, 1440 Wilson ave. Today they will all go to Redfield to spend the day with Mr. and Mrs. Glenn Cave.

Mr. and Mrs. Henry White and son, Artie, 1212 Penn ave., left Friday for Kansas City, Mo., and Hutchinson, Kan., where they are spending the holidays.

Dr. and Mrs. Cecil C. Jones, 3303 Lincoln Place drive, have as their Christmas guests, Mr. and Mrs. Howard A. Jones of Topeka, Kan. Thursday and Friday Mr. and Mrs. Van Crawford of Iowa City were guests at the Jones home.

Wallace Hainline left Saturday morning for Paola, Kan., to spend the holidays with his parents, Mr. and Mrs. W. M. Hainline. They will return with their son to attend his marriage to Miss Dorothy Rose Erbacher which will take place Wednesday.

Alex Archy, a student at the University of Iowa, is spending the Christmas holidays with his parents.

Mr. and Mrs. F. C. Davenport, 615 Prospect road, have as their guests today Mrs. Davenport's parents, Mr. and Mrs. Frank Fox of Woodburn, and her brothers and their families, Mr. and Mrs. W. B. Fox and daughter, Ruth, of Newton, and Mr. and Mrs. J. D. Fox and children, Gloria, Jean, Billy and Cordelia, of Kansas City, Mo.

Miss Mary Kayner, principal of Crocker school, is spending the holidays in Kansas City, Mo.

Elliott Woodruff of Chicago, Ill., arrived Friday to spend several days with his parents, Mr. and Mrs. Fred P. Woodruff, at the Chamberlain hotel. The three are spending today in Knoxville with Mr. and Mrs. Carl C. Gamble and family. Mr. Elliott will return to Chicago tonight.

Dr. and Mrs. Daniel F. Crowley and family have returned from Omaha, Neb., where they attended the funeral of Mrs. Crowley's mother, Mrs. Martin Langdon.

70. "Score Theory Dakota Twins Had 2 Fathers,"
accompanied by a photo of Dr. Erwin von Graff,
The Des Moines Register, December 28, 1933, p. 1
www.newspapers.com/image/128032527/
[Accessed August 8, 2025]

The text reads:

Score Theory Dakota Twins Had 2 Fathers

Iowa physicians and gynecologists Wednesday scouted the theory of dual male parentage of the twins born to Mrs. Ewald Peddie, defendant in a South Dakota divorce action which was decided Wednesday in favor of her husband.

Dr. Erwin von Graff, gynecologist from Vienna, Austria, now on the teaching staff at State University of Iowa, declared over long distance telephone that two different conceptions, as recognized by the trial judge "never have been proved by medical science."

"Some deductions as to parentage of the twins might be made from blood tests of both children, the mother and the two fathers," he said.

"However, little could be deduced unless the principals were of distinctly different blood groups, and the fusion of blood strains makes the whole experiment largely a matter of conjecture," he added.

Basis for Decision.
The South Dakota court based its decision on Mr. Peddie's story that the twins were unlike and that they were born several hours apart. His wife had admitted relations with a neighbor, Mr. Peddie testified.

In the South Dakota case, the judge at Yankton, S. D., gave Mr. Peddie custody of the twin which he claimed was his, but left the other of disputed parentage to the mother.

Physicians Testify.
Mrs. Peddie did not appear in her own defense, and physicians subpoenaed by Mr. Peddie testified that in the case of what they termed "fraternal twins" the matter of two fathers could be possible.

"Twins can be born as long as 20 hours apart," said Dr. von Graff, "and similarity of appearance is in no way an essential characteristic, even though it is usually the case."

Further View.
"Furthermore," he added, "twins could develop from one female cell or from two, which fact alone would preclude the possibility of accepting dual male parentage as an unqualified theory, because of the obvious uncertainty."

Consensus of Des Moines physicians interviewed is that the case has no scientific precedent and no authentication of medical knowledge.

Bierring's Comment.
Dr. Walter L. Bierring, state health commissioner, said "I doubt very much that such a thing is possible, and I know of no scientific test which would prove or disprove the findings of the court."

Dr. Fred Moore, president of the Polk County Medical society, said the difference in appearance, the interval of several hours between the birth of the twins was quite possible in normal cases involving twins.

Others Skeptical.
Others expressed their skepticism and said they knew of no scientific substantiation of the theory on which the court based its decision."

News Reports of His Death in 1935

In March 1935, several Austrian media outlets reported that Graff had died in Ohio.[134] After working for several years in Ohio as a practitioner and university lecturer, he was said to have taken his own life with a revolver.[135]

When the news from Austria reached Graff, he responded quickly, telling the press that this was the third time he had been reported dead. The first time was thirty-four years earlier, in 1901, and the second time in 1914. In 1901 he was climbing with a friend in the Dolomites. Two tourists hiking in the same area were killed by rockfall, and their bodies could not be recovered for several days. The press immediately reported that Graff and his friend were the victims. The second purported death occurred in September 1914 in the first days of World War I. He was responsible for a hospital on the Serbian front. A retreat was ordered but the hospital personnel and patients were forgotten. Graff waited until it was dark and then, guided by local Muslims, crossed a remote mountain pass with 100 cars and 300 people. They left the lights burning in the hospital and private residences to fool the Serbian troops. When he arrived at army headquarters eighteen hours later, they were surprised because they had assumed he was dead. Graff learned about his third supposed death in 1935 from two private detectives who showed up at his practice one day and, laughing, found him alive after all. They had been hired by the Austrian consulate in Chicago to verify the report of Graff's death. Relatives and friends in Austria could not believe the account of Graff's suicide and asked the Foreign Ministry to clarify it, which in turn contacted the consulate in Chicago. Graff's mother, who had been in deepest mourning for four days and had already received several expressions of condolences, was overjoyed when she heard that it had been a false report. The source of this report could not be identified.[136]

The Austrian media had to revoke the report as well: according to messages from the Federal Ministry of Foreign Affairs to Graff's family, he was healthy and working. And it was added that he was not living in Ohio, as erroneously reported, but in Des Moines in Iowa.[137]

The Des Moines Register

The Newspaper Iowa Depends Upon

COLD BRINGS DEATH TO 100 IN U. S.

ATE SALE OF L LIQUOR BUT 2 BEER IS AIM

mittee Ignores 'Party' Permits; Bill in Revision.

By Rider Richmond.

ges in the state monopoly forbid sale of all liquor except beer in any establishment than a state store were upon by the Iowa house control committee late nday night.

ting at Hotel Kirkwood a hectic afternoon session which efforts to vote out bill for floor consideration house failed, the committee over the monopoly bill until ht.

A Subcommittee.

he conclusion of the night which ended, temporarily differences over where d wine of over 3.2 percent uld be sold, the committee ne over the entire bill section.

result, a subcommittee pointed to work today revise the bill and incorporating ed changes.

Provides for Penalties.

changes included the elimof the sections which alseer and wine up to 10 per he sold in hotels, restaund clubs.

r changes were made in ording of the bill and profor penalties added.

man Fabritz of the comsaid no further meeting whole committee would be till the subcommittee had ed redrafting the bill.

No "Party" Permits.

e developments were beo mean that the commitid not be afforded an opty of voting a bill out bey and perhaps not be New Year recess.

ions for special "party" for hotels and clubs, preeliminated, will not be back in the measure by the mittee.

ption Not Discussed.

option was not discussed committee and will not be

Liquor.
(Continued on Page 3.)

NS ON CORN S 18 MILLION

More Farmers Get $850,000.

Table on Page 10.

the cold and the Inh just to hit back and enduring the holidays, Iowa Wednesday recorded corn that totaled more than

rum pushed the total loans roducers have negotiated government on their corn med a: 45 cents a bushel than 18 million dollars.

Near Half.

weekend, they will have nd, or become eligible to nearly half of the 45 milars corn loan program disestimate will be disbursed 1, the deadline for filing loans.

eday 1,328 farmers reeans throughout the state 1,362. In all, 28,518 corn n have qualified to bor-,779,584.

hontas Nears Million.

ontas county Wednesday as less than $50,000 short llion dollar loan total. In nty, 1,087 corn producers ompleted loans totaling and dealers reported they y plenty of work ahead of care for loan applicants. sday the county was far fore when 96 farmers reoans totaling $82,211.

Hamilton Second.

ton county farmers were e the day. In this counroducers recorded loans 088. In Kossuth county, ers completed loans for

thoun county 35 farmers d loans for $18,324 to total loans completed in ity to more than $600,000. counties, Dallas, Greene, ster and Wright, Webster had more than $500,000 recorded.

Six Others.

hers, Benton, Boone, Fre-Hamilton, Kossuth and y, stood in the $400,000 t

counties have more than in loans completed.

Trio in Home Held Prisoner For 3 Hours

Picture on Page 3.

Menaced by a hysterical former house employe who occasionally threatened them with a gun, Dr. Harold N. Anderson, his wife and a maid were held prisoner three hours at the Anderson home, 692 Forty-fourth st. Wednesday night, they told police.

Dr. and Mrs. Anderson and the maid, Betty Wheeler, finally escaped through a ruse, and the alleged assailant, Lorenz S. Reinecke, 35, was arrested by police at the physician's home at 9.30 p. m.

Held at Bay.

Reinecke entered the home sometime Wednesday afternoon, and when Mrs. Anderson returned to the home about 4.30 p. m. she was met at the door by Reinecke, armed with a gun, and held at bay, she told police.

Earlier in the day he had forced his way into the physician's office and demanded $10, threatening the physician at that time, Dr. Anderson said. Dr. Anderson gave him the money, he said, and police believed he used it to purchase the gun.

Police Called.

After Reinecke had been in the house about four hours, Dr. Anderson suggested they go to South Des Moines to get some rabbits ordered earlier.

Reinecke agreed, according to Dr. Anderson, insisting that Mrs. Anderson accompany them. During their absence the maid called police, and a squad car was sent to the home and another into South Des Moines.

Returns to House.

At the south end of the Seventh st. viaduct, Dr. Anderson stopped the car and Reinecke agreed to obtain the rabbits. When he left the car, Dr. and Mrs. Anderson sped to the home of J. F. Malloy, 1123 Pleasant View drive, where they notified police they were safe.

Reinecke returned to the Anderson residence immediately in a taxicab, where officers were awaiting him. He was arrested without a struggle.

Discharged.

Reinecke was discharged two or three days ago for his failure to cease smoking cigarets around the Anderson home, use of which, according to Dr. Anderson, aggravated the man's high-strung temperament. Reinecke, Dr. Anderson said, immediately became hysterical.

According to Dr. and Mrs. An

Held.
(Continued on Page 3.)

Affidavit for Tax Experts Is Studied

WASHINGTON, D. C. (AP)—Treasury officials have under consideration a proposal by which experts preparing income tax returns for taxpayers would be required to sign an affidavit of their accuracy.

World News At a Glance

(By The Associated Press.)

DOMESTIC.

WASHINGTON, D. C. — Emergency recovery expenditures send treasury deficit past billion dollar mark, but normal expenses are balanced; export trade strengthens; present recovery program to continue another year.

WASHINGTON, D. C.—Navy will ask congress to bring fleet up to full treaty strength by 1939.

WASHINGTON, D. C. — Federal pool guaranteeing 97 per cent of nation's bank deposits called mandatory, despite Chicago bank's objection.

NEW YORK, N. Y.—Soviet quickens American buying program; wants credit and reciprocal trade agreement.

SPRINGFIELD, ILL.—Illinois becomes first state to rely entirely on sales tax: real and personal property levies abolished.

MARLIN, TEX.—Robbers loot bank of $41,000; kidnap three employes.

PHILADELPHIA, PENN.—Experts agree that world economic situation is improving.

FOREIGN.

PARIS, FRANCE—France, rejecting German rearmament demands, will offer to scrap half of its bombing planes as peace gesture; other powers must do likewise.

LONDON, ENGLAND—Other nations disregarding naval treaties, say British, explaining big keel laying program.

HAVANA, CUBA—$20,000,000 debt contracted under Machado held illegitimate; repayment suspended pending study.

800 MILLIONS U. S. SURPLUS IN '35 SLATED

Billion and Half for Recovery, With No Tax Hike, in Sight.

WASHINGTON, D. C. (AP)—A federal budget for 1934-35 which would provide an $800,000,000 surplus and supply possibly $1,500,-000,000 for emergency outlays was discussed Wednesday on Capitol hill.

Members close to the administration mentioned figures which

To the Country

President Roosevelt will speak to the country tonight when he addresses the first national dinner of the Woodrow Wilson Foundation, commemorating the war president's birthday anniversary.

The address will be carried over nationwide hookups of the two leading broadcasting systems beginning at 9:30 p. m., central standard time.

indicated a return part way to the "pay-as-you-go" basis of meeting recovery demands without any tax rate boosts.

Set Income at 3 Billion.

The talk intimated that some administration quarters were relying on Reconstruction Corp. loan repayments of $750,000,000 to add to the $800,000,000 ordinary operating surplus to make a huge fund available for such recovery expenditures as relief and public works.

Those involved in the conversations mentioned $3,400,000,000 as a close estimate on federal revenue during the fiscal year which will begin next July 1 and for which congress soon will begin appropriating.

Expect 800 Million Surplus.

The cost of operating the government was placed at a little below $2,600,000,000, leaving an expected surplus of $800,000,000.

If Reconstruction Corp. repayments meet expectations and the corporation's own demands for more cash are met by the treasury chiefly in this fiscal year, some party members look to this source for hundreds of millions more.

There was a sentiment that budget balancing efforts would not disturb the sinking fund but would depend on borrowed money to fill this nearly $500,000,000 gap.

Roosevelt Checks Up.

President Roosevelt spent the day scanning his entire recovery campaign and exploring new fields preliminary to drafting his program for congress, meeting a week before.

Meantime administration officials noted an increase in the federal deficit to $1,024,121,667. The rise was expected, and it was made known that the president is interested only in making sure that receipts will cover ordinary expenditures, which is being done.

Ordinary Costs Slashed.

The $1,024,121,667 deficit, which includes emergency expenditures, compares with a deficit of $1,593,-694,753 a year ago.

As compared with Dec. 22, 1932.

Roosevelt.
(Continued on Page 2.)

Willard $100 Poorer, Glendale, Cal., Richer

GLENDALE, CAL. (U.S.) — Jess Willard, former world heavyweight champion boxer, was $100 poorer Wednesday.

He failed to file an appeal on his conviction on charges of battery growing out of a street fight with a husky truck driver.

Death of Mother Clouds Cheers for Mistinguette

PARIS, FRANCE — Mlle. Mistinguette, the girl with the million -dollar legs, had an internation a l a u d i e n c e at t h e Folies Bergere cheering h e r W e d nesday night as the star of the show.

She laughed and smiled, but took her bows with a tear, because her mother died Wednesday.

Mme. Marianne Bourgeois,

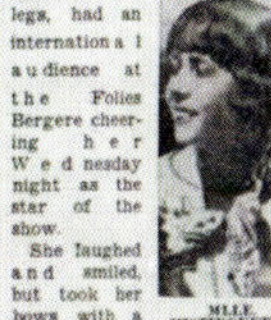

Mistinguette's mother, the widow of a former innkeeper, was 78. She had been ill some time, but her life was always brightened by the new fame her dancing daughter gained.

Mistinguette, former partner of Maurice Chevalier on the French stage, attained great prominence when her legs were selected as the most beautiful of any Parisienne.

She capitalized on this and became one of the highest paid performers in Paris.

Though there are stories Mistinguette is 60, the dancer recently produced a birth certificate giving her age as only 56.

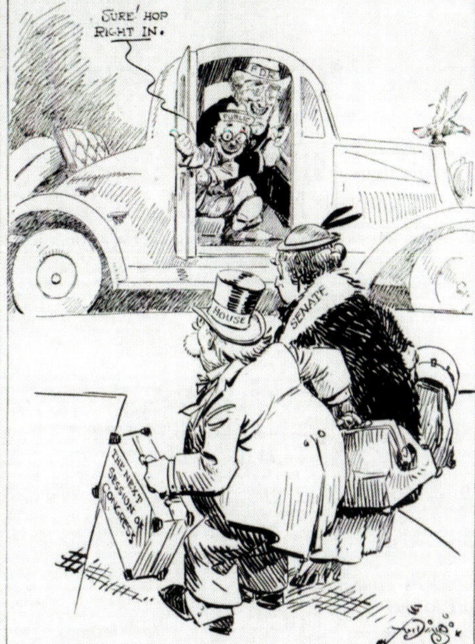

PLENTY OF ROOM IN THE RUMBLE SEAT.

POLK CWA JOB PROBE STARTED

Frauds in Application Are Alleged.

Other CWA News on Page 4.

Twenty relief workers are investigating civil works administration employes to determine whether they are eligible to be on the CWA payrolls, it was announced Wednesday at a meeting of Polk county CWA and relief officials.

Numerous written complaints have been received alleging misrepresentations and unfairness on the part of certain CWA employes, it was revealed.

Other Checkup.

These are being investigated along with a routine checkup in the city and county.

Several cases have been found, it was announced, where persons had obtained CWA work through falsification of their applications or otherwise. Some of these had been holding other permanent jobs and in some cases other members of the family were working.

Removal Set.

Where it has been definitely established that individuals are not entitled to CWA work, they will be removed from the payrolls and other more deserving persons will be given work, it was announced by K. G. Carney, Polk county relief chairman, who presided at the meeting.

An explanation of the program of the state CWA safety program was made by C. W. McFarland, safety director, and of the provisions of the CWA workmen's compensation provisions by L. J. Cowen, claim department director.

Bank Refuses U. S. Insured Deposit Plan

WASHINGTON, D. C. (AP)—The first instance of a national bank refusing to participate in the federal deposit insurance pool Wednesday evoked from treasury officials a statement that the institution had no choice in the matter.

In formed that J. M. Nichols, president of the First National bank of Englewood, Chicago, had announced his institution would not join unless compelled to do so by the government, Walter J. Cummings, president of the Deposit Insurance Corp, said:

"Congress decided that long ago for Mr. Nichols, and his bank will participate along with every other national bank."

Charges "Injustice."

"We are flatly opposed to this deposit insurance scheme," Nichols said, "the only way we will have anything to do with it is through government coercion. Our bank's deposits are secured 84 per cent by cash and government bonds and we can make our bank 100 per cent liquid on a week's notice."

He said "a gross injustice would be committed against the management of this bank and our customers were we compelled to make good the losses of mismanaged banks."

Plan Unrevealed.

Cummings would not answer questions as to what might be done to compel the Nichols bank to come in. However, in other quarters it was said the institution could not qualify for its charter as a national bank or for membership in the federal reserve system unless it complied.

In announcing 7,749 nonfederal reserve member state banks had applied for membership in the deposit corporation and that most of them would meet requirements, Cummings said:

"This has been made possible through the co-operation of the Reconstruction Finance Corp. Millions of dollars have been poured into the nonmember banks at the nation by the R. F. C. in purchase of the preferred stock and capital notes of such institutions, thereby strengthening the financial structure of such banks."

R. F. C. Purchases.

"Up to the close of business Dec. 23, a total of 2,756 state non-member banks had applied to the R. F. C. to buy their preferred stock or capital notes; while purchases by the R. F. C. of such applications had aggregated $171,797,000 in 2,515 of these institutions."

"Purchases by the R. F. C. of capital obligations of all banks amounted to more than $650,000,-000 up to Dec. 23."

Others were bound to the grand jury.

3 KIDNAPED IN HOLDUP FREED

Released by Bandits in $41,000 Robbery.

MARLIN, TEX. (AP)—The three first instance of the bandits, who looted the bank of $41,000, were freed Wednesday.

Several other employes of the First State bank of Marlin, kidnaped by two robbers, Wednesday had been released uninjured near Rogers.

The other two who had been held by the bandits, who looted the bank of $41,000, were Miss Andrew Peyton, bookkeeper, 28; and Lee Humphries, Negro porter.

Wait on Time Lock.

The three employes were made prisoners when they reported for work. The robbers waited until the time lock opened the vault, which they looted of $41,000 in cash, and then fled with their captives.

Half a dozen persons saw the party leave the bank.

Sees Speeding Auto.

A filling station operator and two Negro helpers saw the automobile as it sped west through the edge of Marlin.

FASTER STILL, GARNER SAYS

Sees New Congress Moving 'Big Things' More Rapidly.

DALLAS, TEX. (AP)—Vice President Garner told friends Wednesday that, while the last session of congress was the most important in history, the coming session would, in his opinion, see "big things happen faster."

CWA's 'Navy' Due to Begin Work Today

Des Moines' CWA "navy" aboard the barge that is to deepen the river through the civic center will go to work today, maybe.

It has taken no long to bring the barge from the forks of the rivers due to low water that every statement as to time pumping was to start has been cautiously qualified by Streets Commissioner MacVicar.

However, workmen started laying pipe across the pontoons Wednesday to carry off the flow of pumpings from the river bed, and actual pumping is expected to be started today.

U. S. Refuses Tax Compromise Plea

WASHINGTON, D. C. (AP)—The government Wednesday rejected offers of Moe Rosenberg, west Chicago Democratic leader, to compromise the alleged $64,000 income tax deficiency for which he is now under indictment in Chicago.

The tax division of the department of justice said Rosenberg would go on trial Jan. 2.

New Rum Ordinance Brings $100 to City

Of six cases in municipal court Wednesday afternoon wherein defendants were charged with driving while intoxicated, one was tried under the new city ordinance and added $100 to city coffers by a fine.

Score Theory Dakota Twins Had 2 Fathers

Iowa physicians and gynecologists Wednesday scouted the theory of dual male parentage of the twins born to Mrs. Ewald Peddie, defendant in a South Dakota divorce action which was decided Wednesday in favor of her husband.

Dr. Erwin von Graff, gynecologist from Vienna, Austria, now on the teaching staff at State University of Iowa, declared over long distance telephone that two different conceptions, as recognized by the trial judge "never have been proved by medical science."

"Some deductions as to parentage of the twins might be made from blood tests of both children, the mother and the two fathers," he said.

"However, little could be deduced unless the principals were of distinctly different blood groups, and the fusion of blood strains makes the whole experiment largely a matter of conjecture," he added.

Basis for Decision.

The South Dakota court based its decision on Mr. Peddie's story that the twins were unlike and that they were born several hours apart. His wife had admitted relations with a neighbor, Mr. Peddie testified.

In the South Dakota case, the judge at Yankton, S. D., gave Mr. Peddie custody of the twin which he claimed was his, but left the other of disputed parentage to the mother.

Physicians Testify.

Mrs. Peddie did not appear in her own defense, and physicians subpenaed by Mr. Peddie testified that in the case of what they termed "fraternal twins" the matter of two fathers could be possible.

"Twins can be born as long as 20 hours apart," said Dr. Von Graff, "and similarity of appearance is in no way an essential characteristic, even though it is usually the case."

Further View.

"Furthermore," he added, "twins could develop from one female cell or from two, which fact alone would preclude the possibility of accepting dual male parentage as an unqualified theory, because of the obvious uncertainty."

Consensus of Des Moines physicians interviewed is that the case has no scientific precedent and no authentication of medical knowledge.

Bierring's Comment.

Dr. Walter L. Bierring, state health commissioner, said "I doubt very much that such a thing is possible, and I know of no scientific fact which would prove or disprove the findings of the court."

Dr. Fred Moore, president of the Polk County Medical society, said the difference in appearance, and the interval of several hours between the birth of the twins was no evidence against a single twin.

Others Skeptical.

Others expressed their skepticism and said they knew of no scientific substantiation of the theory on which the court based its decision.

ZERO WEATHER TO GRIP STATE AGAIN TONIGHT

Blaze Guts Home of Willford Family at Waterloo.

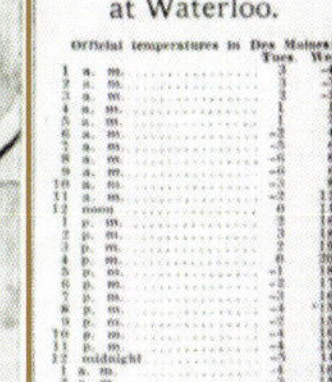

The weather bureau Wednesday night predicted temperatures today will reach 15 above zero today and zero weather will clamp down on Iowa again tonight.

The cold wave which swept over the nation on Christmas day already has been a direct or contributing cause for 100 deaths in the nation.

Two Sports Accidents.

Two serious winter sport accidents occurred in Iowa Wednesday.

Leonard Meyer, 10, was in a Davenport hospital in a critical condition after his sled had struck

Needs It Now
(The Register's Iowa News Service.)

MARSHALLTOWN, IA.—While Ralph Scott was shivering with cold and wishing for some way to get a warm coat, his telephone rang. It was a fur storage firm.

"That muskrat coat you left here is ready for delivery," the voice said. Scott reflected, and decided it should be—by now.

He left it there 15 years ago.

a fire hydrant at the bottom of a coasting hill. He suffered a fractured skull.

At Fort Dodge, Joseph Hinch, 14, of Somers, Ia., was in serious condition at the Lutheran hospital following a skiing mishap in which a splinter from a broken ski penetrated his abdomen.

Willfords Have Fire.

Congressman A. C. Willford and his family were driven out of their Waterloo, Ia., home into 25 below zero weather early Wednesday morning by fire.

The house was gutted. Damage was estimated at $2,000. The family was awakened in time to escape the flames by the barking of a Chesapeake hunting dog owned by the congressman's grandson.

CWA Work Delayed.

Work on CWA projects in Dubuque county was stopped Wednesday by the cold but will be resumed today. At Cedar Rapids, only 14 of 450 CWA workers failed to report for work Wednesday despite the cold, and many of those could not report because of illness. Officials said the work will continue.

Temperatures which warmed to 20 degrees above zero at Des Moines Wednesday afternoon failed to bring comfort because of a wind of increased velocity. The thermometer is expected to remain below 16 degrees today.

28 Below at Waterloo.

The lowest temperature recorded at Des Moines early Wednesday was 5 degrees below zero. Waterloo recorded the lowest temperature, 28 degrees below zero, with Charles City next with 25 below.

Comparatively warm weather is expected for most of today with increased cold toward evening. A low of 10 degrees above zero was predicted for Des Moines this morning.

56 Below in Canada.

Cold weather deaths included the drowning of four fishermen in Lake Michigan. Although some CWA projects over the country were hampered by the cold, snow aided employment in other sections, giving work to 28,000 clearing the Vermont-Quebec highways.

White River, Canada, was the coldest spot on the official weather map with 56 degrees below zero.

Denver, Colo., interrupted the otherwise nearly uniform cold-gripped nation by an unseasonable touch of spring with temperatures as high as 57 degrees.

KING BORIS ILL.

BUCHAREST, RUMANIA (THURSDAY) (AP) — Dispatches from Sofia reported today that King Boris is confined to his bed with a mild case of influenza.

Private Practice in Des Moines

After resigning as university professor, Graff opened a private practice in Des Moines on July 1, 1934.

In August 1935, he took a road trip along the East Coast and visited New York City and Long Island.[138] In October, he participated in the seventh annual meeting of the Central Association of Obstetricians and Gynecologists.[139] During the convention he was a guest in the home of Dr. and Mrs. Karl Robert Werndorff.[140]

Graff was close friends with Mr. Allan Friedlich (1893–1949), owner and president of Utica Clothing Co. in Des Moines, and his wife, the author Ruth Friedlich. In 1935, it was reported that Ruth Friedlich had been commissioned by the New York publisher Random House to ghostwrite a book on child-bearing for which Graff would provide the technical knowledge.[141] It could not be determined whether that happened.

In December 1935, Graff published a lengthy review of James Strachey's translation of the autobiography of Sigmund Freud, in which he emphasized that Freud himself had suffered from a devastating complex triggered by the persecution to which his ancestors had been subjected in the fourteenth and fifteenth centuries and to which he himself had been subjected since childhood. Graff judged the translation itself to be "uninspired and sometimes inept," and ended his review by noting that Freud's accomplishments in the field of psychotherapy had produced valuable results.[142]

On May 11, 1936, Graff became an American citizen.[143]

In 1936, Graff took a public position on a transgender operation. The Czech track-and-field athlete Zdenka Koubková (1913–1986) broke several world records at the Fourth Women's World Games in London in 1934, whereupon the media raised doubts about her true sex. Only after a psychological crisis and withdrawing from sports in 1935 did she undergo medical evaluations, begin hormone therapy, and choose a male identity. To raise the funding necessary, she toured the United States and told her story. Just how little was known about transgender issues is clear from Graff's assessment of the operation: "Her only choice, by means of surgery, was whether or not she would retain the outward appearance of a sexless female or accept her possible male heritage."[144] The surgery was performed in March 1936 and from then on Zdenka called himself Zdeněk Koubek.

There were also reports of a private nature in the newspaper that Graff was an enthusiastic cello player,[145] that he stayed physically fit by playing handball regularly,[146] and that he could cook an exquisite Italian risotto, for which a recipe and instructions were published.[147]

New York City

Allan and Ruth Friedlich moved to New York City with their children around 1936. At the same time, Graff chose to live in New York City. On December 12, 1936, a farewell dinner was held for him at the Des Moines Club,[148] and on December 19 he traveled to New York City. He complained that shortly before his departure a film cannister with a 60 mm film had been stolen in which he performed the complicated "Wertheim" operation (a radical hysterectomy with removal of lymph nodes for the treatment of cervical cancer) on a woman at the State University Hospital. The film had been taken four years earlier to demonstrate the method at meetings with other physicians. That was also the reason

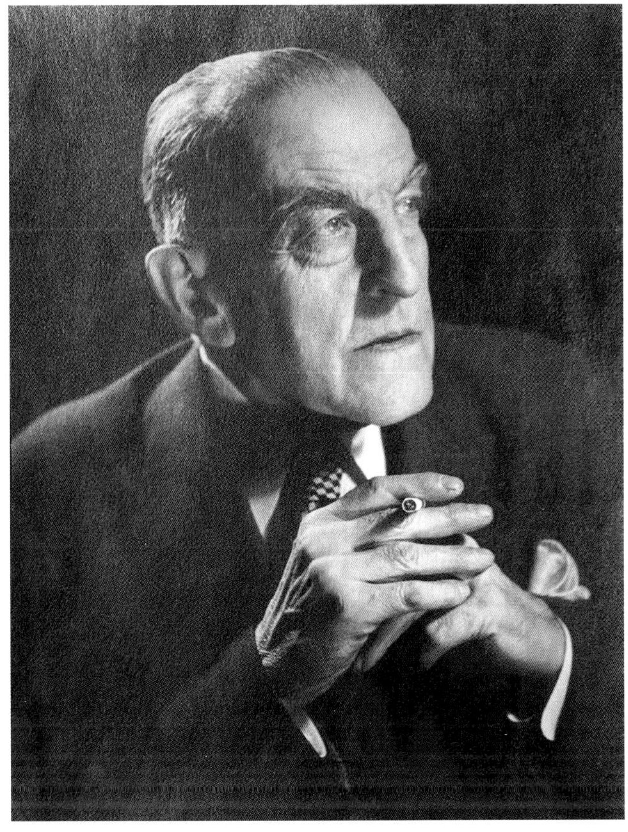

that Graff had borrowed the film. Graff was desperate and offered a reward and assurance that no questions would be asked. He sold his practice in Des Moines to Dr. Lawrence D. Smith and denied that the move to New York was just the first step in his return to Austria.[149]

In the *Medical Directory of New York, New Jersey, and Connecticut, 1938*, Graff was listed as a specialist in obstetrics and gynecology at 728 Park Avenue, with office hours from 11 a.m. to 1 p.m. and by appointment. He was a member of the American Medical Association.[150] He was listed at the same address in the directory for 1939–40,[151] but then from 1941–42 at the address 172 East 82nd Street,[152] which he also entered on his World War II Registration Card in 1942 and listed it as the address of his practice. Graff gave his height as 5 feet, 11 $1/2$ inches and his weight as 186 pounds. As a contact person who would always know his address, he noted Allan Friedlich at 57 East 80th Street.

The New York City telephone directory of 1944 listed his new residence as 139 East 66th Street.[153] He presumably had his practice there as well, since in 1949 this address is given in the medical directory of New York, New Jersey, and Connecticut.[154] It is remarkable that Graff never became a member New York Academy of Medicine.[155]

On his seventieth birthday in 1948, Graff had his portrait taken by the Austrian émigré photographer Trude Fleischmann in New York [Fig. 71]. It is reasonable to assume that the two Austrians in exile knew each other personally.

Death in Berlin

On July 20, 1951, Graff traveled with the *S.S. Wild Ranger* via Cherbourg to Bremerhaven in Germany, giving his residence as 31 West 71st Street, with the intention of remaining abroad for six months.[156] He extended his stay by several months due to illness and was no longer able to travel to Graz, his hometown. According to his family, he was sick and impoverished. On May 2, 1952, he suffered a heart attack and died in the Städtisches Krankenhaus am Knie, Berliner Strasse 37–38, in Berlin-Charlottenburg at age seventy-three.

The American Consulate in Berlin prepared a report on Graff's death that gave his final address in New York City as 139 East 66th Street. His body was cremated, and the urn kept in the crematorium in Wilmersdorf in Berlin until further notice. Coloman Graff, who was residing in North Plainfield, New Jersey, had been informed of his father's death. Margarethe Wrobel is mentioned as a companion who had traveled to Berlin with Graff.[157] This was his last life partner. She travelled with him (under the name Frieda Margarethe Wrobel, aged forty-eight) on the *S.S. Wild Ranger* on July 20, 1951, from New York City to Germany.[158] On departure Graff gave her address as 31 West 71st Street.

Graff's ashes were buried in the family grave in Graz. In a letter of June 12, 1952, Erwin's sister Friederike reported on this to their sister Dorothea:

> *We have had sad days; Erwin's urn arrived, Olga [Erwin's first wife] and I buried it in our parents' grave. Some roads had been traveled before that, and I cannot even say how sorry I felt for Olga as she stood before Erwin's ashes so miserable and unappreciated for her devotion to him with a bouquet of red roses, which he loved so much! Now we will have his name engraved on the plinth because this once promising life has come to a final, sad end. Peace to his ashes!!*[159]

Olga poured out her heart to Dorothea, her friend and former sister-in-law:

> *I am very, very sad about dear Erwin's sad end and that I can no longer show him anything nice and was so out of contact with him during his poor final months because of his unfortunate stay in Berlin. How we would have spoiled and cared for him if he had been with us. As it was, he never reached his longed-for homeland, only his ashes lie in the earth he loved. Friedl [Friederike] and I were deeply moved as we stood together at the grave.*[160]

Wrobel, Graff's final companion, was also in contact by letter with his sister Dorothea after his death. Olga warned Dorothea about her:

> *Dorli, watch out in your correspondence with Margaret Wrobel: she is a notorious communist and dragged poor Erwin into an early death, stole everything he owned, left him freezing and starving, and she is a superficial person. I know everything about her from an acquaintance who has lived in New York for twenty-seven years and knew her well.*[161]

Wrobel presumably married before 1957 because her letters have Margarethe Davis with a return address of 5422 14th Avenue, Brooklyn.

It is not known how Graff's estate was distributed.[162] As noted below, his Schiele drawings went to his two ex-wives and the painting to Coloman von Graff.

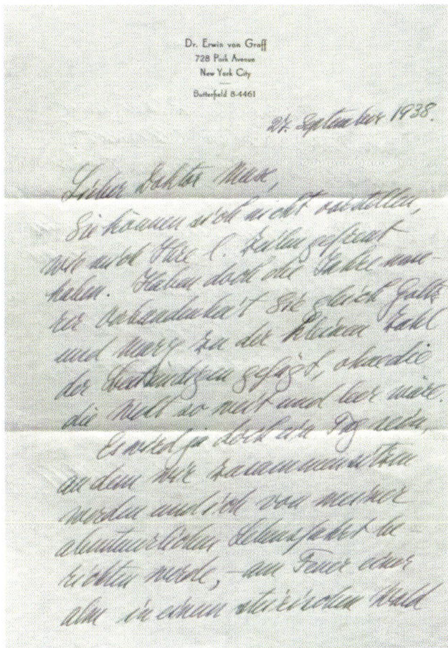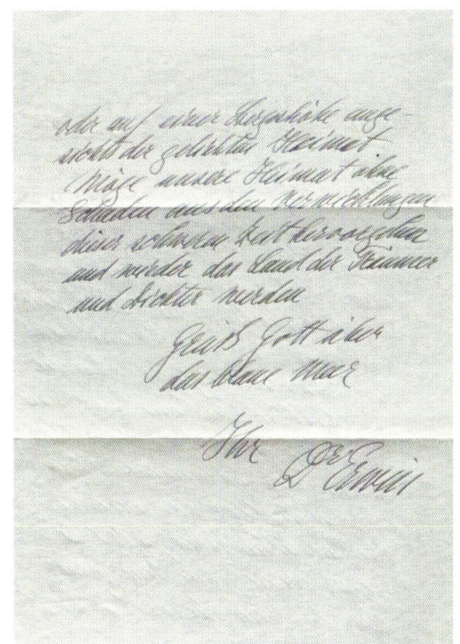

Friendship with Max Mell

Graff mentioned his friend the writer Max Mell several times in his diary of 1918–19. He met him four times from June to November 1918: once Mell went to Graff's home, giving him a bottle of spirits and sending his regards to his ex-wife, Olga; once, even though they were separated, Graff went to dinner with her and Mell; and the two friends went to the theater twice to see George Bernard Shaw's *Fanny's First Play* and Shakespeare's *Pericles, Prince of Tyre*, respectively.

The fathers of the two friends taught science in Graz at the same time and presumably knew each other: Ludwig Graff zoology and Alexander Mell natural history and chemistry. Mell was also in contact by letter with Graff's mother, Jenny. In Mell's papers, there is a letter from her in which she thanks him for congratulating her on his eightieth birthday.[163] There are also two letters from Graff there, including an announcement of his wedding to Adele von Fedrigoni in 1920 and two letters that Graff sent from New York City.

The letter of September 27, 1938, is full of melancholy and homesickness [Fig. 72]:

Dear Doctor Max,

You cannot imagine
how much your kind lines
please me. After all, the years
of our bond have added you, like Goltz[164]
and Mary,[165] *to the small number*
of stable friends without whom
the world would be so vast and empty.
The day will come
when we sit together,
and I will tell you
of the adventurous journey
of my life—next to a fire

in a hut in a Styrian forest
or on a mountaintop with a view
of our beloved homeland.
May our homeland emerge
unscathed from the imbroglios
of this difficult time
and once again be the land
of dreamers and poets.
Greetings to you
across the blue sea

Your Dr. Erwin

Ten years later, he sent Christmas greetings [Fig. 73]:

> *Dear Dr. Max and*
> *the entire Mell family,*
> *who have accepted*
> *and accept so well*
> *my unforgettable "singer."*
> *All joy and all happiness*
> *for Christmas and in 1949*
>
> *from your grateful*
> *Dr. Erwin*

With "singer" Graff meant his first wife, Olga, who had taken singing lessons. As is clear from numerous letters,[166] Mell had visited Olga and her sister, who lived together, for several days almost every year.

Elliott Roosevelt

A mistake that comes up repeatedly in Eleanor Roosevelt's biography must be corrected here. It is claimed that her father, Elliott Roosevelt, who was sent to Europe to treat his alcoholism, consulted with Erwin von Graff in Vienna, who recommended a stay at the Sanatorium Mariengrund.[167] Because Elliott's trip to Europe took place in 1891, it cannot have been Graff, who was only thirteen at the time. Neither is there a Sanatorium Mariengrund in Vienna. It can only be a confusion of names: Not Dr. Graff but rather Dr. Krafft (Richard von Krafft-Ebing) was consulted, a respected psychiatrist and neurologist who had the Sanatorium Mariagrün built in Graz, which was very progressive for its time, to treat patients for all sorts of nervous ailments and for detoxification.

73. Letter from Erwin von Graff to Max Mell, postmarked December 13, 1948. Vienna City Library, ZPH-891/8

The letter reads:

Ihnen lieber Dr. Max und
der ganzen Familie Mell,
die Ihr Euch so gut
meiner unvergesslichen
„Sängerin" angenommen
habt und annehmt.
Alle Freude und alles
Glück für Weihnachten
und 1949
von Ihrem dankbaren
Dr. Erwin

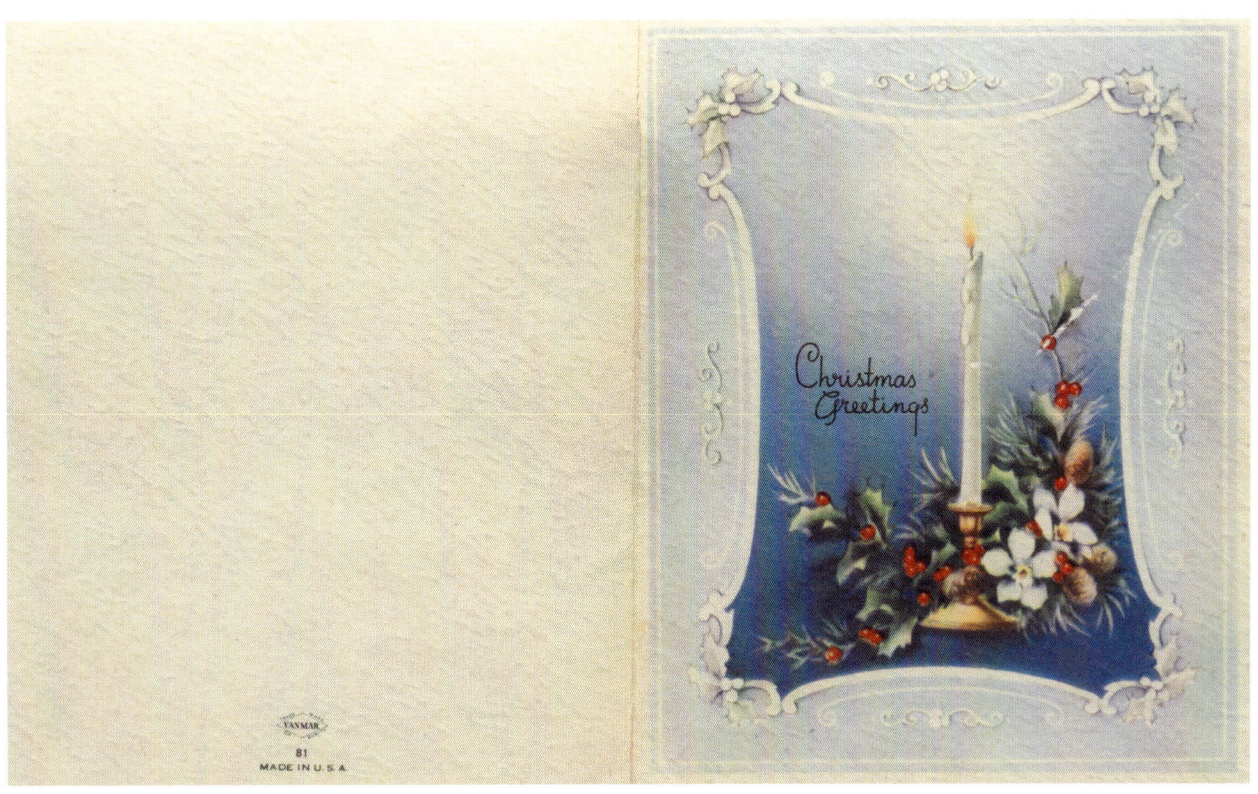

Christmas
Greetings
VANMAR
81
MADE IN U.S.A.

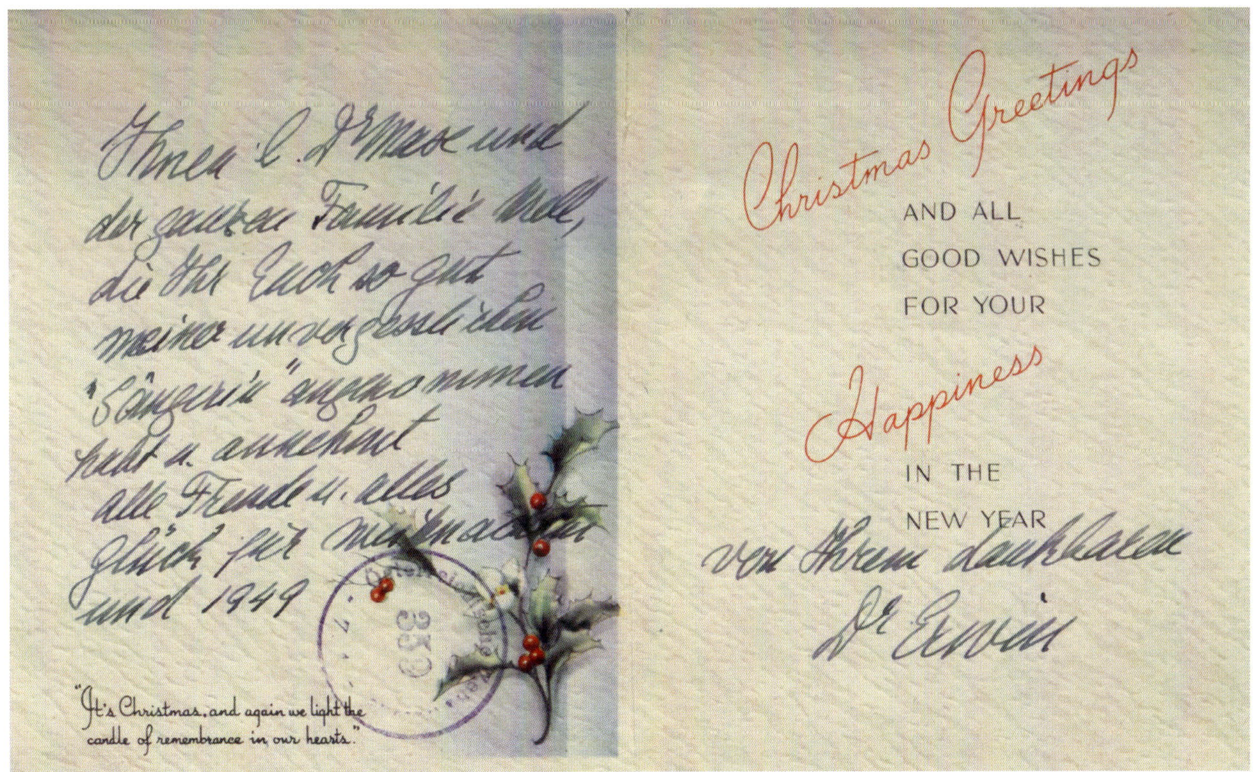

Christmas Greetings
AND ALL
GOOD WISHES
FOR YOUR
Happiness
IN THE
NEW YEAR
"It's Christmas, and again we light the
candle of remembrance in our hearts."

In addition to his portrait from 1910, several Schiele drawings were also in Graff's possession. Without exception, they were all from 1910, and most were therefore presumably connected to the clinic drawings. As mentioned above, they may have been Schiele's payment for Graff having arranged for pregnant women and newborns to pose as models. Several sheets are labeled identifying Graff as owner. But because there are also drawings that have only been traced back to Graff thanks to provenance research, such as *The Painter Max Oppenheimer* [Fig. 74] in the Albertina Museum, Vienna, it can be assumed that he may have owned additional works by Schiele of which we are unaware.

Girl with Folded Hands (Gerti Schiele), 1910[168]*
Leopold Museum, Vienna, inv. no. 1389, Kallir D509

Standing Nude with Black Stockings, 1910[169]*
Neue Galerie am Landesmuseum Joanneum, Graz, inv. no. 11/10.809, Kallir D567

Sitting Nude Girl with Stockings and Shoes, 1910[170]*
Leopold Museum, Vienna, inv. no. 1390, Kallir D576

Baby in Swaddling Clothes, 1910[171]*
Neue Galerie am Landesmuseum Joanneum, Graz, inv. no. II/10.808, Kallir D390

Standing Nude Boy, from the Knees Up, 1910[172]*
Neue Galerie am Landesmuseum Joanneum, Graz, inv. no. II/10.805, Kallir D459

Seated Female Nude with Bent Knees and Green Pillow, 1910[173]*
Neue Galerie am Landesmuseum Joanneum, Graz, inv. no. II/10.807, Kallir D520

Semi-Reclining Nude Girl, 1910[174]*
Neue Galerie am Landesmuseum Joanneum, Graz, inv. no. II/10.804, Kallir D574

The Painter Max Oppenheimer, 1910[175]** [Fig. 69]
The Albertina Museum, Vienna, inv. no. 32438, Kallir D587

Portrait of Dr. Erwin von Graff, 1910
Private Collection, USA, Kallir P161

* Adele von Lička (Graff's second wife) sold these works to the Neue Galerie am Landesmuseum Joanneum, Graz, in 1956. She had presumably inherited them after Graff's death.

** Olga Graff (Graff's first wife) put this work up for auction in 1956 at the Dorotheum in Vienna, where the Albertina Museum, Vienna, acquired it. She had presumably inherited this work from Graff.

Graff also owned a portrait that the Viennese painter Ferdinand Kitt (1887–1961) had painted of him. It shows him pale and clean-shaven, wearing an enormous wig on his head, a lace jabot under his chin, and a scholar's coat. His hands are energetically gripping the silver handle of a cane. It depicts Graff dressed in a medieval costume for an artists' party that the Künstlerhaus, more properly known as the Gesellschaft bildender Künstlerinnen und Künstler Österreichs (Artists' House, Society of Fine Artists of Austrian)—organized for decades, which earned a legendary reputation. The portrait was in Graff's salon in 1927,[176] but its current whereabouts are unknown.

Translated from the German by Steven Lindberg.

74. Egon Schiele, *The Painter Max Oppenheimer*, 1910, charcoal, ink and watercolor on kraft paper, 45.1 × 29.8 cm (17 3/4 × 11 3/4 in.), Kallir D587. The Albertina Museum, Vienna, inv. no. 32438. Photo Credit: The Albertina Museum, Vienna

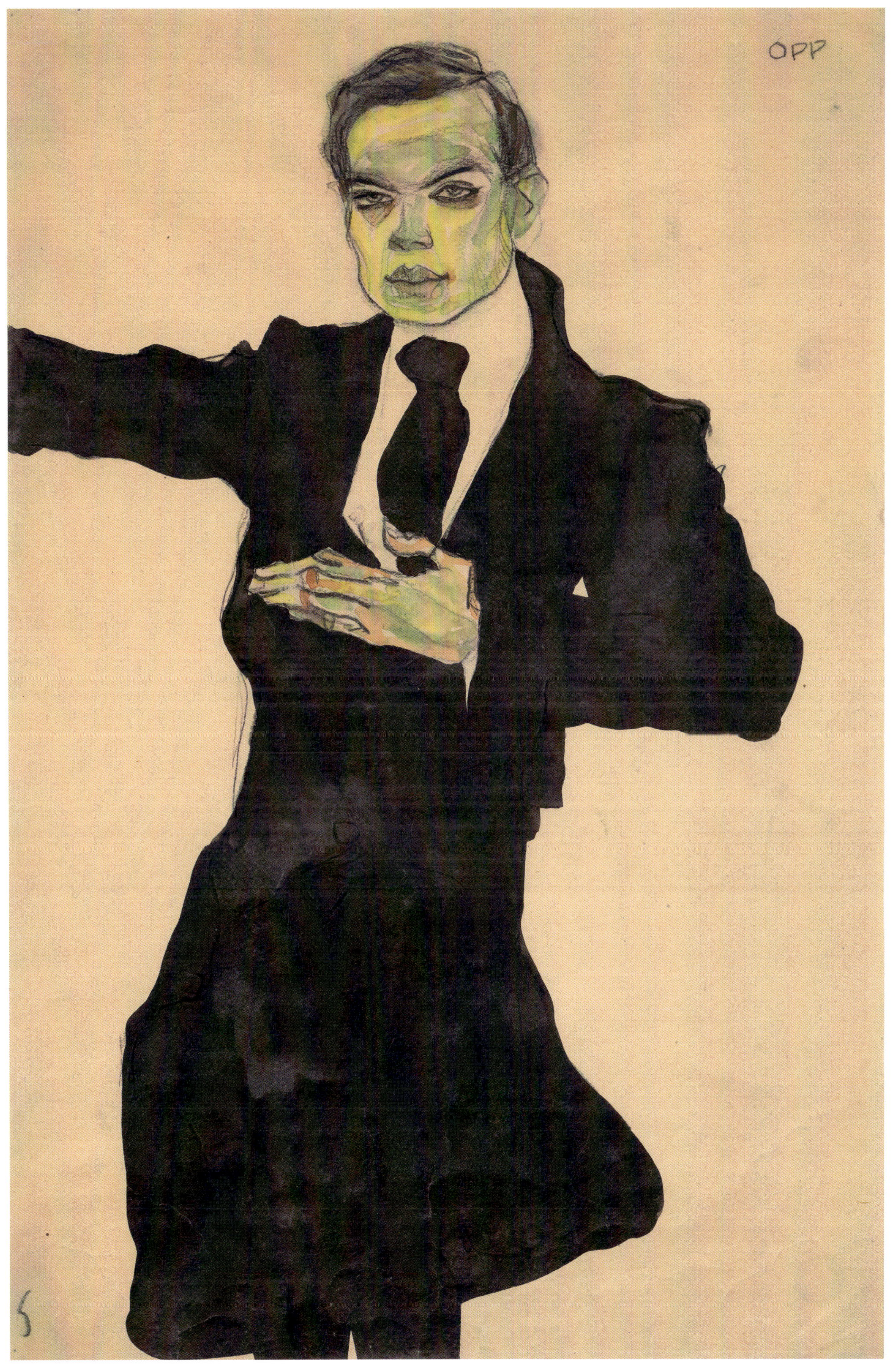
ÖPP

"Eine Ersteigung des Grossvenedigers auf norwegischen Schneeschuhen," lecture, 1901.

"Ein Fall von primärer Lungenaktinomykose von der Spitze der linken Lunge ausgehend," *Zeitschrift für Heilkunde* 25, no. 10.

"Zur Therapie der operativen Verletzungen des Ductus thoracicus," *Wiener klinische Wochenschrift* 18, no. 1 (1905).

"Angeborene Hyperplasie der einen Lunge bei gleichzeitiger rudimentärer Bildung der anderen," *Münchener medizinische Wochenschrift* 52, no. 13 (1905).

"Zur Kasuistik und Therapie der Hämangiome," *Zeitschrift für Heilkunde* 27, no. 6.

"Experimentelle Beiträge zur Erklärung der Wirkungsweise der Bierschen Stauung," *Münchener medizinische Wochenschrift* 55, no. 6 (1908).

"Klinische und experimentelle Beiträge zur Bierschen Stauung," *Brun's Beiträge zur klinischen Chirurgie* 59, no. 3.

"Über eine endochoriale amniotische Zyste," *Archiv für Gynäkologie* 89, no. 1.

"Haben wir von der prophylaktischen Anwendung der Nukleinsäure unter der Geburt und im Wochenbett eine Verbesserung der Morbidität zu erwarten?" *Zentralblatt für Gynäkologie* 34, no. 27 (1910).

"Zur Frage der Immunisation gegen Puerperalinfektion," *Zentralblatt für Gynäkologie* 34, no. 51 (1910).

"Zum Nachweis hämolytischer Stoffe in der Plazenta," *Monatsschrift für Geburtshilfe und Gynäkologie* 32, no. 2.

"Klinische und experimentelle Beiträge zur Vorbehandlung von Laparotomien mit subkutaner Injection von Nukleinsäure" (with Bernhard Aschner), *Mitteilungen aus den Grenzgebieten der Medizin und Chirurgie* 22, no. 1 (1910).

"Atresie und Torsion einer Tube," *Archiv für Gynäkologie* 93, no. 1.

"Über die Wirkung des Plazentarserums und des Serums Gravider auf menschliche Karzinomzellen" (with R. Kraus), *Wiener klinische Wochenschrift* 24, no. 6 (1911).

"Biologische Studien über mütterliches und Nabelschnurblut," (with I.v. Zubrzycki), *Archiv für Gynäkologie* 95, no. 3.

"Über neuere serologische Methoden zur Diagnose maligner Tumoren" (with R. Kraus und E. Ranzi), *Wiener klinische Wochenschrift* 24, no. 28 (1911).

"Diskussion zu dem Vortrag Dr. Neumann und Hermann: Biologische Studien über die weibliche Keimdrüse," *K. k. Gesellschaft der Ärzte in Wien*, meeting of March 31, 1911.

"Experimentelle Beiträge zum Mechanismus der Toxin-Antitoxinwirkung" (with Dr. Menschikoff), *Zentralblatt für Bakteriologie*, 1. Abt. Originale 61, no. 3.

"Weitere Beiträge zur Vorbehandlung der Laparotomien mit subkutaner Injektion von Nukleinsäure," *Mitteilungen aus den Grenzgebieten der Medizin und Chirurgie* 24.

"Die Kobragift-Pferdebluthämolyse in der Schwangerschaft und bei Karzinom" (with I.v. Zubrzycki), *Münchener medizinische Wochenschrift* 58, no. 11 (1912).

"Ein Fall von primärem Sarkom des Magens, Resektion, Heilung," *Wiener klinische Wochenschrift* 25, no. 26 (1912).

"Experimentelle Beiträge zur Serumtherapie des Tetanus (intravenöse Injektion)," *Mitteilungen aus den Grenzgebieten der Medizin und Chirurgie* 1912, 25.

"Zur Frage der Immunisierung gegen maligne Tumoren" (with E. Ranzi), *Mitteilungen aus den Grenzgebieten der Medizin und Chirurgie* 25, no. 2, p. 278.

"Über den Antitrypsingehalt des Blutes bei Schwangerschaft und Karzinom" (with I. v. Zubrzycki), *Zeitschrift für Geburtshilfe und Gynäkologie* 72.

"Zur Technik der Röntgentherapie in der Gynäkologie," *Wiener medizinische Wochenschrift* 63, no. 16 (1913).

"Schilddrüse und Genitale (Habilitationsschrift)," *Archiv für Gynäkologie* 102, no. 1 (1914).

"Schilddrüse und Gestation," lecture at the fifteenth meeting of the Deutsche Gesellschaft für Gynäkologie.

"Basedow und Genitale" (with I. Novak), *Archiv für Gynäkologie* 102, no. 1.

"Basedow und Genitale," lecture at the fifteenth meeting of the Deutsche Gesellschaft für Gynäkologie.

"Karzinomatöser Uteruspolyp," *Zentralblatt für Gynäkologie* 57, no. 32 (1913).

"Röntgenstrahlen, Mesothorium und Radium, Referat auf der 85. Versammlung deutscher Naturforscher und Ärzte in Wien," *Fortschritte auf dem Gebiete der Röntgenstrahlen* 21 (1913).

"Die Serodiagnose maligner Tumoren," *Zentralblatt für
die Gesellschaft für Geburtshilfe und Gynäkologie* 3
 (summary report).

"Über den Einfluss der Gravidität auf das Wachstum maligner
Tumoren," *Wiener klinische Wochenschrift* 27, no. 1 (1914).

"Die Behandlung der nichtklimakterischen Meno- und
Metrorrhagien," *Strahlentherapie* 4, no. 1.

"Röntgentherapie in der Gynäkologie," *Fortschritte auf dem
Gebiete der Röntgenstrahlen* 21.

"Über Versuche, die Heilungsdauer bei der Myombehandlung
durch Steigerung der verabreichten Röntgenmengen noch weiter
abzukürzen," *Zentralblatt für Gynäkologie* 38, no. 11 (1914).

"Die Basedowsche Krankheit als Kontraindikation gegen
gynäkologische Röntgentherapie," *Wiener klinische
Wochenschrift* 27, no. 5 (1914).

"Über die bisherigen Erfahrungen mit Radium und
Röntgenstrahlen bei der Krebsbehandlung," *Strahlentherapie* 5,
Originale.

"Eine neue Röhrenblende für therapeutische Bestrahlungen,"
Strahlentherapie 4, no. 2 (1914).

"Über die Verdauung von Plazentarpepton durch Serum,
gemessen mit der Formeltitration" (with P. Saxl), *Medizinische
Klinik* 10, no. 33 (1914).

"Geheilte Beckenfraktur mit Harnröhrenzerreissung,"
Militärsanitätswesen, Wiener klinische Wochenschrift 29,
no. 45 (1916).

"Gasphlegmonen, Harnröhrenschuss, Lues des Rückenmarkes,"
Militärsanitätswesen, Wiener klinische Wochenschrift 29,
no. 42 (1916).

"Zur Kasuistik der entzündlichen Bauchdeckentumoren,"
Wiener klinische Wochenschrift 30, no. 16 (1917).

"Über Schädelschüsse," *Archiv für klinische Chirurgie*
110 (1918).

"Zur Kenntnis der Fettsucht der Frauen," *Wiener medizinische
Wochenschrift* 75, no. 23 (1925).

"Über Abortusbehandlung," *Wiener medizinische Wochenschrift*
75, no. 42 (1925).

"Blutungen in Geburtshilfe und Gynäkologie," *Wiener
medizinische Wochenschrift* 76, no. 38 (1926).

*Die Unfruchtbarkeit der Frau: Bedeutung der Eileiterdurchblasung
für die Erkennung der Ursachen, die Voraussage und die
Behandlung.* Vienna: Springer, 1926.

"Behandlung der Sterilität," *Medizinische Klinik: Wochenschrift
für praktische Ärzte* 24, no. 31 (August 3, 1928).

"Ursachen und Behandlung der Sterilität," *Wiener medizinische
Wochenschrift* 78, no. 6 (1928).

"Frühsymptome des Krebses," lecture, 1928.[177]

"Die Fruchtbarkeit der Ehe," lecture, 1928.[178]

"Die kinderlose Ehe," lecture, 1928.[179]

"Hormonbehandlung mit Thelygan in der Frauenheilkunde,"
Medizinische Klinik: Wochenschrift für praktische Ärzte 25,
no. 13 (March 29, 1929).

"Bedeutung der Blutgruppen für Mutter und Kind," *Stunde
der Volksgesundheit: Wöchentliche Beilage von "Radio-Wien,"*
no. 39, November 5, 1929, pp. 279–82, and *Stunde der
Volksgesundheit: Wöchentliche Beilage von "Radio-Wien,"*
no. 40, November 15, 1929.

Die Geburtshilfe des Praktischen Arztes. Vienna: Ars Medici,
1930.

"Sole-Anwendung in der Frauenheilkunde," Vortrag bei einem
ärztlichen Fortbildungskurs in Bad Ischl, *Medizinische Klinik:
Wochenschrift für praktische Ärzte* 26, no. 32 (August 8, 1930).

"Etiology of Prolapse," *American Journal of Obstetrics
and Gynecology* 25, no. 6 (June 1933).

"A Plea for the Early Recognition of Uterine Cancer,
with Some Remarks on Treatment."[180]

"Bilateral Ureterovaginal Fistula: Successful Implantation
of Both Ureters into the Bladder Seven and Eleven Months
Following Total Hysterectomy," *American Journal of Obstetrics
and Gynecology* 29, no. 4 (April 1935).

"Tubal Sterilization by the Madlener Technique,"
American Journal of Obstetrics and Gynecology 38,
no. 2 (August 1939).

Provenance

1910–52   Erwin von Graff, Vienna/New York

1952–59   Coloman von Graff, North Plainfield, NJ

1959–71   Galerie St. Etienne, New York

Since 1971   Private Collection, United States

Selected Exhibition History

Vienna 1930, Neue Galerie, "Unbekanntes von Egon Schiele," October 29 – November 30, 1930

1959 New York, Galerie St. Etienne, "European and American Expressionists,"
September 22 – October 17, 1959

1960–61 Boston/New York/Louisville/Pittsburgh/Minneapolis, Institute of Contemporary Art/
Galerie St. Etienne/J.B.Speed Art Museum/Carnegie Institute/Minneapolis Institute of Arts, "Egon Schiele,"
October 6, 1960 – May 21, 1961

1963 Berkeley/Pasadena, University Art Gallery of the University of California/Pasadena Art Museum,
"Viennese Expressionism 1910–1924," February 5 – April 21, 1963

1964 New York, Galerie St. Etienne, "Twenty-Fifth Anniversary Exhibition, Part I,"
October 17 – November 14, 1964

1980 New York, Galerie St. Etienne, "Gustav Klimt, Egon Schiele," November 11 – December 27, 1980

1986 New York, The Museum of Modern Art, "Vienna 1900: Art, Architecture & Design,"
July 3 – October 21, 1986

2001–02 New York, Neue Galerie New York, "New Worlds: German and Austrian Art, 1890–1940,"
November 11, 2001 – February 18, 2002

2005–06 New York, Neue Galerie New York, "Egon Schiele: The Ronald S. Lauder and Serge Sabarsky
Collections," October 21, 2005 – February 10, 2006

2011 New York, Neue Galerie New York, "Birth of the Modern: Style and Identity in Vienna 1900,"
February 24 – June 27, 2011

2014–15 New York, Neue Galerie New York, "Egon Schiele: Portraits," October 9, 2014 – January 9, 2015

2018 Vienna, Leopold Museum, "The Jubilee Show," February 23 – November 4, 2018

VI. SELECTED BIBLIOGRAPHY

Gemma Blackshaw. "The Pathological Body: Modernist Strategising in Egon Schiele's Self-Portraiture." *Oxford Art Journal* 30, no. 3 (2007), pp. 377–401.

Christian Bauer. *Egon Schiele*: *Der Anfang*. Munich, 2013.

Rudy Chiappini (ed.). *Egon Schiele*. Exh. cat., Museo d'Arte Moderna della Città di Lugano, Villa Malpensata. Milan, 2003.

Alessandra Comini. *Egon Schiele's Portraits*. Berkeley, 1974.

Jane Kallir. *Egon Schiele*: *The Complete Works*. New York, 1998.

Gianfranco Malafarina. *Egon Schiele*. Vienna/Geneva/New York, 1990.

Tobias G. Natter. *Die Welt von Klimt*, *Schiele und Kokoschka*: *Ihre Sammler und Mäzene*. Cologne, 2003.

Tobias G. Natter/Ursula Storch (eds.). *Schiele & Roessler*: *Der Künstler und sein Förderer*, *Kunst und Networking im frühen 20. Jahrhundert*. Exh. cat., Wien Museum. Ostfildern-Ruit, 2004

Tobias G. Natter (ed.). *Egon Schiele*: *The Complete Paintings*, *1909–1918*. Cologne, 2017.

Christian M. Nebehay. *Egon Schiele*, *1890 – 1918*: *Leben*, *Briefe*, *Gedichte*. Salzburg/Vienna, 1979

Sonja Niederacher. *Dossier Leopold Museum-Privatstiftung*: *Egon Schiele*, *Mädchen mit aneinander gelegten Händen* (*Gerti Schiele*), *LM Inv. Nr. 1389 und Egon Schiele*, *Sitzendes nacktes Mädchen mit Strümpfen und Schuhen*, *LM Inv. Nr. 1390*. Vienna, December 31, 2012.

Arthur Roessler. *Erinnerungen an Egon Schiele*. Vienna, 1948

Anton Schaller. *Die Wertheim-Klinik*: *Eine Geschichte der II. Universitäts-Frauenklinik in Wien*. Vienna, 1992.

Anton Schaller. "Egon Schiele und die Wiener Frauenklinik." *Psychopraxis*: *Zeitschrift für praktische Psychotherapie und Grenzgebiete* 2 (2007), pp. 28–33.

Friedrich Schauta/Rudolf Chrobak. *Geschichte* und *Beschreibung des Baues der neuen Frauenkliniken in Wien*. Vienna, 1911.

Walter Schübler. "Geniale Sprüche im Literatencafé: Bibiana Amon stand nicht nur für Romanfiguren von Robert Musil und Franz Werfel Modell, sondern auch für den Maler Egon Schiele, Ein Recherche-Zickzack zwischen Fakten und Fiktion. *Frankfurter Allgemeine Zeitung* no. 70 (March 23, 2019), p. 16.

Walter Schübler. *Bibiana Amon*: *Eine Spurensuche*. Vienna, 2022.

I am deeply grateful to Renée Price for the idea and enthusiasm for this project, and to Janis Staggs for her energetic support in conducting research and writing.

I would like to thank everyone who supported me in this project, especially the Graff family, the daughter of Adele Lička and the descendants of Liliana Amon, who all welcomed me warmly and generously provided me with information, letters, photographs and diaries. Most appreciated was the help and competent technical information in medical and medical history questions, as well as in other scientific areas. My thanks go to, in alphabetical order: Christian Bauer, Alessandra Comini, Herwig Czech (Institute for Ethics, Collections and History of Medicine at the Medical University of Vienna, Josephinum), Elisabeth Draxler, Andreas Dutz, Michael Freissmuth (Head of the Center for Physiology and Pharmacology at the Medical University of Vienna), Verena Gamper, Ralph Gleis (Director General of the Albertina Museum, Vienna), Elisabeth Graff de Pancscova, Alexander Graff de Pancsova, Gerhard Jenisch, Ingrid Jenisch, Kerstin Jesse, Jane Kallir, Herbert Kiss (Head of the Department of Obstetrics and Gynecology at the Medical University of Vienna), Ursula Kreuzbauer, Sonja Niederacher, Mauricio Olivares Díaz, Brigitte Schwarzer-Daum (Deputy Head of Department of Clinical Pharmacology at the Medical University of Vienna), Arlene Shaner (the Historical Collections Librarian at the New York Academy of Medicine), Marcella Sigmund-Graff, Christa Simon and Harald Sitte (Center for Physiology and Pharmacology at the Medical University of Vienna).

1 "*Ausserordentlich*" (extraordinary, special) is used to describe a professorship that is not associated with a specific chair.

2 Prof. Dr. Michael Freissmuth to the author, e-mail, June 11, 2025.

3 Alessandra Comini, *Egon Schiele's Portraits* (Berkeley: University of California Press, 1974), 72–73.

4 Report by the daughter of Adele Fedrigoni von Etschthal, July 8, 2021, and February 28, 2025.

5 Prof. Dr. Michael Freissmuth to the author, e-mail, June 11, 2025, also providing a link to this source: John A. O'Donnell and Judith P. Jones, "Diffusion of the Intravenous Technique among Narcotic Addicts in the United States," in "Recreational Drug Use," special issue, *Journal of Health and Social Behavior* 9, no. 2 (June 1968), 120–30.

6 Dr. Alexander Graff de Pancsova provided me with this information and the corresponding links, personal interview on September 1, 2025.

7 Manuela C. Warscher, "Die 'neue Art von Strahlen,'" *Österreichische Ärztezeitung*, no. 21 (November 10, 2021): 48–51, esp. 49.

8 Dr. Alexander Graff de Pancsova, personal interview on September 1, 2025.

9 It was the psychoanalyst Sigmund Freud who gave this phenomenon its name. He was inspired to do so by numerous legends about women with vaginas equipped with teeth or other weapons and linked this myth to his theories on castration anxiety and the idea of "eat or be eaten."

10 N. F. Karlins, "Drawing Notebook," Artnet online, n.d.; www.artnet.com/magazineus/reviews/karlins/karlins11–10–05.asp (accessed September 3, 2025).

11 Jenny Graff to her daughter Dorothea, April 21, 1904, Private Collection.

12 Jenny Graff to her daughter Dorothea, May 13, 1904, Private Collection.

13 Jenny Graff to her daughter Dorothea, June 2, 1904, Private Collection.

14 Arthur Roessler, *Erinnerungen an Egon Schiele*, 2nd ed. (Vienna: Wiener Volksbuchverlag, 1948), 5.

15 Ibid., 27.

16 Christian M. Nebehay, *Egon Schiele, 1890–1918: Leben, Briefe, Gedichte* (Salzburg: Residenz, 1979), 519.

17 Tobias G. Natter, *Die Welt von Klimt, Schiele und Kokoschka: Ihre Sammler und Mäzene* (Cologne: DuMont, 2003), 169.

18 Austrian State Archive, AT-OeStA/AVA Unterricht UM allg. A 624.17, Curriculum vitae of Erwin von Graff, April 22, 1914. As an assistant physician, one was a licensed doctor who was undergoing specialist training. In addition to Graff, several assistant physicians were employed at the clinic, who were responsible for caring for patients on the ward and for routine tasks.

19 Jakob Lehne, Peter Husslein, and Petra Kohlberger, "Die Frauenheilkunde in Wien von ihren Anfängen bis in die Jetztzeit," *Speculum: Zeitschrift für Gynäkologie und Geburtshilfe* 37, no. 3 (2019): 3–21, p. 8.

20 Prof. Dr. Herbert Kiss to the author, e-mail, August 31, 2025.

21 Comini, *Egon Schiele's Portraits* (see note 3), 72.

22 Ibid., 212n64.

23 Nebehay, *Egon Schiele, 1890–1918* (see note 16), 251, 519.

24 Anton Schaller, "Egon Schiele und die Wiener Frauenklinik," *Psychopraxis: Zeitschrift für praktische Psychotherapie und Grenzgebiete*. 2 (2007), 28–33, p. 29.

25 Ibid., 29–30.

26 The operating theaters and studio were demolished after the gynecological clinics were merged and relocated to the new general hospital in 1996.

27 The photographic studio belonged to the Institute for X-ray and Photography. It is not known how it was furnished, but we do know what equipment it contained: a Goerz Anastigmat camera, an enlarger, a plate display case, an electric plate dryer, a metronome for measuring time, an Osmium lamp, various auxiliary instruments, and a Zeiss microphotography camera. Friedrich Schauta and Rudolf Chrobak, *Geschichte und Beschreibung des Baues der neuen Frauenkliniken in Wien* (Vienna: Urban & Schwarzenberg, 1911), 75.

28 Schaller, "Egon Schiele und die Wiener Frauenklinik" (see note 24), 30.

29 Schauta and Chrobak, *Geschichte und Beschreibung des Baues der neuen Frauenkliniken in Wien* (see note 27), 32.

30 Ibid.

31 Jane Kallir, *Egon Schiele: The Complete Works* (New York: Abrams, 1998), D528, D529, D531–40.

32 Walter Schübler, "Geniale Sprüche im Literatencafé: Bibiana Amon stand nicht nur für Romanfiguren von Robert Musil und Franz Werfel Modell, sondern auch für den Maler Egon Schiele; Ein Recherche-Zickzack zwischen Fakten und Fiktion," *Frankfurter Allgemeine Zeitung*, no. 70 (March 23, 2019): 16; followed by idem, "Bibiana Amon: Eine Spurensuche," Vienna 2022.

33 Ignatius Taschner (1871–1913) was a German sculptor and medallist.

34 Eduard Stella (1884–1955) was a Viennese painter.

35 This refers to the exhibition "I. Internationale Jagd-Ausstellung" from May–October 1910 in the Rotunde at the Prater, a public park in Vienna, where the 1873 World Exposition took place. Exhibition halls with the Rotunde at its center were constructed, and at that time it was the world largest dome at about 355 feet in diameter. Egon Schiele participated with a large nude whose whereabouts are unknown (Kallir P170).

36 This refers to works from the Künstlerhaus, the conservative Vienna Artists' Society, from which several artists broke away in 1897 to found the Vienna Secession.

37 Marie Amon, *Barrières* (Paris: Denoël, 1939). The novel *Barrières* was published only in French, in a translation from German by Albert Paraz. The German manuscript has been lost. Ursula Kreuzbauer provided the German translation of the French text.

38 This probably refers to the Café Museum on the Karlsplatz in Vienna.

39 For Fyodor Dostoyevsky, life itself is a continuous process of finding meaning.

40 Recognizably a barely encrypted Dr. Graff.

41 Amon, *Barrières* (see note 37), 61–64.

42 Lehne, Husslein, and Kohlberger, "Die Frauenheilkunde in Wien" (see note 19), 5.

43 Letter of the Vienna City and State Archives, Magistrate Department 8, no. MA 8 – B-AP–343925–2021, dated May 25, 2021.

44 Erwin Osen (1891–1970) was a Viennese painter and close friend of Schiele at the time. See Christian Bauer, *Erwin Osen: Egon Schieles Künstlerfreund* (Munich: Hirmer, 2023).

45 On May 12, 1910, he sent a telegram from Český Krumlov to his uncle Leopold Czihaczek in Vienna (Egon Schiele Database of Autographs, ESDA ID 233).

46 Egon Schiele Database of Autographs, ESDA ID 244.

47 Postcard from Arthur Roessler to Egon Schiele, July 21, 1910, The Albertina Museum, Vienna, inv. no. ESA531.

48 Letter from Egon Schiele to Thomas Csmarich, August 1, 1910, Vienna City Library, Manuscript Department, inv. no. H.I.N. 154832.

49 Egon Schiele Database of Autographs, ESDA ID 249.

50 Information from Liliana Amon's grandson, interview, September 12, 2025.

51 She was probably the model for Alpha in Robert Musil's *Vinzenz und die Freundin bedeutender Männer* (translated as *Vinzenz and the Mistress of Important Men*), 1924.

52 She was the model for Angelika in Franz Werfel's *Barbara, oder Die Frömmigkeit* (Barbara, or Piety), 1929.

53 Interviews with Marie Liliana Amon's son on July 31, 2021, and September 12, 2025.

54 Letter from Marie Schiele to Egon Schiele, November 14, 1913, Leopold Museum, Vienna, inv. no. 8054.

55 In Austria, it was customary to announce an upcoming church wedding publicly three times. These announcements were intended to ensure that there were no impediments to the marriage.

56 Letter from Marie Schiele to Egon Schiele, November 23, 1913, Leopold Museum, Vienna, inv. no. 8052.

57 At the age of seventeen, she was admitted to the Steinhof Hospital for the first time and subsequently received treatment there on numerous occasions. During the Nazi era, the facility became a place of horror, where Gerti Peschka died in 1944. This was only recently uncovered. For more information, see Kerstin Jesse, Jane Kallir, and Hans-Peter Wipplinger, eds., *Changing Times: Egon Schiele's Last Years, 1914–1918*, exh. cat. Leopold Museum, Vienna (Cologne: Verlag der Buchhandlung Walther und Franz König, 2025).

58 It claimed between 25 and 50 million lives worldwide, with some estimates putting the death toll as high as 100 million. It spread across the globe through troop movements during World War I.

59 Diary of Erwin von Graff, October 24, 1918.

60 Diary of Erwin von Graff, November 10, 1918. I presented this diary entry at the fourth Egon Schiele Symposium at the Leopold Museum in Vienna on December 3, 2021, believing it to be the diary of Adele Saxl, née Fedrigoni von Etschthal, as her daughter assured me in 2021. In 2021, I only had two pages of the diary at my disposal. It was only when I was given the entire diary in 2025 that it became clear that it was from Erwin von Graff.

61 Comini, *Egon Schiele's Portraits* (see note 3), 73.

62 Nebehay, *Egon Schiele, 1890–1918* (see note 16), 519, 527.

63 Prof. Dr. Michael Freissmuth to the author, e-mail, June 11, 2025. Dr. Andreas Dutz provided me with a newspaper article from the *Deutsches Volksblatt* of January 12, 1911; there were specialized clinics such as the Bellevue Sanatorium in Hacking, near Vienna, that used morphine injections and oxygen inhalation to treat respiratory distress.

64 Prof. Dr. Harald Sitte, e-mail, May 30, 2025.

65 Prof. Dr. Brigitte Schwarzer-Daum, email, October 7, 2025.

66 Prof. Dr. Brigitte Schwarzer-Daum, email, October 7, 2025.

67 Dr. Alexander Graff de Pancsova, interview, September 1, 2025.

68 Dr. Adolf Kronfeld, "Universitätsprofessor Doktor Erwin Graff: Ein Porträt," *Neues Wiener Journal*, February 13, 1927, 16.

69 Kulturstiftung der deutschen Vertriebenen, biography of Ludwig Bartholomäus Graff Edler von Pancsova: kulturstiftung.org/biographien/graff-edler-von-pancsova-ludwig-bartholomaus–2 (accessed July 20, 2025).

70 Baptismal register Aschaffenburg, Parish St. Agatha (Innenstadt), scan 06–0011: data.matricula-online.eu/de/deutschland/wuerzburg/aschaffenburg-sankt-agatha-innenstadt/00260/?pg=192 (accessed July 20, 2025).

71 *Grazer Tagblatt*, November 21, 1896, 14.

72 Letter from Jenny Graff to her daughter Dorothea dated March 4, 1900, Private Collection.

73 Letter dated January 20, 1902, Private Collection.

74 *Grazer Tagblatt*, March 16, 1903, 3.

75 Karl Doménigg, *Ein Bergsteigerleben: Einer von der "Gilde zum groben Kletterschuh"* (Vienna: Österreichische Bergsteiger-Zeitung, 1949), 217.

76 Ibid., 173–80.

77 *Innsbrucker Nachrichten*, January 4, 1901, 3; *(Salzburger) Fremden-Blatt*, January 12, 1901, 6; *Ischler Wochenblatt*, January 13, 1901, 3, etc. Even today, the tour is mentioned in history books on alpinism.

78 *Nebraska Staats-Anzeiger,* February 14, 1901, 3.

79 *Grazer Tagblatt*, January 17, 1891, 4.

80 The Vienna Medical School has its origins in the second quarter of the eighteenth century with the appointment of Gerard van Swieten as personal physician to the Viennese court. It lost its significance during World War I. In between, there were around 200 years of significant medical achievements in research, treatment, and academic teaching.

81 *Innsbrucker Nachrichten*, May 11, 1908, 2; *Neue Freie Presse*, May 30, 1908, 27.

82 Austrian State Archive, AT-OeStA/AVA Unterricht UM allg. A 624.17, Curriculum vitae of Erwin von Graff of April 22, 1914.

83 Lehne, Husslein, and Kohlberger, "Die Frauenheilkunde in Wien" (see note 19), 9.

84 *Wiener medizinische Wochenschrift* 63, no. 16 (1913): 999.

85 *Wiener medizinische Wochenschrift* 63, no. 16 (1913): 1002.

86 Kronfeld, "Universitätsprofessor Doktor Erwin Graff" (see note 66), 16.

87 This is surgical adage suggesting that surgical intervention offers an opportunity to remove disease or repair an injury.

88 Vienna University Archive, Zl. 1338 ex 1913/14.

89 Austrian State Archive, AT-OeStA/AVA Unterricht UM allg. A624.17, Z. 11121.

90 Note in *Monatsschrift für Geburtshilfe und Gynäkologie,* Stuttgart 1916, 567: https://karger.com/mgg/article-pdf/43/6/566/3085139/000294196.pdf (accessed July 20, 2025).

91 *Wiener medizinische Wochenschrift* 76, no. 47 (1926): 1411.

92 Kronfeld, "Universitätsprofessor Doktor Erwin Graff" (see note 66), 16.

93 Jenny Graff to her daughter Dorothea, May 7, 1904, private collection.

94 *Der Schnee: Wochenschrift des Alpen-Skivereines* 6, no. 5 (November 12, 1910): 3.

95 Letter dated April 9, 1959.

96 Diary of Erwin von Graff, August 24–29, 1918.

97 Diary of Erwin von Graff, October 8, 1918.

98 Diary of Erwin von Graff, October 11, 1918.

99 Diary of Erwin von Graff, October 17, 1918.

100 His residential address during the war years 1914–1918 is listed in the Lehmann telephone directory as Vienna, Neustiftgasse 18.

101 Diary of Erwin von Graff, June 29, 1918.

102 Diary of Erwin von Graff, June 23, 1918.

103 Austrian State Archives, AT-OeStA/HHStA HA OrdK Kartei 4–1166, Z 4015.

104 Dr. Fritz Falk (1880–1912) was a physician and friend of Erwin von Graff.

105 Diary of Erwin von Graff, October 8, 1918.

106 Diary of Erwin von Graff, October 17, 1918.

107 Diary of Erwin von Graff, November 7, 1918.

108 Diary of Erwin von Graff, November 21, 1918.

109 Diary of Erwin von Graff, May 2, 1919.

110 Warscher, "Die 'neue Art von Strahlen'" (see note 7), 49.

111 Unpublished life notes, Private Collection.

112 Memories of Adele Lička, unpublished typoscript, 83, Private Collection.

113 "Die Vaterschaftsbestimmung auf Grund der Blutgruppen," *Juristische Blätter*, no. 8, April 21, 1928, 171.

114 Erwin von Graff, "Behandlung der Sterilität," *Medizinische Klinik: Wochenschrift für praktische Ärzte* 24, no. 31, (August 3, 1928): 1145–51.

115 Erwin von Graff, "Die Fruchtbarkeit der Ehe," lecture on February 16, 1928, at the Urania, a public educational institute in Vienna. See *Neue Freie Presse*, February 22, 1928, 1.

116 Günter K. Kodek, *Unsere Bausteine sind die Menschen: Die Mitglieder der Wiener Freimaurerlogen (1869–1938)* (Vienna: Löcker, 2009), 124.

117 "Vienna Doctor Will Talk Thursday Noon," *Marshfield News-Herald*, April 1, 1931, 1.

118 "Vienna Medic Here," *Kansas City Journal*, April 30, 1931, 11.

119 "Vienna Doctor to Visit His Pupils," *Los Angeles Evening Express*, April 4, 1931, 2.

120 "Vienna Doctor Here," *Stevens Point Journal*, April 4, 1931, 3.

121 "Child Expert Lauds Clinics," *Los Angeles Evening Express*, April 23, 1931, 6.

122 "Physician Urges Birth Control," *Los Angeles Evening Express,* April 17, 1931, 9.

123 "Patient Not a Machine," *The Kansas City Times,* May 1, 1931, 15.

124 "Doctor Warns of Sterility in Use of Liquor," *The Los Angeles Times*, April 24, 1931, 19.

125 "Prohibition Said to Have Aroused Desire to Drink," *The Sacramento Bee*, April 24, 1931, 15.

126 "Patient Not a Machine," *The Kansas City Times,* May 1, 1931, 15.

127 Vienna University Archive, Zl. 1324 ex 1903/31

128 "'Favorite Persons' Frolic at Fancy Dress Party," *The Des Moines Register*, December 25, 1933, 16.

129 "Score Theory Dakota Twins Had 2 Fathers," *The Des Moines Register*, December 28, 1933, 1.

130 According to Adele Lička's daughter, Graff's skills as a surgeon had deteriorated, and he was showing symptoms of tremors.

131 "Dr. von Graff Will Leave S. U. I. Staff," *Iowa City Press-Citizen*, May 21, 1934, 2.

132 "Colomon Von Graff," *Kennebec Journal* (Augusta, Maine), July 2, 1987, 14.

133 According to Coloman's son Kurt von Graff, June 15, 2025.

134 *Medizinische Klinik: Wochenschrift für praktische Ärzte* 31, no. 11 (March 15, 1935): 364; "Selbstmord eines Grazer Gelehrten in Amerika," *Allgemeiner Tiroler Anzeiger*, March 29, 1935, 4; "Selbstmord eines Grazer Gelehrten in Amerika," *Salzburger Chronik für Stadt und Land*, March 29, 1935, 6.

135 "Freiwilliger Tod eines Gynäkologen," *Freie Stimmen*, March 8, 1935, 5.

136 "Doctor Alive Third Time," *Des Moines Tribune*, April 3, 1935, 3.

137 *Freie Stimmen*, March 16, 1935, 3; "Professor Dr. Erwin Graff lebt," *Die Stunde*, April 4, 1935, 3.

138 *Des Moines Tribune*, August 8, 1935, 20.

139 "Doctors Say Fortitude to Make Childbirth Safer," *Omaha World-Herald*, October 10, 1935, 4.

140 *The Daily Nonpareil*, October 11, 1935, 5.

141 *The Des Moines Register*, June 9, 1935, 32.

142 "Even the Dream Doctor Had a Little Complex All His Own," *The Des Moines Register*, December 1, 1935, 26.

143 District Court, Central Division, Iowa, National Archives and Records Administration, www.ancestry.de/imageviewer/collections/61198/images/0077957 61_00016?rc=&queryId=be24630c–23be–4150–a1dd–6623be3f7b3a&usePUB=true&_phsrc=NID6&_phstart=successSource&pId=16929 (accessed August 11, 2025).

144 Quoted in Helen Bond, "21-Year-Old Girl Becomes a Man," *The Des Moines Sunday Register*, February 16, 1936, 42.

145 *Des Moines Tribune*, October 17, 1934, 8.

146 *The Des Moines Register*, June 21, 1936, 38.

147 "Des Moines Families Like Genuine Foreign Foods," *Des Moines Tribune*, March 31, 1936, 9–10.

148 "Dr. von Graff Honored," *Des Moines Tribune*, December 14, 1936, 16.

149 "Dr. von Graff to Leave City," *The Des Moines Register*, December 16, 1936, 9.

150 Arlene Shaner provided this information.

151 *Medical Directory of New York, New Jersey, and Connecticut, 1939–1940* (New York: Medical Society of the State of New York, 1940), 488.

152 Arlene Shaner provided this information.

153 *City Directory, Manhattan, New York, 1944*, 1092.

154 *Medical Directory of New York, New Jersey and Connecticut, 1949* (New York: Medical Society of the State of New York, 1949), 368.

155 Arlene Shaner provided this information.

156 The National Archives at Washington, D.C.; Washington, D.C.; Series Title: *Passenger and Crew Lists of Vessels and Airplanes Departing from New York, New York, 07/01/1948–12/31/1956*; NAI Number: *3335533*; Record Group Title: *Records of the Immigration and Naturalization Service, 1787–2004*; Record Group Number: *85*; Series Number: *A4169*; NARA Roll Number: *128*.

157 National Archives at College Park; College Park, Maryland, U.S.A.; NAI Number: *302021*; Record Group Title: *General Records of the Department of State*; Record Group Number: *Record Group 59*; Series Number: *Publication A1 205*; Box Number: *1060*; Box Description: *1950–1954 Germany S – Z.*

158 The National Archives at Washington, D.C.; Washington, D.C.; Series Title: *Passenger and Crew Lists of Vessels and Airplanes Departing from New York, New York, 07/01/1948–12/31/1956*; NAI Number: *3335533*; Record Group Title: *Records of the Immigration and Naturalization Service, 1787–2004*; Record Group Number: *85*; Series Number: *A4169*; NARA Roll Number: *128*.

159 Letter dated June 12, 1952, Private Collection.

160 Postcard dated June 19, 1952, Private Collection.

161 Letter dated October 22, 1953, Private Collection.

162 Coloman von Graff's son Kurt does not know anything about it and does not have any papers from his father or Erwin von Graff.

163 Vienna City Library, Manuscript Department, inv. no. ZPH–891/8.

164 This was Alexander Demetrius Goltz (1857–1944), an Austrian painter and stage designer, who created the panel paintings in the auditorium of the University of Graz.

165 Maria (Mary) Mell (1885–1954) was the sister of Max Mell and married to Alexander Demetrius Goltz. She was a famous actress at the Burgtheater in Vienna.

166 Various letters from a Private Collection.

167 David Michaelis, *Eleanor* (New York: Simon & Schuster, 2020), 23.

168 Sonja Niederacher, Dossier on two sheets by Egon Schiele with provenance Erwin von Graff dated December 31, 2012, 3–6.

169 Inscribed "Prof. Dr. Graff", verso (Kallir 1998)

170 Sonja Niederacher, Dossier on two sheets by Egon Schiele with provenance Erwin von Graff dated December 31, 2012, 3–6.

171 Inscribed "Prof. Dr. Graff 6." (Kallir 1998)

172 Inscribed "Prof. Dr. Graff 7," verso (Kallir 1998)

173 Inscribed "93/Dr. von Graff," verso (Kallir 1998)

174 Inscribed "Graff 3," lower right (Kallir 1998)

175 After Erwin von Graff it belonged to Olga Graff, his first wife, until 1956. Then it was sold in an auction on March 15, 1956, at the Dorotheum, Vienna, where the Albertina Museum, Vienna, bought it.

176 Kronfeld, "Universitätsprofessor Doktor Erwin Graff" (see note 66), 17.

177 *Neues Wiener Tagblatt (Tages-Ausgabe)*, February 16, 1928, 8.

178 *Neues Wiener Tagblatt (Tages-Ausgabe)*, February 21, 1928, 11.

179 *Neues Wiener Tagblatt (Tages-Ausgabe)*, October 9, 1928, 9.

180 "Seventy Physicians Hear Gynecologist," *The Courier*, April 19, 1933, 5.

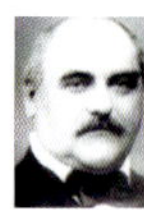

Wilhelm Herrmann Graff de Pancsova

BIRTH: Sept. 21, 1813, Pancsova, Banat
DEATH: June 14, 1893, Pancsova, Banat
MARRIAGE: Nov. 19, 1839, Lazarevo, Banat

Elisabeth Zoldy de Zold

BIRTH: Nov. 27, 1822, Lazarevo, Banat
DEATH: May 12, 1898, Pancsova, Banat
MARRIAGE: Nov. 19, 1839, Lazarevo, Banat

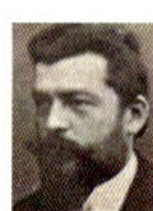

**Univ. Prof. Dr. Ludwig Bartholomäus
Graff de Pancsova**

BIRTH: Jan. 2, 1851, Pancsova, Banat
DEATH: Feb. 6, 1924, Graz
MARRIAGE: Aug. 5, 1874, Břeclav, Moravia

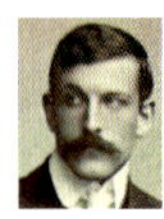

Dr. Erwin Graff de Pancsova

BIRTH: Sept. 23, 1878, Aschaffenburg
DEATH: May 2, 1952, Berlin-Charlottenburg
MARRIAGE 1: Oct. 4, 1902, Graz
DIVORCE 1: June 7, 1915, Vienna
MARRIAGE 2: Feb. 14, 1920, Vienna
DIVORCE 2: Oct. 9, 1929, Vienna

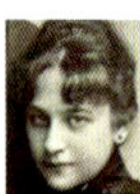

Olga Fayenz

BIRTH: Nov. 5, 1880, Fiume, (Rijeka, Croatia)
DEATH: Oct. 17, 1971, Graz
MARRIAGE: Oct. 4, 1902, Graz
DIVORCE: June 7, 1915, Vienna

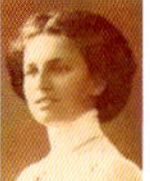

Adele Fedrigoni von Etschthal

BIRTH: Aug. 1, 1891, Bruck an der Mur, Styria
DEATH: Oct. 11, 1981, Vorarlberg
MARRIAGE: Feb. 14, 1920, Vienna
DIVORCE: Oct. 19, 1929, Vienna

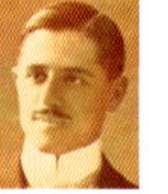

Konrad Alois Saxl

BIRTH: Aug. 3, 1877, Cheb, Bohemia
DEATH: Oct. 1914
MARRIAGE WITH ADELE: Oct. 5, 1910, Ljubljana

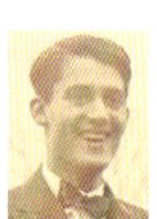

**Dr. Peter Franz Konrad Maria Graff de
Pancsova, né Saxl**

BIRTH: Oct. 24, 1911, Ljubljana
DEATH: Feb. 10, 1944, Vienna

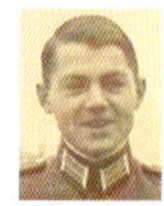

**Dipl. Ing. Kurt Anton Julius Maria Graff de
Pancsova, né Saxl**

BIRTH: Feb. 2, 1913, Ljubljana
DEATH: April 26, 2004, Vienna

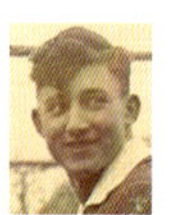

Coloman von Graff, né Saxl

BIRTH: Sept. 2, 1914, Gorizia
DEATH: June 29, 1987, Portland, ME

ADOPTED

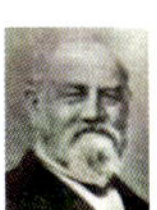

Robert August Schorisch

BIRTH: March 25, 1814, Wicina
DEATH: July 18, 1889, Graz
MARRIAGE: July 13, 1846, Ostrovačice, Moravia

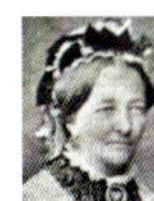

Ludovica Aloisia Kier zu Oberbojanowitz

BIRTH: Sept. 29, 1828, Ostrovačice, Moravia
DEATH: April 26, 1911, Graz
MARRIAGE: July 13, 1846, Ostrovačice, Moravia

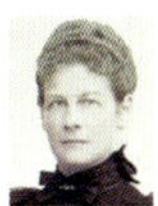

Eugénie "Jenny" Schorisch

BIRTH: Sept. 16, 1855, Szentmikló
DEATH: Feb. 8, 1943, Graz
MARRIAGE: Aug. 5, 1874, Břeclav, Moravia

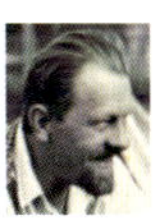

Wilhelm Anton von Lička

BIRTH: May 14, 1897, Vienna
DEATH: Sept. 28, 1971, Salzburg
MARRIAGE WITH ADELE: 1932

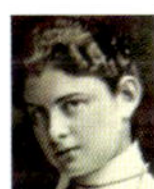

Rosa Friederike Graff de Pancsova

BIRTH: Jan. 10, 1876, Munich
DEATH: March 28, 1965, Lassnitzhöhe, Styria

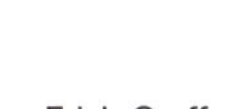

Erich Graff de Pancsova

BIRTH: June 1, 1877, Munich
DEATH: March 25, 1878, Vienna

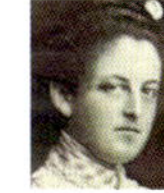

Dorothea Elisabeth Graff de Pancsova

BIRTH: Oct. 20, 1880, Aschaffenburg
DEATH: May 12, 1963, Graz

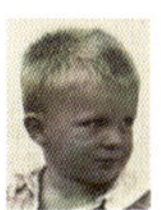

S. Lička

BIRTH: Dec. 18, 1925, Vienna
DEATH: July 20, 2020, Vorarlberg

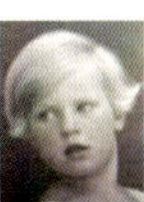

E. Lička

BIRTH: Feb. 13, 1927, Vienna

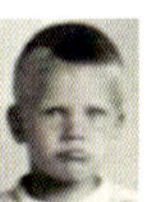

M. Lička

BIRTH: Dec. 24, 1936, Graz

This catalogue has been published in conjunction with the exhibition

EGON SCHIELE ■ PORTRAIT OF DR. ERWIN VON GRAFF

Neue Galerie New York
February 12 — May 4, 2026

Curator
Renée Price
Janis Staggs

Author
Elisabeth Dutz

Director of Publications
Scott Gutterman

Managing Editor
Janis Staggs

Editorial Assistant
Liesbet Van Leemput

Book Design
William Loccisano

Translation
Steven Lindberg

Project Coordinator
Anja Besserer

Production
Martina Effaga

Separations
Schnieber Graphik, Munich

Printing and Binding
Longo AG, Bolzano

© 2026 Neue Galerie New York;
Prestel Verlag, Munich · London ·
New York; and authors

Prestel Verlag, Munich · London ·
New York
A member of Penguin Random House
Verlagsgruppe GmbH
Neumarkter Strasse 28 · 81673 Munich

1st edition 2026

produktsicherheit@penguinrandomhouse.de
(The above information is mandatory information
according to GPSR and should be used for all
queries relating to the safety of our books)

The publisher expressly reserves the right to
exploit the copyrighted content of this work for the
purposes of text and data mining in accordance
with Section 44b of the German Copyright Act
(UrhG), based on the European Digital Single
Market Directive. Any unauthorized use is an
infringement of copyright and is hereby prohibited.

A CIP catalogue record for this book
is available from the British Library.

Library of Congress Control Number is available.

Paper: 170 g Galaxi Supermat

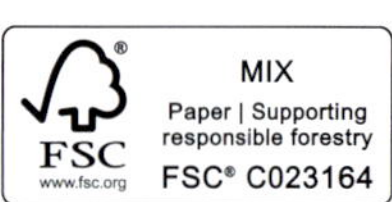

Penguin Random House
Verlagsgruppe FSC® N001967

Printed in Italy

ISBN 978-3-7913-9419-0

www.prestel.com

PAGE 2: Egon Schiele (detail), 1914.
Private Collection. Photograph by Anton
Josef Trčka (Antios)

PAGE 3: Erwin von Graff (detail), 1927.
Private Collection

PAGE 4: Erwin von Graff in his office at the
Second University Women's Clinic, 1918.
Private Collection

PAGE 6: Erwin von Graff in Panscova (detail),
August 1899. Private Collection

PAGE 8: Egon Schiele at his studio on Hietzinger
Hauptstrasse in Vienna's thirteenth district with
the painting *Death and the Maiden*, 1915, vintage
silver gelatin contact print. Private Collection.
Photograph by Johannes Fischer

[illegible handwritten text]